WRITING DISSERTATIONS AND THESES

COVENTRY UNIVERSITY LONDON CAMPUS
East India House,
109-117 Middlesex Street, London, E1 7JF
Tel: 020 7247 3666 | Fax: 020 7375 3048
www.coventry.ac.uk/londoncampus

INSIDE TRACK

WRITING DISSERTATIONS AND THESES

Neil Murray

Senior Lecturer in Applied Linguistics and
Senior Consultant English Language Proficiency,
University of South Australia

David Beglar

Director of the Graduate TESOL Program, College of Education,
Temple University, Japan Campus

PEARSON

Longman

Harlow, England • London • New York • Boston • San Francisco • Toronto
Sydney • Tokyo • Singapore • Hong Kong • Seoul • Taipei • New Delhi
Cape Town • Madrid • Mexico City • Amsterdam • Munich • Paris • Milan

Pearson Education Limited

Edinburgh Gate
Harlow
Essex CM20 2JE
England

and Associated Companies throughout the world

Visit us on the World Wide Web at:
www.pearsoned.co.uk

First published 2009

© Neil Murray and David Beglar 2009

ISBN: 978-0-273-72170-3

British Library Cataloguing-in-Publication Data
A catalogue record for this book is available from the British Library

Library of Congress Cataloging-in-Publication Data
A catalog record for this book is available from the Library of Congress

10 9 8 7 6 5 4 3 2
13 12 11 10

Typeset in 9/12.5 pt Helvetica Neue by 73.
Printed in Great Britain by Henry Ling Limited., at the Dorset Press, Dorchester, DT1 1HD

The publisher's policy is to use paper manufactured from sustainable forests.

This book is dedicated to our parents,
Terence and Audrey Murray, and
David and Margie Beglar

GET THE INSIDE TRACK TO ACADEMIC SUCCESS

INSIDE TRACK

SUCCESSFUL ACADEMIC WRITING

ANDY GILLETT, ANGELA HAMMOND & MARY MARTALA

INSIDE TRACK

SUCCEEDING IN EXAMS & ASSESSMENTS

EDDIE BLASS

INSIDE TRACK

WRITING DISSERTATIONS & THESES

NEIL MURRAY & DAVID BEGLAR

Written by a team of highly experienced authors, this series will equip students with effective and practical ways to improve their academic skills across all subject areas.

CONTENTS

Contents

5 THE RESEARCH PROJECT   141

ACKNOWLEDGEMENTS

Authors' acknowledgements

This book is the result of the support, goodwill and insight of a number of people all of whom deserve our sincere thanks. The first round of applause should go to Steve Temblett, Editor-in-Chief, Skills and Vocational Publishing, who took on the project, saw its potential and was always positive, encouraging . . . and patient. Katy Robinson, Editorial Assistant, and Anita Atkinson, Senior Editor, were invaluable in being our eyes and ears at Pearson, keeping us informed of progress, and generally being highly efficient and always delightful to deal with. Our thanks also extend to Chris Klinger and Adam Simpson for kindly agreeing that we could use extracts of their work as examples of good practice, and to Jackie Knowles for help with some of the book's graphics. Finally, we absolutely must acknowledge the forbearance, love, support and encouragement of our families.

Publisher's acknowledgements

We are grateful to the following for permission to reproduce copyright material:

Figures

Figure 4.6 adapted from *English Legal System*, Pearson Education Ltd (Elliott, C. and Quinn, F. 2008).

Tables

Table on page 121 from *Accounting: An Introduction*, Pearson Education Ltd (McLaney, E. and Atrill, P. 2008) p. 369.

Text

Extracts on pages 41, 147, 154, 168, and 181 from The influence of daily conflict on perceptions of creativity: a longitudinal study, *The International Journal of Conflict Management*, 16(4) (Kurtzberg, T.R. and Mueller, J.S. 2005) © Emerald Group Publishing Limited all rights reserved; Extract on page 46 adapted and reprinted from *Cognitive Psychology*, 55, Lombrozo, T., Simplicity and probability in casual explanation, pp. 232–57, Copyright 2007, with permission from Elsevier; Extract on page 61 from http://www.mantex.co.uk/ou/resource/eval-01.htm; Example on pages 83–4 adapted from the website accompanying *The New Century Handbook*, 3rd ed., Pearson Education Inc. (Hult., C.A. and Huckin, T.N. 2005) Copyright Pearson

Acknowledgements

Education 2005, http://wps.ablongman.com/long_hult_nch_3/0,9398,1483997-,00.html, Reprinted by permission; Box on pages 91–4 from Turnitin.com and Research Resources with permission; Extract on page 112 adapted from *News and Journalism in the UK*, Routledge (McNair, B. 1994) pp. 121–2; Extracts on pages 121 and 122, Activity 4.11 (adapted) and Answers to Activities 4.11 (adapted) from *Psychology*, Pearson Education Limited (Martin, G., Carlson, N. and Buskist, W. 2007); Example on page 139 and extracts on pages 207–11 and 212–14 from Klinger, C. (2005) Process physics: bootstrapping reality from the limitations of logic. PhD thesis. Flinders University; Extracts on pages 114–5 and 121, Activity 4.2, and Answers to Activity 4.2 adapted from *Social Work: An Introduction to Contemporary Practice*, Pearson Education Limited (Wilson, K., Ruch, G., Lymbery, M. and Cooper, A. 2008); Activity 4.3, Activity 4.11 (adapted), Answers to Activity 4.3, and Answers to Activity 4.11 from *Principles of Marketing*, Pearson Education Limited (Kotler, P., Armstrong, G., Wong, V. and Saunders, J. 2008); Activity 4.3 (adapted) and Answers to Activity 4.3 from *The Essential Guide to Teaching*, Pearson Education Limited (Davies, S. 2006) pp. 19, 55; Activity 4.5 (adapted) and Activity 4.11 and Answers to Activity 4.11 from *English Legal System*, Pearson Education Limited (Elliott, C. and Quinn, F. 2008); Activity 4.10 adapted from Traversing more than speed bumps: green politics under authoritarian regimes in Burma and Iran, *Environmental Politics*, 15(5), pp. 763–4 (Doyle, T. and Simpson, A. 2006), reprinted by permission of the publisher (Taylor & Francis Group, http://www.informaworld.com); Extract on page 148 from Graesser, A.C. and Person, N.K., Questions asked during tutoring, *American Educational Research Journal*, 31(1), p. 105, Copyright © 1994 American Educational Research Association. Reprinted by permission of SAGE Publications; Extract on page 177 adapted and reprinted from *The Leadership Quarterly*, 18, Sosik, J. and Dinger, S., Relationships between leadership styles and vision content: the moderating role of need for social approval, self-monitoring and need for social power, p. 145, Copyright 2007 with permission from Elsevier; Extracts on page 180 adapted from Wittrock, M.C. and Alesandrini, K., Generation of summaries and analogies and analytic and holistic abilities, *American Educational Research Journal*, 27(3), pp. 499, 500–501, Copyright © 1990 American Educational Research Association. Reprinted by Permission of SAGE Publications; Extract on page 186 adapted with kind permission from Springer Science + Business Media: *Motivation and Emotion*, Turning fantasies about positive and negative futures into self-improvement goals, 29(4), 2005, pp. 264–5, Oettingen, G., Mayer, D., Thorpe, J.S., Janetzke, H. and Lorenz, S., © 2005, Springer Netherlands.

In some instances we have been unable to trace the owners of copyright material, and we would appreciate any information that would enable us to do so.

INTRODUCTION

Writing a dissertation or thesis is a long process in which writers can face intellectual and emotional challenges at every step. Among the questions you may have to wrestle with are: What's an acceptable topic? What literature should I read? How can I organise my literature review? What writing conventions should I use? What's my supervisor's role in the process? What are the components of a methods section? How can I present my results? How can I relate my findings to previous research?

One of the purposes of this book is to provide initial answers to these and many other questions that you might have about the dissertation and thesis writing process. While everyone's situation differs to some degree, our experience tells us that almost all dissertation and thesis writers encounter certain predictable challenges. Thus, we've tried to provide you with strategies and ideas that you might find useful when you encounter those challenges. While no textbook can solve your problems for you, we believe that the ideas in this book will at least provide you with ways to keep moving forward, and that's one of the keys to successfully completing a dissertation or thesis!

A second purpose of this book is to help you become a more autonomous dissertation or thesis writer. While it's natural to depend on your supervisor to a degree, you'll probably find that your supervisor is extremely busy and can offer you limited guidance. We hope that the ideas in this book will allow you to become more independent and will support you in your attempts to formulate responses to the challenges that you face. This will also allow you to approach your supervisor with plans and possible solutions, not just questions, when you speak with him or her. This will clearly show your supervisor that you're engaged in perhaps the most important task of any dissertation or thesis writer – becoming an independent researcher.

The third purpose of this book is to support you with the affective challenges that you are likely to face. While some dissertation or thesis writers seem to have 'smooth sailing' from start to finish, that is not the norm. In fact, as we've already hinted, because of the unfamiliarity, complexity and length of the dissertation and thesis writing experience, most people will go through periods of frustration, anxiety or stress. One way to minimise these kinds of negative feelings is to be in control of your own destiny, and the way to do that is to formulate and enact a plan that you believe in. We hope that this book will support you in your efforts to do that.

So what's in this book? Chapter 1 alerts you to some of the challenges that you'll face and provides you with some ideas on how to deal with them. In addition, we let you know a bit about becoming a member of an academic community, and how to work with one very important member of that community, your supervisor.

Chapter 2 provides you with information that you should think about before you put pen to paper, including finding an acceptable topic and determining an effective research approach. Indeed, careful planning is one of the most crucial keys to doing good research. Chapter 3 presents some of the fundamentals of clear and effective writing. This is one of the greatest challenges that dissertation and thesis writers face because writing academic papers at a highly professional level is difficult for all but the most talented and experienced writers. In Chapter 4 we walk you through various parts of a research paper. While you may not include all of these parts in your dissertation or thesis, you'll find them useful because they'll help you to think about your study from a wide variety of perspectives. Finally, in Chapter 5, we'll give you some information about important issues that occur at the end of the process: selecting examiners, preparing for a successful oral examination and publishing your research.

Although writing a dissertation or thesis is a time-consuming and sometimes difficult process, it can be a fascinating one as well. In the best cases, students find it to be a peak intellectual experience during which they had the opportunity to explore and understand an issue of interest to them in greater depth than at any other time in their lives. So don't forget that it's OK to enjoy the experience, and good luck!

Neil Murray and David Beglar

About the Authors

Dr Neil Murray is Senior Lecturer in Applied Linguistics and Senior Consultant English Language Proficiency at the University of South Australia. He has taught academic English and Applied Linguistics at undergraduate and postgraduate level for twenty-five years.

Dr David Beglar is the Director of the Graduate TESOL Program in the College of Education at Temple University, Japan Campus. He has taught graduate level courses in Applied Linguistics for fifteen years and has been the primary advisor to over thirty doctoral dissertation writers.

1 ACADEMIC RESEARCH: AN OVERVIEW

This chapter looks at what is involved in conducting academic research: the demands and expectations it brings with it, the kinds of decisions required of you, the intellectual and personal challenges it can present, and strategies for dealing with those challenges. It will help ensure that you not only complete your research successfully but also enjoy the process itself and feel enriched for having engaged in it.

The chapter will cover:

- conducting academic research: common concerns
- the similarities and differences between a thesis and a dissertation
- developing independence as a researcher and finding your voice
- meeting the challenges of academic research
- becoming a member of an academic community
- choosing and working with your supervisor
- the upgrading process.

USING THIS CHAPTER

CONDUCTING ACADEMIC RESEARCH: COMMON CONCERNS

Conducting research for the first time represents an important milestone in a student's academic career. For many, though, it can be a daunting prospect and one that's often approached with some trepidation. Typically, concerns centre around one or more of the following:

- uncertainty about what research actually is and what it entails
- lack of understanding about the research process itself – how to carry out research
- inability to identify a suitable research topic and focus
- lack of knowledge of research methodology and research study design
- lack of ability to take control of a project and work autonomously
- little sense of the time commitment required.

All of these concerns are perfectly understandable and it can be reassuring to know that, despite appearances to the contrary, most researchers – including the most seasoned and capable – have at some point experienced similar feelings. The fact is that the more research you do, the better you become at doing it. It gradually loses its mystique and becomes an accessible, engaging and stimulating activity; for some, it becomes the basis of their whole career.

The purpose of this book is to help de-mystify research by talking you through all the aspects involved in preparing for, designing, conducting and writing up a research project. We have tried to present the material in a way that is accessible and that answers the concerns of those of you, in particular, who are about to engage in research for the first time. To this end, the material has been organised serially so as to mirror your progress through the various stages of your project. The idea is that while we would recommend you read the complete book prior to setting out, particular sections can be referred to as and when they become relevant. The examples are an important part of the book in that they will help to clarify the ideas discussed and, by making them more concrete, give them greater meaning. The tasks give you the opportunity to consolidate your knowledge and test your understanding through applying the ideas presented. As such, we strongly recommend that you take the time to read the examples and work through the tasks.

The chances are that you have picked up this book because you will shortly be embarking on an undergraduate or postgraduate dissertation, or perhaps a PhD thesis. Therefore, before looking in more detail at what research means for you as an individual and some of the challenges you will face as you begin your research project, let's clarify the distinction between a dissertation and thesis.

THE SIMILARITIES AND DIFFERENCES BETWEEN A THESIS AND A DISSERTATION

Despite having different names, a thesis and a dissertation are, in fact, very similar in most respects. First, both are expected to follow the principles of sound research design and implementation – aspects we will return to in greater detail in Chapter 2, *Preparing your research*. Both also follow the same principles of good academic writing style and are written up in much the same way, sharing as they do similar structure, organisation and formatting conventions. Finally, both require you, as a researcher, to produce a piece of work that is original and adds to the body of knowledge in the field with which your research is associated. One university's book of rules and regulations for PhD research students puts it like this:

Criteria for examination

Examiners shall examine the candidate's thesis according to the following criteria:

(a) Capacity to demonstrate critical analysis and original thought in all aspects of the study;

(b) The extent to which the thesis makes a significant original contribution to knowledge and/or the application of knowledge within the field of study.

(University of South Australia, 2008)

And here's another example:

The thesis shall form a distinct contribution to the knowledge of the subject and afford evidence of originality by the discovery of new facts and/or by the exercise of independent critical power.   (King's College London, 2006)

Having read this, students often ask the question, 'How original does my research need to be?' or 'When can a contribution be said to be "significant"?' Although both originality and significance are, admittedly, difficult to define and measure in anything other than vague terms, they do nevertheless provide one basis for distinguishing a thesis from a dissertation. Although both types of research project should offer original and significant contributions to their fields, the extent to which they are expected to do so differs. A dissertation will normally be submitted as just one of a number of written requirements of a Bachelors or Masters degree (BA, BSc, MA, MSc, MEd, MPhil) and may well be the product of only two or three months' work. As such, it will be shorter than a thesis (typically 10,000 to 15,000 words), probably contain a simpler design and methodology, and report on a smaller-scale project that is more manageable given the greater time constraints. Its originality may be limited to replicating a previous study in a somewhat different context, or perhaps employing a slightly different methodology, for example. In contrast, a PhD thesis is generally the product of three or more years' work, and often considerably more. It will normally extend to at least 100,000 words and constitute the sole written requirement for the PhD degree. It is reasonable to expect, therefore, that the study will be more in-depth, the design and methodology adopted more sophisticated, and the insights generated more profound and far reaching than those of a dissertation.

This is not to say, of course, that all PhD research is earth-shaking in its impact! Instances where research findings are profound enough to shake the foundations of a field, trigger a paradigm shift or even provoke the re-evaluation of a major principle or theory are few and far between. Indeed, in the vast majority of cases doctoral research is much smaller scale in the sense that it is far more focused, has less 'reach' and serves to add one tiny piece to the jigsaw puzzle that provides a picture of the state of the field and where it is in its evolution. However, this does not mean that the research is not original and significant. It will probably have involved intensive and detailed work and/or perhaps employed a unique methodology or technique in an effort to shed new light on an area previously unnoticed or neglected. Furthermore, its findings may subsequently provoke new avenues of inquiry or have other implications that were not necessarily anticipated. Similarly, while a dissertation will be much shorter, its impact may be considerable, particularly if it gets published in a well-respected journal.

TIP When you submit your thesis or dissertation proposal, your supervisor or receiving department will give you guidance on whether or not your study is suitable in terms of its size and scope, given the academic degree toward which you are working.

Originality, then, is a key criterion against which your research is evaluated. There are, however, a number of other expectations that apply to both dissertations and theses, some of which are listed below. Once again, though, in certain cases, these expectations are subject to differences of degree according to whether your research project is a dissertation or a thesis. This is true, for example, of item 3 in the box opposite – your review of the literature (➡ see Chapter 5, p. 158) would need to be more extensive in the case of a thesis.

TIP Although you do not need to commit it to memory, we would nevertheless strongly urge you to familiarise yourself with the content of your university's book of rules and regulations concerning the conduct and submission of research.

Some requirements of a dissertation/thesis

1 Capacity to demonstrate critical analysis and original thought in all aspects of the study.

2 The extent to which the thesis makes a significant original contribution to knowledge and/or the application of knowledge within the field of study.

3 Ability to demonstrate a comprehensive and detailed knowledge of the literature and theoretical understandings relevant to the field of study.

4 Capacity to apply appropriate research methodologies.

5 The quality of the presentation of the dissertation/thesis, including:
- the clarity of expression
- the accuracy and appropriateness of presentation of results
- the quality and relevance of illustrative material (such as graphs, tables, illustrations)
- the relevance and accuracy of citations, references, etc. and the development of a coherent argument where relevant to the field of study.

6 The quality of artefacts, if any, including:
- the conceptual understanding of the relevant field
- the ideas and/or imagination demonstrated
- the technical competence
- the resolution of the artifacts, and
- the complexity and difficulty demonstrated.

7 The worthiness of the dissertation/thesis for publication in any appropriate form.

DEVELOPING INDEPENDENCE AS A RESEARCHER AND FINDING YOUR VOICE

Developing independence is an essential and integral part of becoming an effective researcher, and there are two key ways in which that independence will need to be demonstrated. First, you will be expected to 'carry' your project; in other words, to exercise initiative and a considerable degree of autonomy in its design, implementation and final presentation in the form of a dissertation or thesis. In the case of research degrees in particular, what gives these degrees value in the eyes of future employees is not merely the fact that you have demonstrated the ability to conduct a substantial study, but have also shown yourself capable of leading a project, operating independently and on your own initiative, and bringing it to a successful conclusion. In this respect, successful research says almost as much about the researcher as it does about the quality of the study itself. Yes, your supervisor will be there to support you and help keep you on the straight and narrow, but they will expect *you* to run the show and keep them informed of your progress.

As we saw ➡ on page 2, this idea of having to take control of a research project can be a source of real anxiety for many students, the majority of whom will be facing this situation for the first time. However, there are ways of alleviating this anxiety, some of which we'll visit in the following sections.

The second way in which you will need to show independence is in the way you approach ideas. What do we mean by this? Although an important objective of university education is to nurture individuals who are able to think critically about ideas rather than simply take them at face value, it is nevertheless true that much of what students actually do during the course of their university careers consists of locating, reading, selecting and making notes on information obtained from journals, books and lectures, often with a view to writing an essay or perhaps presenting a summary of that information. While there may be some critiquing of the content, this is often minimal and the process of writing becomes, in reality, little more than a process of regurgitation, of showcasing what they have read and learnt. Although, on occasions, this may be precisely what they have been instructed to do, more often than not it is the result of a lack of self-confidence and an aversion to what is seen as risk taking, when the stakes can be unacceptably high. The thinking is that it is better to do a rather tame assignment and get a moderate mark than to stick your neck out and risk a poor one because your ideas are naïve, misguided or misinformed. Furthermore, students often feel that they do not have the authority to question or take issue with respected and prolific scholars whose names grace the covers of books and journals. As a researcher embarking on a dissertation or thesis project you simply cannot afford to approach ideas in this way.

If your research is to be original, interesting and exciting to read, and if you are to gain the respect of your peers, it is crucial that you 'find your own voice'. In other words, you must be prepared to adopt a critical view toward those ideas with which you come into contact, and decide where you stand on particular issues in your field of study, especially those that relate to the subject of your research. As a researcher and a true scholar, you cannot simply accept the word of others at face value; you must evaluate it on the basis of evidence and sound argument and be prepared to disagree and criticise. This is a fundamental part of what it means to exercise your independence and autonomy, and as we've seen, it requires self-confidence. Let's consider, for a moment, what underlies such self-confidence.

Most importantly, for you to feel comfortable advocating a particular position, and to legitimately criticise the stance taken by others, you need to be well-informed. Your knowledge of the relevant literature and your understanding of the concepts involved needs to be comprehensive – an issue we will revisit in ➡ Chapter 5, p. 158. Furthermore, your own position needs to be well thought out and cogently argued, for it too will be subjected to the scrutiny of others. Its intellectual and methodological rigour will be tested and it will need to prove itself robust enough to withstand such critical appraisal.

TIP This ethos of peer evaluation and critical appraisal serves an important purpose: ultimately, it forces disciplines to evolve and progress by maintaining their academic integrity. Develop your ability to consider ideas critically but fairly from the moment you set out on your dissertation or thesis.

'Finding your own voice' means more than positioning yourself and having a clear perspective on ideas. It refers also to the way in which you express that perspective and 'voice' your views. In other words, finding your voice is, in part, about developing your own style – your distinct writing identity, if you will. This, of course, is not something that happens overnight, but it is something that you should nonetheless strive towards as it helps to give you an 'academic personality', something which helps set you and your work apart. The way in which any of us writes is a product of everything we have ever read: however, it is a fact that those writers whose work we particularly enjoy and admire are more likely to influence our own writing style. Often, unwittingly, we incorporate elements of their particular style into our own writing, ending up with a hybrid of sorts. It can be a useful exercise, therefore, to try and identify a scholar whose work you particularly respect and to consider what gives their writing its particular tone. What makes it readable, accessible and enjoyable? Although we would not suggest that you strive to emulate it (the idea is certainly *not* to copy), the process of noticing its particular characteristics may influence your own style, one that is unique to you but coloured by some of the qualities you find particularly effective in the writing of others. Without forcing it, you will gradually find yourself merging styles and naturally creating a style that is yours and which will eventually also come to represent what you stand for.

Activity 1.1 Your strengths and weaknesses as a researcher

Below is a list of ways, discussed above, in which you can develop yourself as an independent researcher. Which do you consider to be your strengths and weaknesses? Decide how you rate on each one by ticking the appropriate box.

Method	Good	Average	Poor
Exercising initiative			
Thinking critically about ideas			
Not taking things at face value			
Questioning the ideas of established scholars			
Questioning established wisdom			
Overviewing and distilling ideas			
Establishing my own perspective			
Having confidence in my own ideas			
Arguing my case cogently			
Developing my own style			

MEETING THE CHALLENGES OF ACADEMIC RESEARCH

We have looked at two key and related aspects of conducting research: the need to work independently and the importance of finding your own voice. We have also noted that these things can present significant challenges, particularly for the novice researcher who may well lack confidence and feel insecure, particularly in the initial stages of their project.

In this section, we will consider some other types of challenges you may face during the course of your research and look at ways of coping with them. Of course, different individuals will perceive these challenges differently and have their own strategies for dealing with them, and our purpose in presenting them to you is certainly not to increase your levels of anxiety but to help prepare you. The fact is that all too often students undertake research unaware of the kinds of difficulties they will come up against in the weeks, months or years ahead and, as a result, sometimes react badly – and often over-react – when they hit a difficult patch. Their reaction can range from mild surprise or frustration, to panic and despair. In extreme cases, they may feel unable to continue with their studies and consequently withdraw. This is always sad and disappointing for all concerned, particularly as, in most cases, their problems are actually commonplace, not as severe as they may think, and frequently solvable. So, our thinking in putting together this section is to pre-empt any feelings of negativity you may have further down the line, thereby offsetting their potentially damaging effects to your confidence and sense of perseverance. Our basic message is: forewarned is forearmed.

> **TIP** Partly as a result of anxiety, insecurity and lack of confidence, research students' perceptions of their challenges often exaggerate those challenges; their response, therefore, tends to be disproportionate. It can be reassuring to know that all students face similar such challenges, whether or not they choose to show it. When you face difficult moments, try to remember that you're in good company!

Many of the issues touched on below will be addressed in greater detail in other contexts later in the book.

Intellectual challenges

Needless to say, the job of conducting research can be an intellectually demanding one and the challenges that present themselves can come from a number of quarters, including the following.

Identifying a problem

Identifying a problem or research question is one of the first pressure points a new researcher will experience. While this is discussed in detail in Chapter 2

(➡ see p. 38), it is worth pointing out here that in order to identify a gap in the literature which your research might address, you first need to have a comprehensive overview and understanding of that literature so as to be sure that there is indeed a gap, that the problem you wish to address is indeed a problem, and that by addressing the problem you have added something significant and worthwhile to the body of knowledge which constitutes your field of inquiry (➡ see also the first section of this chapter on p. 3).

Understanding concepts

Clearly, before you begin any process of inquiry, you need to have an excellent grasp of the concepts pertinent to that inquiry; to feel intellectually in control of the material with which you are dealing. In certain cases, where concepts are particularly abstract or complex, this can be an extremely demanding task. However, it's an essential one, because if concepts are not clear in your own mind your research will almost certainly be vague, ambiguous and disorganised – qualities that will subsequently be reflected in your dissertation or thesis, the writing of which will be a painful and probably fruitless process.

Designing the research

As we shall see, the most critical factor governing the success of any research project is the soundness of the design of that research; after all, the findings generated by your study are only as valid as its research design is sound. In other words, if your methodology is flawed, then your results will necessarily be called into serious question and the study fatally undermined. If that is not to occur, then considerable energy and intellectual application needs to go into the process of designing a study that is rigorous in every respect and as elegant, suitable for purpose and effective as it can possibly be. This, as we shall see, is something your supervisor can play a key role in ensuring.

Resolving unexpected problems

One of the things you can always count on as a researcher is that things will never go entirely according to plan; this is a fact of life that you'll need to come to terms with early on! The unexpected can, of course, happen during the course of your data collection (if you're doing an empirical study) or it can happen while you're pondering the project or writing it up, or when you come across a new idea – possibly in a journal article of which you were previously unaware, or at a conference. One quite common scenario is for a student suddenly to spot an inconsistency in their thinking. This can be very disconcerting and really can cause momentary panic, although, the 'collateral damage' usually proves, subsequently, to be fairly minimal and such inconsistencies can be resolved or at least neutralised. Whatever the circumstances though, you will need to have the intellectual wherewithal to face such problems head on, perform some mental acrobatics and, hopefully, resolve them.

Breaking new ground

The very fact that your research seeks to be original means that, to a degree at least, you will need to think beyond what is already known, what has already been discovered. This means that you'll not only need to know what's already out there and to understand it, you'll also need to have the vision to analyse it, to deconstruct it, to see its strengths and weaknesses, and to perceive where there are gaps and where there would be value in pursuing research. Although all research is derivative to some extent and originality does not necessarily mean a radical new direction, nevertheless in certain cases a project can represent a major departure in thinking and you will need the intellectual capacity to work it through in your mind and the confidence to trust in your own critical faculties. This would be the case, for example, if you were constructing and applying a unique methodological approach or analytical technique – a situation in which there would be few points of reference, or 'anchor points' in the literature.

Making sense of large bodies of complex and often conflicting literature

As you read around your subject you will probably hit a number of problems. First, the work you read may contain ideas that are inherently complex and require intense mental application and a very clear and organised mind to penetrate them. There will be occasions when you find that you are simply not up to the task. Rather than struggling fruitlessly, it is usually best to move on and return to it later with a fresh mind.

Then there are occasions when articles – even books – are written in a way that is dense and inaccessible. It can be a struggle to get through them and to understand the ideas their writers are attempting to convey.

Sometimes, concepts you thought you had clear in your mind suddenly become confused as you read the literature and find that different writers understand them differently. On occasion, different takes on the same idea may actually conflict and contradict each other, leaving you pulling your hair out in frustration. This can be particularly problematic for new researchers who often mistakenly believe that everything 'out there in the literature' is black and white and neatly packaged, and all they need to do as researchers is familiarise themselves with it and then build on it in some way. Not so! You will need to learn to tolerate ambiguity and to understand that there are inconsistencies, inaccuracies and contradictions evident in the literature which can be the result of bad writing, personal agendas, poor research or carelessness. Do not assume that because something appears to you to be inconsistent or unclear, for example, you must be misunderstanding it or lacking the necessary insight or background knowledge. While that may be true of course, it may equally be true that the inconsistency or lack of clarity is real. While you will need to follow up such cases, learn to have confidence in your own perceptions. Just because something is in print doesn't mean that it's faultless and unquestionable. Clearly, this issue of confidence bears strongly on the idea of developing independence as a researcher and finding your own voice, as discussed in a previous section (➡ see p. 5), and it's one to which we'll be returning at a number of junctures in this book.

Making sense of your findings

Having completed your research, you will face the task of having to make sense of your findings; to interpret them and evaluate their significance. Once again, this requires the ability to step back and be objective. You will need to be able to analyse the data you have collected, to determine the best means of doing so, and perhaps have the wherewithal to perform statistical analyses. You will also need to think about the implications of your findings and the ways in which future research might usefully build on them.

Mastering 'research tools'

Students new to research often express concern over their ability to work with research tools such as statistical packages used for analysing data. Most of their anxiety comes from never having worked with such tools before – a fear of the unknown. It may be that you will need to master a number of such instruments in the course of your research, and this is something your supervisor may be able to help you with. Alternatively, departments and schools will often hold a series of research seminars designed to introduce the new researcher to the process and demands of conducting research. Such programmes frequently include seminars on working with particular types of research tools. Furthermore, there are numerous 'An Introduction to . . .' and 'The Idiot's Guide to . . .' sort of publications available – as well as more scholarly works – designed to address the concerns of the uninitiated! Once you are familiar with them, you will find that many of these tools are actually quite simple and straightforward to use.

Organising information logically

As we'll see in Chapter 3 (➡ see p. 76), if your research is to read well, carry conviction and 'carry your reader along' with it, then it needs to develop a powerful argument structure. It can only do this if it has been very carefully thought out and the information it presents bolted together in a way that is logical and gives your work coherence, fluency and flow. In long dissertations and theses, this can present a particular challenge as the amount and complexity of information tends to be greater. The trick is to ensure that you:

- have a complete understanding of what you are writing about and how the various elements relate to one another
- have a clear vision at the outset of how you intend to structure your discussion
- have the audience for whom you are writing in mind. Always put yourself in their shoes and ask yourself whether you have presented your information in a way that is most easily understood.

Emotional challenges

It would be unrealistic to discuss the challenges of conducting a research project without making some reference to the emotional ups and downs you are likely to experience from time to time. And you *will* experience ups and downs. When your project is progressing well you will enjoy a real sense of satisfaction, achievement and even excitement. This, after all, is something of your own creation and over which you have ownership, something original that will, hopefully, bring new and unique insights to your field. Every time you have a new insight, solve a problem, conclude a particular part of your research or complete a section of your dissertation or thesis, you will get a buzz. As you feel things coming together and the goal of completion and a degree looming on the horizon, your sense of anticipation will increase. It is these moments that make research worthwhile and you need to savour them and remind yourself of them during those periods when things are not going as smoothly as you would wish.

So what kinds of things might present you with emotional challenges during the course of your research? There are, of course, a myriad different things that might crop up and it would be impossible for us to cover them all here. However, it is possible to identify a few broad areas where problems tend to arise and lead to feelings of disenchantment, doubt or even depression. Obviously, one of these is the project itself; the kinds of intellectual challenges discussed earlier can, on occasion, be so acute as to lead to a sense of losing control of your research. Suddenly it feels as though everything is unravelling, and this can be very unnerving, particularly for a novice researcher who has not experienced it before. At these moments it is important to remind yourself that you are breaking new ground and that unforeseen problems are an inevitable part of the process – it's a very rare research study that goes exactly according to plan, without any hitches!

Research requires great dedication, particularly in the case of a research degree lasting three years or more. For it to come to fruition and not drag on forever takes great discipline and single-mindedness and this can often present a problem, particularly for those who have families. For these individuals, time spent on their research can mean time not spent with their partners or children, and this sometimes leads to feelings of guilt or failure, regardless of how supportive their families may be. In other words, creating a research–family life balance can prove difficult. For those who are not partnered, they risk cutting themselves off from their social circle – a situation which can be unhealthy and bring its own emotional challenges. One solution is to be well-organised and to schedule time to be with friends and family. And remember, getting away from your research periodically is important as it allows you to refresh yourself and see your project with 'new' eyes.

Loneliness and isolation can be a cause of distress for both researchers who have family around them, as well as those who do not. As we have seen, conducting research with a view to obtaining a degree involves working alone and this sometimes leads to a feeling of dislocation and isolation, of being in your own world, one that no one else is privy to and fully understands. To a certain extent this is inevitable as you are working on a project over which you have sole ownership and which, to some extent at least, is isolating by virtue of its originality. Only you fully understand what it is you are doing; only you are truly immersed in it and fully aware of its strengths and weaknesses (and their significance), the joys and the problems it presents and their effect on your feeling of well-being. The fact is that while, as we shall see in moment, there are ways of mitigating the effects of these things, research is essentially a very private pursuit in the context of a degree and can therefore be a very cloistering experience, one where you may feel out of touch with those around you and frustrated – even disturbed – by the fact that others do not really have a window into your world or know what you are going through.

Sometimes, students experience a crisis of confidence. Suddenly, for a variety of different reasons, they lose faith in themselves and feel they are simply not up to the task; it is beyond them. It is all too easy, particularly for more tentative students, to believe that they have fluked it up to this point, and to convince themselves that they're neither capable nor worthy of the degree toward which they are working. They believe either that they must somehow have duped the system or that the department's screening process somehow failed to weed them out at the time of their application for entry to the degree programme. As we shall see, it is at these times that the support and reassurance of those around us can be crucial, and often it's all that's needed to get us back on track and into the correct mindset. It is also important to keep faith with yourself and believe in the system – chances are you're there because you deserve to be there. Others have faith in you, so you should have faith in yourself.

Although it is unlikely, one final emotional challenge you may face concerns your relationship with your supervisor. As we we'll see in a later section (➡ see p. 19), your choice of supervisor can be absolutely critical to your development as a researcher and the success of your project; as such, you need to select your supervisor very carefully indeed. Unfortunately, even then, this important relationship can run into problems and be a cause of great stress and anxiety.

Whatever problems you face, you will have access to your university's counselling service. Here, you can talk through and get advice on how to deal with your problems in the knowledge that whatever you choose to discuss will remain confidential. Many students use this service for a wide variety for reasons and there's no stigma attached to it. So, if you feel you need to offload some of your problems or anxieties and may benefit from the advice of a trained counsellor with an alternative perspective, don't hesitate to use it.

Motivational challenges

Particularly for longer research projects, it can sometimes be difficult to maintain momentum, especially if you have many other commitments in your life. We have already looked briefly at the difficulty of balancing your research commitments with those of your immediate family, but research students typically come with an enormous range of other pressures each of which can potentially distract them from their academic work. Typical scenarios include a death in the family, a family member who needs to be cared for, health problems, visa difficulties, work-related problems such as the loss of a job or a significant increase in workload, financial difficulties and accommodation problems. Each of these things can and often will interrupt your research, forcing you to disengage with it and, in extreme cases where you may not be able to re-engage for weeks or even months, distancing you from it. This latter situation is a particularly challenging one because you will have to 'waste' time re-familiarising yourself with what it was you were doing and what you were thinking prior to the interruption, and it can be difficult to 'get back into the groove'. In the worst case, you may actually forget exactly where you left off and what was in your mind at the time and have to continue on a slightly different track. This can be unnerving, to say the least.

All of these things can greatly affect your motivation level. But the story does not end there. There may well be other forces at work which similarly threaten to sap your enthusiasm for your project. Intellectual dead-ends of the kind mentioned above can leave you feeling disillusioned or disheartened, as can emotional problems arising from tensions between you and your supervisor. At times you may feel that your project is getting bogged down, that you are making little progress or that the findings at the end of it will not really be worthwhile or significant. You may struggle with the collection of your data or find that the data you have is invalid and will need collecting again. This kind of situation is not uncommon but it has the potential to seriously undermine motivation.

Organisational challenges

Given the commitment that conducting research involves and the many, often conflicting academic and personal demands on your time, organisational challenges are sure to present themselves. If you are to keep your head above water and avoid, as far as possible, that sense of intense frustration that this kind of situation can provoke, you will need to be very disciplined and systematic in the way in which you respond to it. First and foremost, stay calm and try not to panic! Prioritise your commitments and try to work out (and write down) a schedule that reflects those priorities and leaves you enough time to keep engaged – at some level at least – with your research. You may well have to accept that during certain periods other commitments may have to take priority for a while. What is important is that you are comfortable with the way in which you've prioritised those commitments, realistic in your scheduling, and unwavering in your implementation of the schedule. Even if you've only scheduled three hours for your research in that particular week, be sure to devote the allocated time to it. This will help you keep engaged with the project. You will also be in a better position psychologically, knowing that you have also met your other commitments as far as possible. If you are *not* organised, you tend to make very little significant progress in anything, and it is that sense of failure and lack of achievement overall which can be lethal to your state of mind and ultimately to the progress of your project.

As you will have realised by now, it's a pretty safe bet that at some point during your research you'll face one or more of the difficulties we've looked at in our discussion. It is important, therefore, to be psychologically prepared and have strategies in place to counter their potentially detrimental effects on you and your research project. Here are a few suggestions:

- Choose a research topic that really inspires you and is likely to keep you interested and motivated to see your project through regardless of the obstacles that will inevitably present themselves.

- Know exactly what you are doing and do not tolerate vagueness and lack of clarity. If your research aims, the concepts with which you are working, the structure of your dissertation or thesis, etc. are in any way fuzzy and ill-defined, do not proceed on that basis for you'll be building your house on sand. Take a step back, take the time to reflect on things, and be absolutely certain that everything is squared away in your own mind before proceeding any further. Time invested now will bring enormous returns later in terms of your productivity and the quality of research.

- If possible take a break from your research for a few days – even two or three weeks. Switch off completely and don't feel guilty about taking time out. Sometimes, putting a little distance between yourself and the project can have a very positive effect by allowing you to recharge your batteries, attend to other matters, and come back to it refreshed and with new ideas.

   While it can be very beneficial to take breaks periodically, try to avoid overextensive breaks as it can be difficult to reconnect with your thinking and re-engage with the project when you return to it. As your research takes shape and you become increasingly immersed in it, you naturally develop an overall sense of 'how it works', how the pieces fit together and where it's going. Lengthy breaks can cause you to lose touch with this sense and it can take time to re-establish it. Sometimes it's impossible to do so, and you effectively end up approaching your research from a slightly different angle or perspective. While this need not necessarily be a problem, in many cases it has the potential to be one.

   Even more crucially, putting your project on hold for a long period of time can result in it getting overtaken by developments in the field and becoming redundant and irrelevant.

- Try to maintain other interests that allow you to switch off briefly but on a regular basis. Physical activities such as sports are particularly good in this respect as they not only provide an excellent distraction but also help maintain your physical health, which in turn impacts positively on your mental health, and stress levels in particular.

- Keep calm, don't panic and keep faith with yourself. Don't lose confidence just because you come up against what might seem to be an insurmountable problem in your research. While you certainly need to be critical of what you are doing, don't automatically assume that the problem and the difficulty of solving it are the result of your own shortcomings. Chances are that you have identified a genuine problem that would present a challenge for anyone.

- Try to establish and maintain a close working relationship with your supervisor; after all, they are the person who will probably have the best understanding of what it is you are doing and the difficulties you are facing, and who will therefore be well positioned to both empathise and, where necessary, sympathise! We will look in more detail at your supervisor's role ➡ on page 20.

- Use all of the support mechanisms at your disposal. Although you supervisor should be a key source of support for you, there will be others to whom you can turn: your family, fellow research students within your own or other departments, research seminar groups, special interest groups, university support services and support groups that you and your fellow researchers may have set up on your own initiative. Conferences can also prove useful events for networking with those who have similar research interests and for gaining clarification on issues and ideas. Furthermore, they can also serve as useful sounding boards for your own ideas.

- Try to be as efficient as possible by actively managing your commitments. This way, you feel in control of things even if at times you are under pressure from various quarters.

- Try to 'read your way out of trouble' by searching appropriate literature for how others have approached the same or similar problems.

- Do not look too far down the road as this can result in you feeling overwhelmed with the size of the project. Set specific proximal goals and learn to think in terms of 'what will I accomplish today?'

- Try to create a good study environment (e.g. a study room at home) or identify one (e.g. a favourite area in a library).

- Study with another person for 2–3 hours. During this time, each of you may well be focused on your own work; nevertheless, many people feel that the presence of the other person makes studying more enjoyable and less daunting. After finishing studying, you can then spend an hour socialising over coffee or tea.

Activity 1.2 Different challenges you will face and strategies for dealing with them

Think about your own personality and circumstances. What are some of the intellectual, emotional, motivational and organisational challenges you will be susceptible to during the course of your research? List them in the table opposite, along with some strategies that you believe will help you address those challenges.

Intellectual challenges	Strategies
1	
2	
3	
Emotional challenges	Strategies
1	
2	
3	
Motivational challenges	Strategies
1	
2	
3	
Organisational challenges	Strategies
1	
2	
3	

BECOMING A MEMBER OF AN ACADEMIC COMMUNITY

As we've seen, becoming a member of an academic community can be an important means of support during the course of your research. When we talk about an 'academic community' we are referring to a number of different groups or 'communities'. Of course, once you become a student you become part of a large academic community of students studying undergraduate and postgraduate degrees, as well as other non-degree courses such as diplomas. However, as a research student there may be a number of other groups you may well have access to and which can be a rich source of information and support. Let's now look briefly at some of these.

Research seminars and conferences

Most departments that offer research degrees also hold research seminars. Although these are primarily, and sometimes only, open to students doing research degrees, occasionally they are open to all members of the academic department concerned – and sometimes, though less commonly, even other departments. The purpose of these seminars is usually to provide a forum where research students are able to talk about their research or, indeed, other issues in the field. Students often present their research, or certain aspects of it, either as a way of clarifying their own thinking (it's difficult to explain something to others unless it's first clear in your own mind) or in order to benefit from the feedback of seminar participants. In the first section, we listed the inability to identify a suitable research topic and focus as one of the problems students frequently face; well, research seminars can also be a rich source of ideas for research projects.

Similarly, conferences can be excellent places to get connected with others in your field, and particularly those interested in areas related to the focus of your research. They are also places where you can share ideas, either informally through casual interactions with others, or more formally via presentations. Those ideas may be things you are mulling over or considering incorporating into your research, and a conference audience can be a very valuable sounding board and a source of inspiration and new directions you may not have previously considered. In fact, it is at professional conferences that many people first get the seed of an idea which they eventually grow into a fully-fledged thesis or dissertation.

Local chapters and special interest groups

Local chapters of professional bodies and special interest groups (SIGs) can also be excellent communities with which to become involved for very similar reasons. SIGs, as their name suggests, are much more focused in their interests, and provided you can identify a group that shares your particular interests, an association with them can be very fruitful and fulfilling.

Networking in person and on the internet

All the events and organisations we've looked at in this section are of course fora that provide opportunities for you to network with others in your field, some of whom will be engaged in their own research projects, and a few may even have interests very closely aligned with your own. The fact is that networking is a way of surrounding yourself with a community of broadly like-minded people. These can collectively or individually serve as a support mechanism when necessary and can help immerse you in your field of study and keep you engaged and switched on. They can stimulate new ideas, provoke new ways of looking at problems and inform you of developments or resources of which you may be unaware.

In this age of the internet and virtual learning environments, the way in which research is conducted has changed quite radically – a fact we shall return to at various points in this book. One of the great benefits of this technology is that it allows us to communicate with one another very quickly, even instantaneously, at the click of a button. And with software such as Skype and MSN we can do these things very cheaply indeed. We can use email to contact people on the other side of the world and expect a response within a day or two, if not hours or even minutes. We can set up conference calls with half a dozen individuals and create a truly interactive environment, much like we would experience in a regular, 'terrestrial' seminar. The long and short of it is that these new technologies provide, as never before, the means to become connected with other individuals and groups who share your research interests and with whom you can build useful dialogues and professional friendships that can prove valuable in numerous ways. They may be sources of new contacts, conduits of useful information, paths to new research subjects or references, and sounding boards.

Creating a support group

All of the individuals, groups, organisations and events we've mentioned in this section can play an important role in supporting you in your research. However, you may also choose to set up your own research group in order to discuss issues of importance to your own project. Members of that group will probably, though not necessarily, be individuals who are working in a similar area and who will benefit both intellectually and emotionally from each other. Groups of this kind can regularly 'get together' online, as discussed above, or in person – every week or month, say.

Activity 1.3 Support networks to help you become part of an academic community

Take a few moments to consider carefully your own situation. List below some of the ways in which you personally can become part of an academic community. What support networks do you have available to you, or which might you be able to initiate?

1	
2	
3	
4	
5	
6	

CHOOSING AND WORKING WITH YOUR SUPERVISOR

If you are working on a thesis, your choice of supervisor is one of the most critical decisions you will have to make. Why? Because it can make or break your research and the sense of enjoyment and satisfaction you derive from the entire process of conducting it. In order to fully understand why this decision is so crucial, let's now look at what a supervisor's role consists of, some of the factors you will want to consider when selecting a suitable supervisor, and some of things that can go wrong in the supervisor–supervisee relationship.

The supervisor's role

The role of a supervisor is essentially supportive in nature. They are there to stimulate you, to keep you on the straight and narrow, and to provide encouragement during difficult periods when you may face challenges of the kind discussed in an earlier section (➡ see p. 8). Their role is not to lead you but to advance your own thinking by challenging your ideas, suggesting other avenues of enquiry or argument, and provoking you into thinking about things in alternative ways. They can also be a valuable repository of information and well positioned to direct you to relevant literature as well as potentially helpful professional connections – both individuals and institutions.

It is expected that you will meet with your supervisor periodically to discuss your work and any progress made, to talk through any difficulties, and to obtain their feedback. It's quite common, prior to the supervision, for students to submit any written work they may have done in order to give their supervisor the opportunity to review it. That piece of work and the supervisor's response to it then constitutes a stepping off point for the discussion.

How often supervisions take place will depend on a number of factors including the following:

- *The nature of the project itself.* If a project is intellectually demanding or particularly original – in its methodology, say – you may well need to meet with your supervisor more frequently in order to work through problems and discuss ways of overcoming unforeseen obstacles.
- *The stage your project is at.* If you are in the process of collecting your data, for example, you may have little need to meet with your supervisor.
- *Your level of self-confidence.* Students who lack self-confidence or who are cautious by nature may appreciate the guidance and reassurance that can come from supervisions; consequently, they tend to schedule them more often. In contrast, those with a good deal of self-confidence may well only feel the need to meet with their supervisors once every few months.
- *Your personal style of working.* Some people relish autonomy and are quite happy to 'go it alone' until they run into a snag. At that point, they may feel it's time to schedule a meeting with their supervisor.
- *Your supervisor's availability.* Your supervisor may have limited availability. A busy schedule may mean that meetings with you may have to be fairly infrequent affairs – a point we shall look at in more detail below.
- *The physical distance between you.* Particularly in these days of quick and easy electronic communication, it's not uncommon for students to live in one country whilst being enrolled in a department located in another country. In extreme cases, where a student is jointly supervised by two academics from different institutions,

personalities are compatible; indeed, this is arguably as important as your supervisor's intellectual prowess. Although there have doubtless been numerous cases where personality incompatibilities or clashes have existed and students successfully gone on to complete their research and receive their degrees regardless, this is not an ideal scenario. Ideally, you should feel at ease with your supervisor and enjoy a good working relationship that brings satisfaction and enjoyment to both of you.

■ *Their interest in you and your project.* If your supervisor is to inspire, motivate and support you, they will need to have a genuine interest in you, your success and your project. Remember: being qualified to supervise a project does not necessarily mean being particularly interested in that project and in you and your success as an individual. Although, for the most part, supervisors select their supervisees because of who they are and because they have a real interest in their research proposal, in a few cases departmental pressures can mean that academics sometimes feel obliged to supervise projects they might not necessarily take on in other circumstances. You, of course, won't know this and will therefore have to judge as best you can their level of genuine interest in what you are doing. Even before you submit a proposal, therefore, try to meet them to discuss your project and get a sense of how well they respond to you and your line of research.

■ *Their professional profile.* Although Bachelors and Masters level students may automatically be assigned a tutor or supervisor for their research studies, PhD students normally select their own supervisor and will often opt for an individual with a strong national or international reputation. While there can be real advantages to doing this, there can also be disadvantages, and it's important to be aware of these. The table below highlights some of the possible advantages and disadvantages of having a high-profile supervisor. As will be apparent, one of the downsides is that your supervisor may often be away and unable to respond to you at short notice. Even if they are able to respond to you, it may be that they are not in a position to offer you a supervision when you would like; in other words, they may have fewer free slots in their diary than might otherwise be the case with a less high-profile supervisor. This can be frustrating, especially if you've reached an impasse in your work and need help in getting past it.

You will have to decide, then, whether the potential advantages of working with an academic heavyweight outweigh the possible disadvantages. In making this decision your own personality and working style should be a factor. As we've seen, some people are more confident than others and perfectly content to work more autonomously without having recourse to the kind of support a supervisor can offer, whereas others can feel a need for and thrive on that support. Furthermore, certain kinds of research either minimise the need for contact with a supervisor or involve certain periods where there is little to be gained from such contact. This may be the case, for example, with an empirical study in which the data collection is a slow, time-consuming process – for example, where fieldwork

Advantages and disadvantages of a high-profile supervisor

Advantages

- High-profile supervisors will often have considerable and wide-ranging knowledge which often extends beyond their own discipline.
- They will often have an extensive knowledge of the literature and therefore be well positioned to refer you to relevant works.
- Because of their knowledge, they will be especially able to identify links between ideas both within and across disciplines.
- Their knowledge and substantial experience of supervising can result in wonderfully stimulating and energising supervisions and a generally rewarding 'research experience'.
- They will probably be well placed to put you in contact with other academics who may be of help to you and your research.
- Once you have completed your research and (hopefully) been awarded your degree, your association with your supervisor may well add weight to your degree and serve to help increase your academic career and professional standing.
- Often, supervisors serve as referees for their students, who may be applying for jobs or for promotions. A good reference from a well-respected academic can be very influential indeed.

Disadvantages

- High-profile academics tend to be very busy – this is almost certainly the reason for and the result of their success.
- High-profile academics are often in demand. They frequently travel nationally and internationally due to conferences (they are often invited as plenary speakers), requests to deliver courses at other institutions (for weeks, perhaps, or even months) and numerous projects with which they are likely to be involved.
- They may take a sabbatical (a period of academic leave) in order to finish writing a book, for example.
- Some well-known academics are so busy and distracted that it's difficult for them to keep track of everything – including your project – and to give you and it the attention you might wish and which it deserves.

might take a few months, or in a longitudinal study which follows the development of a phenomenon over two or three years.

TIP Longitudinal studies tend not to be a popular choice for both students and supervisors because, by their very nature, they take a long time to complete and there is a greater risk of problems occurring.

Finally, while you may know who you want to supervise your research, it may be that the individual you request is unable or unwilling to supervise *you*! They may already be supervising many students and feel unable to take on an additional one.

Alternatively, they may feel that the subject of your particular project is not one in which they have the requisite expertise. They may even be concerned that the physical distance between you would hamper their ability to give you the kind of support they would wish. There are, in fact, numerous reasons why a supervisor may feel unable to take you on as their student; however, that shouldn't stop you from approaching them and sounding them out, even before you have a fully-fledged proposal.

Joint supervisions

Joint supervisions refer to an arrangement where two people supervise your research. This is an option you may wish to consider and tends to arise in the following circumstances:

- The supervisor you request feels unable to take you on due to their workload and other commitments. In this situation they may compromise and agree to jointly supervise you, either as the primary or secondary supervisor.
- The subject of your research may span two disciplines and a single supervisor may therefore not have the necessary expertise in both disciplines to provide you with adequate support.
- You may be moving regularly between two countries and feel you need a supervisor in both. Alternatively, your supervisor may feel that there is another academic overseas who could bring useful expertise to your project and they may therefore recommend a joint supervision.

Many people feel that unless absolutely necessary, joint supervisions are not ideal. Both supervisors need to be kept informed of what is going on and, if possible, keep in touch with one another so as to ensure that they are 'singing from the same hymn sheet'. Problems can also arise if the two supervisors have different perspectives on issues – something that can be confusing and frustrating for all concerned, and particularly the supervisee. On the other hand, when they work well, joint supervisions can provide a very rich learning experience for the supervisee and bring considerable and wide-ranging expertise to a research project.

What can go wrong in the supervisor–supervisee relationship

Occasionally, problems occur in the supervisor–supervisee relationship. This may be the result of a clash of personalities, a major disagreement over the direction your research is taking, dissatisfaction with the amount and/or quality of support you are receiving, or even a fundamental and irreconcilable difference of perspective over a theoretical question or issue. Whatever the reason, you are always at liberty to request a change of supervisor and should not hesitate to take up this option if you no longer feel comfortable with the relationship. After all, it is your time, research and money that are at stake, and if you are not happy this may be reflected in the time taken to complete your research, the enjoyment you derive from doing it, and the quality of the final product.

Activity 1.4 Considering the best supervisor for you

Think about your own personality, your needs and vulnerabilities, your strengths, your personal circumstances, and the nature of the research you are intending to undertake. Describe them as a series of bullet points below. Then, in light of the information presented in this section, consider what type of supervisor would best be able to support you during the course of your research, and why. If possible, try also to think of a particular individual under whose guidance you might feel comfortable working.

My situation:

_____

_____

_____

_____

My ideal supervisor: _____

My reasons: _____

_____

Name of supervisor: _____

THE UPGRADING PROCESS

If you are commencing a PhD, it's very common for a university or individual department to require you, initially, to register as an MPhil student. At a point in your research, normally decided by you in consultation with your supervisor, you will need to go through an 'upgrading' process. This involves being examined or interviewed about your project by a small committee of academics, typically within the same department. The interview is normally fairly informal and conducted in a constructive spirit and in the presence of your supervisor, who may contribute to the discussion. When you choose to upgrade is normally determined by the stage you have reached in your research. When you apply to upgrade you will normally be expected to have your project fully mapped out, to have made some progress in the conduct of your research, and ideally (though not necessarily), have written some of the thesis itself – on the understanding, of course, that this may well change before the thesis is finally submitted in its full form.

The upgrading process exists primarily for your benefit. Most importantly, it forces you to reflect on your project and consider whether your vision for it remains clear and focused, and whether you are happy with the direction it is taking and the progress you have made. During the interview, you will be asked about the project and alerted to potential problems and weaknesses. The purpose here is to check whether you have a good grip on the project, to highlight its strengths and to offer advice about how you can improve it and avoid potential pitfalls. The discussion that takes place can, therefore, be very useful not only to you personally but also to your supervisor, who may also benefit from issues raised and, as a result, be even better placed to support you subsequently. In essence, then, upgrading is a way of evaluating your progress to date and your ability to see the project through to a successful conclusion. This is important for both you and your supervisor and department. For you, a well-received upgrade report on your research, along with a good interview, can be very reassuring by confirming the direction in which you are heading and the quality of the research so far. On the other hand, it can sound alarm bells by identifying serious flaws in your project and/or by casting serious doubt on your ability to conduct research at this level and to bring your thesis to fruition as required. The possibility that you will not be permitted to continue with your research is an essential and valuable part of the process – if an unwelcome one – in that it can save you and the department time and money by cutting losses at a fairly early stage in your research, and spare you from even greater disappointment later on.

There are three possible outcomes of the upgrading process as shown in the box.

Three possible outcomes of the upgrading process

1 The project is given a clean bill of health, along with suggestions for improvements, alerts to possible weaknesses and ideas for addressing those weaknesses. Upon the recommendation of the examiner, the university registry will then enrol you as a PhD student.

2 There are major concerns expressed over the project and you are required to address these as best you can and reapply for an upgrade once you feel confident that the problems identified have been adequately addressed.

3 It is felt that the project is not salvageable and/or you are not capable of completing a PhD. However, this does not necessarily mean you go away empty-handed, having achieved nothing. In these circumstances, rather than terminate your enrolment altogether, the committee may well give you the opportunity to recast your work as an M.Phil submission. It will then be examined according to the criteria for M.Phil degrees. The conditions under which the upgrading committee will offer this option are generally twofold:

- The research project is reasonably sound conceptually but, in light of its initial development, is seen as unlikely to have the scope and depth necessary to justify the award of a PhD degree.
- The project has the potential to produce a good PhD thesis, but it is felt that the researcher lacks the ability to take it forward and develop it to the extent required and expected of a PhD.

Following your interview, a report is submitted by the committee summarising key issues discussed and recommending one of these three options.

Hopefully, you will successfully upgrade and your research will be the better for having been subjected to close scrutiny. Having gone through the process, most students experience an increased confidence and enthusiasm that helps carry them through the following stages of their project.

2 ▶ PREPARING YOUR RESEARCH

This chapter looks at a number of tasks that you will need to consider before beginning to write your dissertation or thesis. Proper planning is the key to avoiding unnecessary problems later on, enjoying the writing process and producing a high-quality final product. The two primary aspects of proper planning concern educating yourself about the university regulations that you must follow and then carefully selecting a topic and a strategy for investigating that topic.

The chapter will cover:

- familiarity with your university's rules and regulations
- ethical considerations
- deciding on a research topic
- identifying a gap in the literature
- generating research questions and research hypotheses
- deciding on the research approach.

USING THIS CHAPTER

INTRODUCTION

Many dissertation and thesis writers are so focused on conducting their study and writing up their results that they fail to pay attention to what is arguably the most important part of the entire process: the planning, thinking and preparation that should be devoted to designing a worthwhile study. Careful and detailed planning is an integral part of any professional research endeavour, because to do otherwise is to rely on either good fortune or the skills of another person, and neither of those options will allow you to maximise your learning. The main purpose of this chapter is to get you thinking about issues that will exert a powerful influence on the quality and value of your project and that should be understood and/or decided before you begin gathering data.

FAMILIARITY WITH YOUR UNIVERSITY'S RULES AND REGULATIONS

It is important that you become familiar early on with the rules and regulations of the university or institution in which you are studying because obeying the rules will help ensure a smooth and trouble-free experience, while wittingly or unwittingly breaking these rules can result in unnecessary problems that can take your attention away from where it should be – on your dissertation or thesis. It's important to understand that the rules and regulations are rarely just the creation of some administrator's mind – quite the contrary – they are nearly always based on years of experience working with many professors and students, and are generally designed to keep students on track, minimise unnecessary problems and keep the quality of the final product at a professional level.

Rules and regulations often cover the following issues:

- who can act as your supervisor
- when you should choose a supervisor
- when to form a proposal committee
- who can serve on the proposal committee
- examinations (e.g. oral preliminary examinations) that must be taken
- when and to whom a research proposal should be submitted
- when and where to present your thesis for your oral defence (viva)
- the amount of time you have to complete any rewrites specified by your committee
- formatting rules for all written products, but especially for the thesis (e.g. the width of margins, the formatting of headings, referencing style, page numbering, figures and tables).

TIP Once you're accepted into a programme, be sure to inquire about your university's rules and regulations for dissertation and thesis writers. Get a copy of the rules and regulations, read them and ask about any areas that are unclear.

Let's look at two short examples to see what form these rules can take. The University of London regulations for a BA degree in Philosophy state that:

> The dissertation to be normally of 5,000 words in length, with a maximum of 7,500 words. It is to be on a subject selected by the candidate and approved by his/her supervisor, and is to be written by the candidate in his/her final year. Two copies should be submitted by the first Monday in the April preceding the final examinations.

An important point to note here is that the dissertation topic must be approved by the supervisor. As this regulation is virtually universal, it's almost a certainty that you will need approval for your topic. If you have adopted a topic proposed by your supervisor, this step will be fast and smooth. However, if it's your responsibility (or you have the autonomy) to select a topic, you should start on this task right away because identifying a topic that both you and your supervisor are satisfied with can be time-consuming and include several failed attempts before you arrive at a mutually-acceptable choice. Giving yourself plenty of time to identify a good topic is also important because you have a greater chance of enjoying the dissertation-writing process and producing a high-quality final product if you identify a topic that truly captures your interest.

Let's look at one more example. Cambridge University's Department of Social Anthropology summarises some of its key regulations as follows:

- Be thinking about your plans for a dissertation during your Part IIA year
- Topic: should not duplicate material on which you will be examined
- Length: 10,000 words excluding footnotes, appendices and bibliography
- Deadline for submission of title: last day of Full Michaelmas term of final year
- Final deadline for revised titles: last Faculty Board of the Lent term
- Deadline for submission of dissertation: second Friday of the Easter term

As you can see from both of these examples, a number of important issues, such as when to seriously consider a topic, permissible topics, dissertation length and deadlines for submission, are clearly stated. It's crucial that you're aware of these rules and that you follow them because failure to do so can jeopardise all of your hard work and effort.

Activity 2.1 Rules and regulations governing dissertations at your university

Gather information about the regulations governing dissertations and theses in your major field of study. Then, summarise your answers to the following questions on a separate piece of paper.

- When should you begin to focus on your dissertation?
- What topics are permissible?
- How can you select an advisor?
- Do you need to submit a proposal? If so, when?
- What is an acceptable length for the dissertation?
- When must you submit the final dissertation?
- What formatting style is appropriate?
- What are the other important issues?

ETHICAL CONSIDERATIONS

Ethical issues are an important part of conducting research and cannot be ignored. Your participants have rights that must be protected and you can best do this by consulting the guidelines for the ethical treatment of research participants that are enforced by the human subjects committee at the university you're attending. The following are general guidelines that are applied at most institutions, so they will give you an idea of some of the issues you may need to consider:

- Obtain permission from appropriate people in order to gain access to your participants. For instance, minors will probably need parental consent to participate in your study.
- Let the participants know that their participation is voluntary and that they have a right not to participate.
- Let the participants know that they have the right to ask questions about the study and their role in the study.
- Inform your participants about the purposes of the study.
- Don't allow your participants to experience physical or emotional distress as a result of participating in your study.
- Protect the confidentiality of all data that you gather.
- Don't divulge the identity of anyone in your study. Use pseudonyms or identification numbers rather than the participants' real names.
- Offer to inform the participants of the results of the study.

If you use a written consent form, consider placing a copy in an appendix to your dissertation so that readers can see exactly what the participants agreed to. If you don't have a written consent form, describe what you told the participants verbally. This information is usually placed in the *Participants* section of your dissertation or thesis.

TIP You should find out whether your university has a human subjects committee and what ethical guidelines you need to follow early in the research process. In many institutions, you cannot conduct your study until the human subjects committee has given you a green light to proceed.

In general, the safest approach is to produce a consent form and have your participants read and sign that form before beginning to gather data. In this way, there will be no question whether the participants understood their rights and the nature of your study from the outset. This can protect you, your supervisor and your university from future problems. Some basic aspects of a consent form are as follows:

- Briefly describe your study in easy-to-understand terms that will make sense to your participants.
- Summarise the objectives of the study.
- Describe the procedures you will use.
- Explain any physical or psychological discomfort that the participants may experience.
- Explain how you will keep their participation confidential.
- Inform them about what will happen to their data once the study is finished.
- Explain the benefits they will receive by participating (e.g. monetary payment and/or a copy of the results of the study).
- Verbally ask if they have any questions or concerns.
- Indicate where the participants can direct any questions or concerns that they feel have not been satisfactorily addressed by you. This will usually be the university human subjects committee or your advisor.
- If the person agrees to participate, have them sign and date the consent form.

When writing the consent form, it's a good idea to check the readability of the form using the readability statistics option built into many modern word-processing software programs. Remember that the consent form is not supposed to be an impressive-sounding academic document. Its purpose is to inform your participants of the nature of your research in a simple and comprehensible way. When dealing with adults, you should aim to write at a level that a GCSE (or similar level) student would understand. (Remember that the readability statistics will provide you with the reading grade level of your document.) This will permit all of the participants to comprehend quickly and easily the information on the form and will therefore minimise misunderstandings and possible problems as the study unfolds.

Activity 2.2 Research ethics policies at your university

Gather information about the research ethics committee at your university and the policies for protecting research participants that are used in your major field of study. On a separate piece of paper, summarise the key policies as they apply to you in the left-hand column of a copy of the table below. Add your comments in the right-hand column.

When I conduct my study I need to . . .	Comments

IDENTIFYING A GAP IN THE LITERATURE

After familiarising yourself with your institution's rules and regulations for dissertation and thesis writers and learning about the ethical considerations that you must employ, you'll be in a good position to begin thinking about the study itself. While reading the literature in your field of study – and you should read widely – you should be searching for areas in need of further study. Because the value of any study lies in its contribution to our knowledge of a particular area, you should strive to show clearly how the previous research is conflicting or lacking in some way. This lack is commonly called a 'gap' in the literature. The gap should flow naturally and clearly from your understanding of the literature and the current state of knowledge about the topic. As you identify gaps in the literature, ask yourself how important they are, why they are important and worthy of investigation, and the benefits of studying that area further. You will need to make a persuasive argument for the importance of the issue that you have decided to study, as it will become the *raison d'être* for your study.

The following are five types of gaps that you can look for:

1 *Knowledge-based.* This is the most common type of gap. It occurs when we don't know about a phenomenon or don't know enough about it.

2 *Relationship-based.* This type of gap occurs when we know about certain issues or variables reasonably well, but we are unsure of their relationships to one another.

3 *Theory-based.* In this type of gap, a theory or an aspect of a theory has not been investigated thoroughly, or the theory has not been tested in a particular context or with a particular group of individuals.

4 *Methodological.* In this type of gap, previous researchers have not applied a particular research design or research methodology in their investigations of a

particular phenomenon. In this case, you would need to make clear the advantages of the design or methodology.

5 *Analytical.* The phenomenon hasn't been investigated using a particular analytical approach. In this case, you would need to explain the advantages of the analytical approach. While a new analytical approach is often some sort of advanced statistical technique, it can also mean the opposite. For instance, in an area where previous researchers have predominantly used quantitative approaches, conducting a qualitative study will provide new forms of data and new ways to analyse that data.

TIP Although identifying a gap is desirable, basing your study entirely on a perceived gap in the literature cannot be the only criterion you use, as there is always the danger that you design a study that addresses a relatively trivial gap. As a result, any gaps in the literature that you identify must be evaluated in terms of their importance to theory and/or practice, their meaningfulness to others in the field, and their applicability to other contexts (➡see also Chapter 1, page 3).

Activity 2.3 Identifying the gaps

What gaps are you currently aware of in the field in which you are studying? While you can answer this question using your own knowledge of the field, it would also be a good idea to talk to your colleagues, fellow students and/or your professors about their ideas, as they will almost certainly be able to provide you with ideas that you not have thought of on your own. Try to list at least five topics using the categories below to help you.

Knowledge-based gaps: _____

_____

Relationship-based gaps: _____

_____

Theory-based gaps: _____

_____

Methodological gaps: _____

_____

Analytical gaps: _____

_____

In addition to a gap, an intellectual controversy or paradox can be a worthwhile area on which to focus your efforts. For instance, one major intellectual controversy concerns disagreements between scientists and philosophers who subscribe to a theory sometimes called traditional or classical objectivism, and those who are sometimes labelled deconstructionists or postmodernists. The first group takes the traditional position that truth, reason and knowledge exist in philosophy, science and history, while the second group frequently denies the existence of truth, reason and knowledge. While this is a major intellectual controversy in academia today, you may choose to focus on a more limited controversy in your field of study. Regardless of the breadth of the controversy, you might find jumping into the middle of a contentious issue exhilarating. If this idea suits your personality, you may wish to discuss the possibility with your advisor.

Activity 2.4 Analysing controversy

What are three intellectual controversies in your field? On what issue do the different parties disagree? What are the basic positions of each side? What are the strengths and weaknesses of each side? Make notes on these three controversies on a separate sheet of paper.

DECIDING ON A RESEARCH TOPIC

As noted above, choosing a topic that 'fits' you is one of the most important steps in the entire dissertation writing process, as your work will generally be of much higher quality when you have a genuine interest in your topic and the knowledge and resources available to do a good job on that topic. For some people, identifying a topic is quite fast and easy, but that's certainly not the norm; instead, you should be prepared to engage in a *process* in which you consider multiple possibilities, and after much thought and discussion, eventually reject all but one. Possible topics can be found in a number of places. First, consider the gaps and intellectual controversies that you've listed in the activities above. Secondly, your supervisor or other academics in the department may have suggestions. Thirdly, other students in the same programme, and particularly those who are already writing dissertations, may be able to tell you about ideas that they considered and rejected. Simply because they didn't use the topic, doesn't mean that it's a poor choice. Indeed, you may spot an interesting angle to the topic that they missed! Yet another excellent place to identify good candidate topics is when you're reading articles in your subject area. Some bit of information in the article may spark an idea or the writer may make suggestions for future research. You might use these suggestions 'as is' or adapt and improve them.

You should avoid the tendency to choose a topic that is very broad or complex; it's better to do a limited study well than a large-scale study poorly. One thing that's true for nearly all dissertation and thesis writers is that they're surprised at how much time the project requires. Projects of this size take more time and energy than you predict simply because the number of unanticipated challenges and details that have to be considered and then handled is so large.

Once you've identified several possible topics, you may want to rate them using some or all of the following criteria:

- the topic is interesting to me
- the topic is acceptable to my advisor
- the topic is not considered trivial by experts in the field
- the topic is researchable because it is reasonably well-focused
- my perspective on the topic is (reasonably) original
- the topic has important implications for theory development
- the topic has important implications for practitioners
- the topic has important implications for research methodology
- there are no ethical problems connected with researching the topic.

Activity 2.5 Rating five possible research topics

List five topics that you're considering researching and rate them on the four criteria listed in the table using the following scale: 1 = poor; 2 = so-so; 3 = good; 4 = very good. Add up the total scores to see how they compare with one another. Then extend the table by adding two or three more criteria that are important to you, rate the topics once again, and see if the order has changed.

Topic	Interesting to me	Acceptable to my advisor	Important for theory or practice	Appropriately focused
1				
2				
3				
4				
5				

Activity 2.6 Refining your top two topics

After completing Activity 2.5, take your two highest-rated topics and work with them further by asking questions such as, 'How can I refine the study to make it more satisfying, more important, and stronger?' Then, using the same criteria listed in Activity 2.5, rate the topics once again.

	Candidate topic 1	Candidate topic 2
How can I make the project more satisfying?		
How can I make the project more important?		
How can I minimise weaknesses?		

The key idea to take away from these activities is that really good studies are generally not formulated quickly and easily; they are the product of reading, discussing, drafting, thinking and rethinking. Allow yourself time to go through this process because time spent carefully planning and designing the study will pay off down the road. Be discriminating – don't settle on a topic until you feel comfortable with it, understand it reasonably well, and you and your supervisor are confident that it is a solid foundation upon which you can build a good study. Finally, regardless of the topic that you select, it's crucial that you feel a sense of ownership of that topic. If you're to do really outstanding work, you need to 'make the topic yours' and put your personal imprint on the study.

GENERATING RESEARCH QUESTIONS AND RESEARCH HYPOTHESES

Once you've decided on a general topic to research, you need to generate a list of possible research questions and/or research hypotheses, unless you're going to conduct a very exploratory type of study. As a first step, you might answer general questions such as those listed in Activity 2.7 on the next page. Note that although some of these questions are very similar to one another, the changes in wording can make you think about the issue from a somewhat different angle, and that is what you want at this stage of the research process.

Activity 2.7 Generating research questions

Consider your research topic and briefly note your answers to the following questions.

Question	Answer
What would I like to know about this topic?	
What aspects of the current literature are unconvincing to me?	
What aspects of the current literature are most interesting to me?	
What do theoreticians want to know about this topic?	
What do practitioners want to know about this topic?	
How can I extend my knowledge of this topic?	
What do I not yet know about this topic?	
What are some controversial issues related to this topic?	

Yet another way to generate research questions involves using classical categories such as definition, description, classification, compare and contrast, and cause and effect. Let's look at some examples of research questions created using these categories:

Definition

How is *X* defined? How might I elaborate on this definition? What is missing in this definition? How might I define *X* in relation to *Y*? How might I define *X* in different contexts?

Example from the literature: *What is a question?* (Graesser and Person, 1994)

Classification

What class does *X* belong to? Does it *not* belong to that class in any sense? What other things are in or not in that class?

Example from the literature: *Should perfectionism be a characteristic of gifted individuals?* (Mendaglio, 2007)

Compare and contrast

How is *X* similar to *Y*? How is *X* different from *Y*? Is *X* more similar to *Y* or *Z*?

Example from the literature: *Do gender differences account for differences in these assessments?* (Ruismäki and Tereska, 2008)

Cause and effect

What causes *X*? What does *X* cause? Is *X* a more important cause of *Y* than *Z*? Is *X* a direct or indirect cause of *Y*?

Example from the literature: *Does economic development help to shorten the length of rivalry (between countries)?* (Prins and Daxecker, 2007)

We can also usefully add the categories of relationship, time and stability to the list.

Relationship

What is the relationship between *X* and *Y*?

Example from the literature: *Might relationships between liberal institutions and rivalry termination be non-linear?* (Prins and Daxecker, 2007)

Time

How does *X* change over time? Is *X* different at different points in time?

Example from the literature: *Where longitudinal data are available, how do average student understandings change over two-, four-, or six-year periods?* (Watson et al., 2006)

Stability

How stable is *X* across factors such as gender, culture, age and socio-economic status? Does the degree of stability vary across different factors, i.e. is *X* more stable in one context than another?

Example from the literature: *Do the variables differ in terms of the amount of change from the beginning to the end of the course?* (Gardner et al., 2004)

If you generate broad questions that are interesting to you, think about how they can be broken down into more detailed, specific questions. Many studies are focused on a single main question that is investigated in greater detail using multiple sub-questions.

Once you have generated a list of possible questions, you should discuss them with other students, colleagues or your advisor, as they will probably have some valuable contributions to make. In addition, once you begin to settle on a set of research questions, take the time to explain to someone who knows about the area why you think they are important or interesting. Justifying your research questions to a knowledgeable person often leads to new questions and a refinement of your initial ideas.

Should you prefer to pose research hypotheses rather than research questions, you'll need to rewrite your questions as statements. If you use null hypotheses, you'll predict no difference between two or more treatments or groups (e.g. *There will be no difference between Groups A and B*), and if you use directional hypotheses, you'll predict which treatment will do better (e.g. *Groups A and B will outperform Group C*). Directional hypotheses are preferred because they show that you have thought about your topic sufficiently to make well-supported predictions. For instance, in a study of the influence of three types of conflict (task conflict, process conflict and relationship conflict) on perceptions of creativity, Kurtzberg and Mueller (2005: 335–6) posed the following hypotheses:

- Higher levels of task conflict will lead to lower levels of perceived creativity the same day.
- Higher levels of task conflict will lead to higher levels of perceived creativity the next day.
- Higher levels of process conflict will lead to lower levels of perceived creativity the same and next day.
- Higher levels of relationship conflict will lead to lower levels of perceived creativity the same and next day.

By presenting directional hypotheses, these authors clearly showed that they had thought about the variables in their study to a degree that allowed them to arrive at a reasoned understanding of the relationships between those variables *before* gathering and analysing their data. This brings up an important point when conducting many types of research: in most cases it is best to 'think first, and analyse second'. This means that you should first read and try to understand the variables and issues that are important in your study, and after carefully designing the study, gather data and then analyse and interpret those data. This approach allows you to avoid the tendency to 'go fishing' for answers because it puts you in the position of looking at your results in a confirmatory way; that is, the results confirm, partly confirm, or fail to confirm your *a priori* hypotheses.

DECIDING ON THE RESEARCH APPROACH

There are many ways to answer most research questions and the approach that you eventually adopt can depend on a number of factors, such as your personal preferences, your knowledge of research methodology, the time you have available to complete the study, and your advisors' preferences. It may also depend on whether you take a pragmatic approach and adopt the research approach that seems most appropriate for your topic or a more philosophical approach in which the choice of research method is dictated by a particular view of reality.

In the following sections, we'll take a look at three general research approaches that involve no data collection (philosophical inquiry), the collection of numerical data (quantitative approaches) and the collection of non-numerical data (qualitative approaches). A final approach, the mixed-methods approach, combines quantitative and qualitative approaches in a single study. In our opinion, all of the approaches are valid, though some are more appropriate than others for investigating certain questions, and all are used extensively throughout the social sciences.

Philosophical inquiry

As noted above, the first research approach, philosophical inquiry, is separate from quantitative and qualitative approaches because it does not involve the collection or analysis of any kind of data. It involves thinking critically about important issues in a field, creating new knowledge, generating new avenues for research, and challenging the status quo. Burbules and Warnick (2006) list 10 'methods' common to many papers in the field of education that fall under the heading of philosophical inquiry. These methods can be paraphrased as follows:

1 Analysing a term or concept in order to clarify its meaning.
2 Deconstructing a term or concept in order to show internal contradictions or ambiguities.
3 Bringing to light the assumptions underlying a particular view.
4 Reviewing an argument in a critical or supportive fashion.
5 Critically analysing a particular practice.
6 Proposing the purposes that should be achieved by a group of people or a social institution.
7 Considering alternative approaches or systems that challenge the current approach or system.
8 Analysing an imaginary situation in order to understand key variables in that situation.
9 Explaining a complex philosophical text or abstract concept.
10 Synthesising research from other fields in order to find meaning for a particular field.

As can be seen from the above list, this can be a particularly challenging type of research as the quality of the paper rests completely on the depth and clarity of the author's understanding of the issues that are being discussed and their ability to think in a logical and persuasive way. Look at the following abstract from an article in which the authors (Hodgkinson *et al.* 2008: 2) expound on the idea of intuition and their opinions about its place in the field of psychology.

The concept of intuition has, until recently, received scant scholarly attention within and beyond the psychological sciences, despite its potential to unify a number of lines of inquiry. Presently, the literature on intuition is conceptually underdeveloped and dispersed across a wide range of domains of application, from education, to management, to health. In this article, we clarify and distinguish intuition from related constructs, such as insight, and review a number of theoretical models that attempt to unify cognition and affect. Intuition's place within a broader conceptual framework that distinguishes between two fundamental types of human information processing is explored. We examine recent evidence from the field of social cognitive neuroscience that identifies the potential neural correlates of these separate systems and conclude by identifying a number of theoretical and methodical challenges associated with the valid and reliable assessment of intuition as a basis for future research in this burgeoning field of inquiry.

Hodgkinson *et al.* reveal their careful thinking about the topic in a number of phrases, including intuition's 'potential to unify a number of lines of inquiry', their intention to 'clarify and distinguish intuition from related constructs', and their review of literature that 'identifies the potential neural correlates of these separate systems'. It is also easy to sense how much the authors have read about the topic, as they are approaching the concept of intuition from a number of interesting angles.

Quantitative approaches

As mentioned above, quantitative approaches are classified as such because they involve gathering and analysing numerical data. In the social sciences, quantitative approaches have been dominant for several decades, in part because of their aura of scientific rigour and clarity. One disadvantage of this approach, however, is the amount of time necessary to receive training in test and survey design and statistical analyses, both of which are integral parts of most quantitative studies. In the following sub-sections, we will briefly outline the three main types of quantitative research: survey research, quasi-experimental studies and true experiments.

Survey research

Some simple types of quantitative research make use of a single intact group that is measured only once. While this may sound odd, it's actually very commonly used. For instance, many published studies in the social sciences are based on data collected using a questionnaire that was administered once to a single (large) group of people. While this approach can be very informative where descriptions of people and situations are sought and in investigations of attitudes and beliefs, it's not a good way to establish causality, as cause and effect relationships can only be convincingly established through experiments.

Survey research is an extremely popular form of research in the social sciences because researchers in these fields are often interested in what people believe about an issue (e.g. *Do you believe in life after death?*), their emotional reactions to various situations (*Which political candidate do you feel more positively about?*), and their opinions about people and events (*Do you agree with the new anti-pollution law?*). Survey research takes many different forms including questionnaires administered in paper-and-pencil format, questionnaires administered through the internet, one-on-one interviews, and focus-group interviews involving several respondents at the same time.

The following abstract by Bye *et al.* (2007: 141) illustrates how they used a questionnaire to investigate students' satisfaction with their university education.

This study compares affective and motivational components of academic life for traditional and non-traditional university undergraduates. Traditional students are defined as those aged 21 and younger, who are most likely to have followed an unbroken linear path through the education system, whereas non-traditional students are defined as those aged 28 and older, for whom the undergraduate experience is not necessarily age normative. A total of 300 undergraduates ranging in age from 18 to 60 years were assessed on measures of intrinsic and extrinsic motivation to learn, interest, and positive affect. Non-traditional students reported higher levels of intrinsic motivation for learning than did traditional students. Intrinsic motivation correlated with positive affect more strongly for non-traditional than for traditional students. For all students, interest and age emerged as significant predictors of intrinsic motivation to learn, and both interest and intrinsic motivation significantly predicted positive affect.

The key to success in survey research lies in carefully thinking about the study and producing a detailed plan of what variables to include in the survey and the exact items that will be used to measure those variables. Producing high-quality items is crucial because the dependability of the results depends entirely on the quality of the data produced by the items. It's also necessary to develop a clear plan of how the data will be analysed *before* the questionnaire is administered. This means that understanding the statistical analyses that will be used and their assumptions (e.g. the number of cases necessary to do the analysis properly) is absolutely necessary.

The advantages of administering written questionnaires are numerous, and this is why they are so commonly used in the social sciences. Among those advantages are:

- Large amounts of data can be gathered quickly.
- Various types of questions can be asked (e.g. questions answered using a rating scale and open-ended questions).
- Response rates are extremely high.
- The cost is very low.

- Photos, drawings and other visuals are easily included.
- Responses can be made on special computer mark sheets, so data entry is fast and easy.

Quasi-experiments

A quasi-experiment generally differs from a non-experiment in three ways. First, more than one group is involved. For instance, imagine a teacher who is conducting research with three classes of students that she teaches. Each class can act as a separate group in her study and this allows her to vary the treatment that the groups receive and then compare the results of the different treatments.

Secondly, quasi-experiments often include a control group that does not receive an experimental treatment. The advantage of including a control group is that it helps the researcher rule out many possible unknown and unknowable causes for their results. For example, if our teacher applied two vocabulary teaching techniques in her second and third classes, but not the first class (because it's the control group), she would expect the students in the second and third classes to show much more vocabulary learning than the students in the first class. If this is indeed the case, she can be reasonably sure that the students in her study did not receive any instruction or exposure to those words that she didn't know about in other classes or outside of school. In addition, she can be more certain that her second and third classes learned because of her vocabulary teaching treatment and not for a different reason.

The third difference is that it is possible to include a pre-test in a quasi-experimental study. The advantage of testing the participants before the experiment begins is that we can then be certain that they don't know what we plan on teaching them and that each group's (lack of) knowledge is similar. By knowing each group's starting point, we can get a clearer picture of how much they change as a result of our treatment.

The following abbreviated abstract from a study by Macaro and Masterman (2006) illustrates what one quasi-experimental study looked like.

This paper investigates the effect of explicit grammar instruction on grammatical knowledge and writing proficiency in first-year students of French at a UK university. Previous research suggests that explicit grammar instruction results in gains in explicit knowledge and its application in specific grammar-related tasks, but there is less evidence that it results in gains in production tasks. A cohort of 12 students received a course in French grammar immediately prior to their university studies in order to determine whether a short, but intensive burst of explicit instruction, a pedagogical approach hitherto unexamined in the literature, was sufficiently powerful to bring about an improvement in their grammatical knowledge and their performance in production tasks . . . Our results support previous findings that explicit instruction leads to gains in some aspects of grammar tests but not gains in accuracy in either translation or free composition.

This abstract displays some of the typical characteristics of quantitative studies: the research focus and important variables are clearly stated, the gap in the literature is identified, the hypothesis being tested is clarified, and the results are explicitly stated.

Although quasi-experimental studies are extremely common in the social sciences, they do have a major weakness – the participants are in intact groups (i.e. not randomised), and intact groups may differ a great deal in many ways that can affect the results of a study. For instance, what if one group is more intelligent or more motivated to learn? Obviously, this characteristic will strongly influence their performance and will make it impossible to know exactly to what degree the treatment affected the results. The solution to this problem is randomisation.

True experiments

As you are probably now aware, the primary difference between quasi-experiments and true experiments involves randomisation. When people are randomly assigned to different groups, we are much more confident that the groups are equal in all ways at the start of the experiment. As noted above, in the example of the vocabulary teaching study, the three classes of students might differ in many ways, and some of those ways might exert a strong effect on the results of the experiment. However, as you would imagine, if the groups are formed randomly, which means that each student has an equal chance of being in each of the three groups, we can probably get a clearer and more accurate idea of the effect of the vocabulary teaching technique used in the experiment because other differences among the groups are minimised. While true experiments are in the minority in some branches of the social sciences, such as education, they are quite common in other fields, such as psychology.

Let's look at part of the abstract from an article in which Tania Lombrozo (2007) reports on a true experiment:

What makes some explanations better than others? This paper explores the roles of simplicity and probability in evaluating competing casual explanations. Four experiments investigate the hypothesis that simpler explanations are judged both better and more likely to be true. In all experiments, simplicity is quantified as the number of causes invoked in an explanation, with fewer causes corresponding to simpler explanation. Experiment 1 confirms that all else being equal, both simpler and more probable explanations are preferred. Experiments 2 and 3 examine how explanations are evaluated when simplicity and probability compete. The data suggest that simpler explanations are assigned a high probability, with the consequence that disproportionate probabilistic evidence is required before a more complex explanation will be favored over a simpler alternative. . . . Finally, Experiment 4 finds that the preference for simpler explanations can be overcome when probability information unambiguously supports a complex explanation over a simpler alternative.

In this case, the author clearly identifies the multiple experiments that she conducted and the results for each one. The strength of this approach is that results from earlier experiments are further refined and tested in later experiments. The final conclusions are more valid and reliable because randomisation should have eliminated intergroup differences and she based those conclusions on multiple lines of evidence (i.e. the results of four experiments). The strength of conducting true experiments is that it is a proven approach that has been used successfully in many fields. Some researchers go so far as to say that the *only* way to conclusively determine cause and effect relationships is by conducting true experiments!

Qualitative approaches

Qualitative approaches to research involve measures that do not use numerical data. Examples are written documents, interview transcripts, observations of a person or situation and the field notes that they may generate, and video and audio recordings. Qualitative approaches are particularly well-suited when you are trying to generate new theories or hypotheses, achieve a deep understanding of a particular issue, present detailed narratives to describe a person or process, and as one component of a mixed-methods study. Examples of qualitative research include ethnographies, case studies, narratives, histories, biographies and non-participant observation. We will briefly take a look at the first three of these.

Ethnographies

Anderson-Levitt (2006: 279) defines ethnography as '. . . an approach to the study of people in everyday life with particular attention to culture, that is, to the processes through which people make (and sometimes impose or contest) meaning.' An ethnographic approach to research is useful when the researcher wishes to understand the meanings that various participants make in a particular situation. As such, ethnography can help us to understand some of the complexity that characterises any situation and the actions and lack of action by the participants in that situation. It's a good approach to adopt to answer questions such as: 'What is happening in this situation?', 'How does this event happen?' and 'What does the event mean to the people involved in the situation?' As ethnographers attempt to answer questions such as these, they focus not on their understanding of the situation, but rather on their participants' understanding. Thus, one of the primary goals is to understand how *insiders* make sense of their world. In order to accomplish this, many ethnographers spend a great deal of time with their participants, as this allows them to establish trust and rapport and to observe how processes unfold over time.

Let's look at part of the abstract of an ethnographic study conducted in Tanzania by Frances Vavrus (2005):

International economic forces increasingly affect policy at multiple levels and in multiple domains. The interplay of three levels – international, national, and local – are under-researched in the social and educational policy fields, which includes educational policy studies. In this article, Frances Vavrus employs ethnography to investigate how these interactions play out in a Chagga community in the Kilamanjaro region of Tanzania. She examines how the lives of

➡

secondary students in Tanzanian schools are affected by structural adjustment policies, adopted by Tanzania at the advice of the International Monetary Fund and the World Bank, in three domains: access to schooling, opportunities for employment, and the risk of HIV/AIDS infection. She makes a convincing case for the importance of understanding the local setting in the development of international and national policy, and for investigating the impact policy change in non-educational sectors has on educational realities.

Like many qualitative researchers, this author shows a strong concern for social issues and her study takes place in the 'real world' rather than in a laboratory or other contrived setting. Unlike experimental researchers, she has not manipulated any variables; her purpose is to investigate how variables at the international, national and local levels interact with one another naturally and to draw conclusions about their impact on the people in the specific area of Tanzania that she is researching. The strength of this type of study is the rich detail about the situation and the ways in which variables and persons interact in complex ways.

Case studies

Case studies can be defined as the intensive, in-depth study of a specific individual or specific context or situation. The real strength of the case study method is its potential to illuminate a 'case' in great depth and detail and to place that case in a 'real' context.

As Yin (2006: 112) stated: 'The case study method is best applied when research addresses descriptive or explanatory questions and aims to produce a firsthand understanding of people and events.' An example of a descriptive question is 'What process do teachers use when planning a course?' and two examples of explanatory questions (i.e. how and why questions) are 'How do teachers use informal meetings to improve instruction?' and 'Why did school principals oppose a new regulation in their school districts?'

Researchers conducting case studies must first define the case(s) that they're studying. For instance, a researcher might be interested in individuals who have learned to speak a foreign language to a very high level of proficiency in order to describe their learning histories and the learning strategies they applied. Once this first step has been accomplished, it is then necessary to do a *single-case study* of one individual or *multiple-case studies* of several individuals. Multiple-case studies can be especially interesting because they can be designed to highlight hypothesised similarities and/or hypothesised variations among cases. Finally, researchers using the case study approach must consider whether they will adopt a theoretical perspective that will guide their study from the outset or whether they will intentionally ignore current theory in the hope of discovering a new approach to the issue that they are studying.

Look at part of the abstract of a case study of a young Yemeni girl attending an American high school (Sarroub, 2001: 390). Notice that this study illustrates how two types of qualitative research can be combined in a single piece of research; the case study is embedded in a larger ethnographic study of a group of Yemeni girls.

In this article, Loukia Sarroub explores the relationships between Yemeni American high school girls and their land of origin. . . . Sarroub begins by providing historical background on Yemeni and Arab culture and international migration. Then, drawing upon a larger ethnographic study set in the Detroit, Michigan area, she presents a case study of one girl's experiences in the contexts of home, school, and community both in the United States and Yemen. Throughout the study, Sarroub makes thematic comparisons to the experiences of five other Yemeni American high school girls. She uses the notion of 'sojourner' to highlight the fact that many Yemenis 'remain isolated from various aspects of American life while maintaining ties to their homeland.' Sarroub describes the relationships between Yemen and the United States as social and physical 'spaces' from which high school girls' networks and identities emerge . . .

In this abstract, we can get a sense of how expansive this study is initially: the focus moves from Yemen to the USA and also includes the historical background of Arab migration to the west. The author then sharpens the focus to a single girl and her experiences moving between two very different cultures. This, then, is the primary strength of the case study approach; readers are able to understand a great many details of a single individual or situation and to see the world from the point of view of the participant(s) in the study.

Narratives

Narrative inquiry, which can be defined as 'the study of experience as story' (Connelly and Clandinin, 2007), is a relatively new approach to conducting research in the social sciences. The underlying justification for narrative inquiry is that people live and perceive their lives and make and interpret meaning in their lives in terms of 'stories' or narratives. Researchers applying the precepts of narrative inquiry use many types of data including stories, autobiographies, personal letters and journals, field notes, interviews, photos and other artifacts.

Narrative inquiry displays the characteristics of other types of qualitative methods in its emphasis on the individual and gaining a detailed understanding of the context that person is in, but it also places a special emphasis on temporality, sociality and place. Temporality concerns the idea that all people and events are in transition and that in order to understand the present, we must know something of the past. Sociality is important in narrative inquiry because all individuals exist in an immediate and extended social context. For instance, an employee in a company has an immediate context made up of persons such as superiors, subordinates, and co-workers, but that person is also affected by company executives who may be thousands of kilometres away, as well as the society in which the person lives. Finally, place is the specific location where the events studied by the researcher occur. Even when studying the same individual or event, the place can change numerous times.

For example, when examining the relationship between the employee and their superior, the workplace may be the key location in the narrative. However, if the focus is on the employee's attitude toward work, the key place may be organisations in which the person worked previously, as this may have been the site where the employee's present attitude evolved. In sum, narrative inquiry is one of the best ways to obtain a well-rounded, in-depth understanding of persons and events.

The following abstract from an article by Amy Tsui (2007: 657) provides an idea about how one narrative inquiry study looks.

This article explores teachers' identity formation through a narrative inquiry of the professional identity of an EFL teacher, Minfang, in the People's Republic of China ... it examines the lived experience of Minfang as an EFL learner and EFL teacher throughout his six years of teaching, the processes that were involved as he struggled with multiple identities, the interplay between reification and negotiation of meanings, and the institutional construction and his personal reconstruction of identities. The stories of Minfang highlighted the complex relationships between membership, competence, and legitimacy of access to practice; between the appropriation and ownership of meanings, the centrality of participation, and the mediating role of power relationships in the process of identity formation.

Because this is a narrative study, it necessarily covers a length of time – in this case, six years. The focus is on a single individual, Minfang, and in that sense, this narrative study is like a case study. One difference, however, is that the emphasis is placed on telling the 'story' of Minfang's growth and development as a teacher and the social situation in which his story unfolded.

Mixed-methods approaches

Mixed-methods approaches are exactly what they sound like: they are a combination of quantitative and qualitative approaches. They are attractive to many researchers because they logically allow them to take advantage of the strengths of each approach while simultaneously overcoming their weaknesses to some degree. Essentially, proponents of mixed-methods approaches propose that, in most instances, researchers who make use of more types of data collection tools and analyses will come to understand the object of inquiry better than those who restrict themselves to a more limited set of purely quantitative or qualitative tools. Cresswell and Plano Clark (2007) list four main types of mixed-methods designs.

The most common mixed-methods design, the *triangulation design*, is used when the researcher wants to directly compare and/or contrast the quantitative and qualitative results or to elaborate on the quantitative results using qualitative methods. For instance, statistical analyses may indicate a reliable difference between two groups, but the reasons for that difference may best be discovered by interviewing a selected number of persons from each group.

The second design, which is called the *embedded design*, is one in which one data set provides a strictly supportive role for the primary data set. This means that the data set playing the supportive role would not be able to stand alone in a meaningful way. For instance, in a quantitative experimental design the researcher might ask the participants to answer open-ended questions about the experimental treatment. The participants' responses would not make a lot of sense, however, without knowledge of the experiment.

The third type of mixed-methods design, the *explanatory design*, is a two-phase design in which qualitative data explain or enhance quantitative data. For instance, a quantitative researcher may need to speak directly with some participants in order to discover why an experiment did or did not work as planned. A second example is when a researcher tests participants' willingness to communicate with others and forms groups based on the test results (e.g. persons with low, mid, and high levels of willingness to communicate) and then selects several participants from each group in order to discover more details about the reasons for their differing levels.

The fourth and final type of design is the *exploratory design*. In this case, the results of a qualitative study are used to help the researcher develop a quantitative study. By approaching the topic in an open, qualitative way, the researcher can search for important variables in the situation, develop an instrument that more accurately measures the variable of interest, or even develop a model or theory based on an in-depth study of the people and research context. Like the explanatory design, this design is also conducted in two phases, with the quantitative phase following a potentially long qualitative phase.

The following abstract illustrates the use of a mixed-methods design for understanding computer users' activities in a virtual world (Feldon and Kafai, 2007: 575).

This paper examines the use of mixed methods for analysing users' avatar-related activities in a virtual world. Server logs recorded keystroke-level activity for 595 participants over a six-month period in Whyville.net, an informal science website. Participants also completed surveys and participated in interviews regarding their experiences. Additionally, the study included online ethnographic observations of Whyville and offline observations of a subset of 88 users in classroom and after-school settings during their participation. A mixed-methods analysis identified a major user emphasis on avatar appearance and customization that was invariant across user typologies. Implications for the use of mixed methods in online environments are discussed with regard to three challenges resolved during the study: (1) appropriate reduction of the vast quantity of data, (2) integrated analysis of online and offline events, and (3) interactions between qualitative and quantitative data.

Note that these researchers employed four approaches to data gathering: server log records, surveys, interviews and ethnographic observations. This allowed them to (a) get a well-rounded understanding of their participants' behaviour and (b) (dis)confirm the results obtained by one method with those obtained using a different method. These are two of the greatest strengths of the mixed-methods approach.

Disciplinary and subject variations

You need to become familiar with the ways in which your area of study differs from other areas, as this knowledge will generally have a profound impact on what is considered appropriate and conventional when you are engaged in writing your dissertation or thesis, as well as the form that the dissertation or thesis takes.

One area that can change dramatically concerns your relationship with your supervisor and the degree to which you are expected to work independently or in close consultation with them. In some cases, you may be expected to have relatively frequent face-to-face meetings and to be well-prepared to engage with your professor in a professional, somewhat formal manner. In other cases, face-to-face meetings may occur rarely, and the meetings themselves may be very unstructured and casual (➡ see also Chapter 1, p. 19).

A second area that often differs involves the length of the dissertation. A dissertation in one particular field may be two to three times longer than one in a different field. In addition, the typical length of the different sections of the dissertation can vary considerably. This can be especially true for the literature review chapter, with some disciplines opting for short, succinct reviews and others favouring long, detailed reviews. A related area is the expected speed of completion; the maximum length of time that you have to complete the dissertation is clearly specified in all programmes that we are aware of. You obviously need to be aware of the time constraints that you are working under so that you can select a topic and research design that will not be too long in terms of the number of words that will be required to do the topic justice and the amount of time that you have to complete the project.

A third area that can differ across disciplines concerns writing style. In some academic disciplines, a terse, factual tone is appropriate, while in other areas, an expansive, literary tone is more common. You may also find that this distinction applies to quantitative and qualitative approaches, with researchers engaged in quantitative studies adopting a more terse, scientific tone and many qualitative researchers a more literary tone. In general, the appropriate tone is reasonably easy to discern by reading the top journals in your field of study, and by focusing specifically on studies that are similar to yours.

One final area that may prove important concerns expectations regarding presenting and publishing your work. In some fields, you will be expected to present your dissertation in some public context, perhaps in your own department or possibly at a conference open to the public. In addition, you may be expected to publish your work in an academic journal. While this is an exciting and challenging prospect, it is one that must be planned for carefully, as publishing in these journals is often highly competitive (➡ see Chapter 6, p. 198).

3 ▶ PREPARING TO WRITE

This unit looks at the very 'hands-on' business of sourcing and organising relevant source material.

The chapter will cover:

- reading and planning before you write
- sources of information
- identifying and selecting appropriate information
- note-making
- creating a plan and organising your argument.

USING THIS CHAPTER

READING AND PLANNING BEFORE YOU WRITE

Sound preparation is the key to good writing. No matter how well conducted your research and how interesting the findings, if you haven't done the necessary ground-work before embarking on the writing process then its impact will be compromised and it will therefore not be as well received as it otherwise might. Careful planning helps ensure that by the time you put pen to paper – or fingers to keyboard! – you will have:

- maximised your knowledge of those areas of inquiry that bear on your research by having comprehensively surveyed the relevant literature
- selected and noted down information that you intend to incorporate into your discussion
- organised the information you have acquired
- developed a sound argument structure
- produced a visual plan/representation of your dissertation or thesis.

The following sections of this chapter will look at ways of ensuring that you have completed this important preparatory work effectively and can therefore move on, with some confidence, to the writing of your dissertation or thesis safe in the knowledge that its foundations are solid.

SOURCES OF INFORMATION

Today, as never before, as a student you have available to you a range of resources that could only have been dreamt about by researchers 20 years ago; furthermore, many of these resources are accessible from your desktop at the mere click of a mouse button. Advances in technology also mean that, in many cases, such electronic resources (e-resources) can be accessed at home – or indeed anywhere else in the world – as well as at the institution where you are enrolled as a research student. This has, of course, transformed the way researchers work. Although empirically-based research projects still require fieldwork, much library-based research can now be conducted in a far more efficient, less onerous way. Thanks to the internet, the many hours once spent tracking down books and journals, travelling between institutions in order to view material, treading the aisles of university libraries or waiting for publications to arrive from other institutions, can today be spent far more productively.

Information literacy

Knowing that there is a vast and rich array of resources available to you as a researcher is, of course, not the same thing as knowing exactly what those resources are and how to access them, whether they are in hard copy or electronic form. Your institution's library will play a pivotal role in helping you develop the *information literacy* skills that will enable you to do this and it is essential, therefore, that you become very well acquainted with your library and the services it provides. As information portals have become more numerous and sophisticated, the role of librarians has become more complex as a result of having to keep up with these developments and they remain well placed to direct students and scholars to relevant search methods and sources quickly and efficiently. As a result, librarians are becoming increasingly specialised, and in many cases take responsibility for specific discipline areas about which they become particularly knowledgeable. Wherever possible, you should take advantage of this expertise.

Most university libraries periodically hold introductory sessions designed to intro-duce new students to the library and the services it offers. Because they will help you become a far more efficient researcher, these sessions are an excellent invest-ment of your time. Typically they cover the following areas:

- how to locate a book, periodical or journal in hard copy or e-journal/book format
- procedures, rules and regulations for borrowing books
- how to use the electronic catalogue to access materials from your own and other libraries
- how to 'order in' hard copies of materials not available in the library
- an explanation of the Dewey decimal system or the Library of Congress System (the two most common ways of organising hard copy resources on library shelves)
- the photocopy facilities available, procedures for using them and copyright regulations
- an overview of other resources, such as microfilm and other archived material, housed in the library.

In addition to these introductory sessions, as library information systems change, new subscriptions are taken out to electronic media or new databases come online, librarians often hold a series of sessions for the purpose of familiarising academic staff and students with these new resources. Most libraries also provide free hard-copy and online guides that give brief instructions on such things as how to use the library, electronic databases available and how to correctly reference sources (➡ see p. 90).

Types of source materials

Generally speaking, the source materials you draw on as you read around your research topic will fit into one or more of the following types shown in the table overleaf.

Reading around your topic: source materials

Monographs	Books written on a particular subject and which usually have a fairly narrow focus. These can include single and multiple author publications as well as edited volumes.
Textbooks	Books offering an overview of a particular field or subject within a field and which, therefore, tend to have a broader focus.
Research papers	Journal articles reporting on both empirically-based and library-based research, as well as conference proceedings (i.e. research presented at conferences which has been re-presented and published more formally as a written article).
Reference works	Works such as indexes, dictionaries, encyclopaedias and yearbooks that provide lists, data collections of different kinds, definitions or concise overviews of particular subjects. These are usually found in a dedicated location in the library and, due to their more general nature, their often wider sphere of application, and (in some cases) the cost and difficulty of replacing them, can only be accessed on the library's premises. They are not normally available for loan.
Reviews	Analyses of research areas, often published annually, which provide a form of commentary on the state of the field.

Electronic sources of information

Electronic sources include electronic books ('e-books'), electronic journals ('e-journals'), indexes and collections of journal articles, reference works and digital collections. As the volume of electronic resources continually expands, the number of databases via which you can access these resources also increases. Although, with time, you will begin to know which databases are most relevant and useful to your own research, and which journals and other particular resources are most productive, when you are just starting out it can be difficult to know where to begin. In this situation, a good strategy is to go to a major multi-disciplinary database and work from there, gradually narrowing your focus. Three such databases are the Web of Knowledge, Cambridge Scientific Abstracts (CSA), and OCLC FirstSearch. The list below gives you an idea of the enormous reach of these databases. The British Library also provides a comprehensive list of databases that can be found at http://www.bl.uk/eresources/main.shtml#dbases

Web of Knowledge – isiknowledge.com

A citation and journal database with access to:

- *Web of Science*. Comprises three databases: Arts and Humanities Citation Index, Science Citation Index and Social Sciences Citation Index. It provides over 30 million references to research from over 9000 journals.

- *Arts and Humanities Citation Index*. Indexes articles in the arts and humanities from over 1400 journals from 1975 to the present. Subject areas include philosophy, history, language, linguistics, music, literature, religion, theatre and the visual arts.

- *Social Sciences Citation Index*. Covers nearly 1800 journals across disciplines from 1956 onwards. Subject areas include political science, women's studies, European studies, history, philosophy of science, anthropology, ethics and applied linguistics.

- *ISI Proceedings – Social Sciences and Humanities*. This indexes the published literature of the most significant conferences, symposia and seminars from 1990 to date. Subject areas covered include art, history, literature and philosophy.

- *Journal Citation Reports*. Providing citation data showing high impact and frequency of use from 1997 onwards in subjects such as political science, women's studies, European studies, history, philosophy of science, anthropology, ethics and applied linguistics.

Cambridge Scientific Abstracts (CSA) – www.csa.com

A database providing access to more than 100 databases:

Arts and Humanities

ARTbibliographies Modern

Avery Index to Architectural Periodicals

BHI: British Humanities Index

Bibliography of the History of Art

DAAI: Design and Applied Arts Index

Design Abstracts Retrospective

Design *Pro*FILES

Index Islamicus

CSA Linguistics and Language Behavior Abstracts

MLA International Bibliography

The Philosopher's Index

RILM Abstracts of Music Literature

Natural Sciences

AGRICOLA

Aqualine

ASFA: Aquatic Sciences and Fisheries Abstracts

Biological Sciences

Biology Digest

BioOne

BioOne.1 Full-Text

BioOne.2 Full-Text

Biotechnology and Bioengineering Abstracts

Biotechnology Research Abstracts

Conference Papers Index

CSA Illustrata: Natural Sciences

EIS: Digests of Environmental Impact Statements

Environmental Impact Statements: Full-Text & Digests

Environmental Sciences & Pollution Management

GeoRef

GeoScienceWorld Millennium Collection

International Pharmaceutical Abstracts

MEDLINE

Meteorological & Geoastrophysical Abstracts

NTIS

Oceanic Abstracts

Physical Education Index

Plant Science

Science and Technology Digest

Scopus Natural Sciences

TOXLINE

Water Resources Abstracts

Zoological Record Plus (1864-Current)

Social Sciences

AgeLine

ASSIA: Applied Social Sciences Index and Abstracts

Communication Abstracts

Criminal Justice Abstracts

EconLit

ERIC

FRANCIS

IBSS: International Bibliography of the Social Sciences

IMID: Institute of Management International Database

Index Islamicus

CSA Linguistics and Language Behavior Abstracts

LISA: Library and Information Science Abstracts

National Criminal Justice Reference Service Abstracts

PAIS International

Physical Education Index

PILOTS Database

PsycARTICLES

PsycBOOKS

PsycCRITIQUES

PsycINFO

Scopus Business and Economics

CSA Social Services Abstracts

CSA Sociological Abstracts

CSA Worldwide Political Science Abstracts

Technology

Aerospace & High Technology Database

ANTE: Abstracts in New Technologies and Engineering

Aqualine

Biotechnology and Bioengineering Abstracts

Biotechnology Research Abstracts

CINDAS MPMD

CINDAS TPMD

Computer Abstracts International Database

CSA/ASCE Civil Engineering Abstracts

CSA Illustrata: Technology

CSA Technology Research Database

Earthquake Engineering Abstracts

Information Technology Case Studies

IRWI: Information Research Watch International

LISA: Library and Information Science Abstracts

Mechanical & Transportation Engineering Abstracts

NTIS

Paperbase/PIRA

Polymer Library (formerly Rapra Abstracts)

Science and Technology Digest

OCLC FirstSearch (Online Computer Library Centre) – oclc.org/firstsearch

A gateway to databases, e-Journals, eBooks, and archived content, including:

ABI/INFORM

AGRICOLA

Alternative Press Index

Alternative Press Index Archive

Anthropological Index

Anthropological Literature

Anthropology Plus

Applied Science and Technology Abstracts

Applied Science and Technology Index

Art Abstracts

Art Index

ArticleFirst

Arts & Humanities Search

ATLA Religion

ATLA Serials Database

Avery Index to Architectural Periodicals

Bibliography of the History of Art

Biological & Agricultural Index

Biology Digest

General Science Index

GEOBASE

GeoRefS

GPO Monthly Catalog

Hand Press Book

History of Science, Technology, and Medicine

Humanities Abstracts

Humanities Index

Index to Legal Periodicals and Books

Index to 19th-Century American
    Art Periodicals

Library Literature

MEDLINE

MLA International Bibliography

Newspaper Abstracts

PAIS Archive

PAIS International

PapersFirst

Periodical Abstracts

Philosopher's Index

Other widely used databases not listed above include the following:

Applied Social Sciences Index and Abstracts
    (ASSIA)

Archive of Americana

Bibliografia de la Literatura Española

Bibliographie de Civilisation Médiévale

Bibliography of American Literature

British Newspaper Index

Central and Eastern European Online Library

Dictionary of Old English Corpus

Early English Books Online (EEBO)

Eighteenth Century Collections Online
    ECCO (multidisciplinary)

French Bibliography 15th Century

Grove Art Online

Grove Music Online

Handbook of Latin American
    Studies Online

Hispanic American Periodicals Index (HAPI)

Index to Theses (covering theses accepted
    in Great Britain and Northern Ireland
    since 1716)

International Medieval Bibliography

International Philosophical Bibliography

Library of Latin Texts (CLCLT)

Literature Resource Center

Middle English Compendium

Oxford English Dictionary

Oxford Reference Online

Oxford Scholarship Online

Russian National Bibliography

Russian/NIS Universal Databases

Social Policy and Practice

Times Digital Archive

Victorian Database Online

ZETOC (British Library Electronic
    Table of Contents).

TIP   Access to these resources is normally made through your academic institution's library and learning services website. The university pays for its staff and students to have access to these resources via a subscription and licensing fee. Your fees help cover the cost involved, so make sure you make the most of this invaluable and convenient resource!

Activity 3.1 Familiarising yourself with library resources

Make a visit to your library, either in person or online. Spend some time familiarising yourself with its online databases. Practise searching for sources related to the subject (or probable subject) of your dissertation or thesis.

Try to locate hard-copy information on using the library's resources and getting the most out of what's available.

Citation indexes and impact factors

When you are using sources, you need to be confident that they are considered credible by other scholars. Obviously, the more credible and respected your sources the more credible will be your own work. A citation index is an article database that indicates how many times the work of an author has been referred to, or cited, by another author, and where. How many times a document is cited by other writers is seen as a good indication of its credibility and/or importance. Citation indexes are a handy way to search for a subject by taking a useful or well-known paper and looking at later work that refers back to it. A Web of Science cited reference search (see table above) will do this.

Similarly, so-called 'impact factors' provide an indication of an article's importance or influence by 'rating' the journal in which it appears. It does this by quantifying the frequency with which the 'average article' published in a given scholarly journal has been cited in a particular year or period. This, in turn, is used in citation analysis.

The internet (World Wide Web)

Just as you need to exercise discretion in selecting your scholarly sources in order to make certain that your own work maintains its integrity, you also need to show great caution in dealing with sources you have consulted on the internet. Indeed, the quality of information available on the internet is so variable that the chances of including inaccurate or misleading information in your work is significantly greater than if you confine yourself to more traditional, scholarly sources. In order to avoid including 'rogue' information in your work, you may wish to ask yourself the following questions:

- Who is the information provider? For example, is it a government or non-governmental organisation? Is it a commercial organisation?
- Is there reason to believe that the provider is a reliable source of information?
- Why is the information provided? For example, is it to inform, to sell, to promote a point of view? In other words, does the provider have a vested interest in painting a certain picture for its audience? Is the presentation of information likely to be biased?
- When was the website/information last updated? Try to locate a date on the page.
- Is the tone of the website casual or flippant, or more formal and serious? Does the content tend to be personal and emotive?
- Does the content feel subjective or objective, more opinion than fact?
- Is the source of the information clear?

Although questions such as these are not necessarily definitive, they can certainly help you evaluate information obtained via the internet. The following websites listed on the Mantex website (http://www.mantex.co.uk/ou/resource/eval-01.htm) also provide useful information on how to check the quality and reliability of web resources:

- How to evaluate a web page – http://manta.library.colostate.edu/howto/evalweb .html
- Evaluating web resources – http://www.science.widener.edu/~withers/webeval .htm
- Evaluation of information sources – http://www.vuw.ac.nz/~agsmith/evaln/ evaln.htm
- Internet detective: an interactive tutorial – http://sosig.ac.uk/desire/internet-detective.html
- Thinking critically about web resources – http://www.library.ucla.edu/libraries/ college/instruct/critical.htm
- Evaluating World Wide Web information – http://thorplus.lib.purdue.edu/ library_info/instruction/gs175/3gs175/evaluation.html
- Evaluating internet research sources – http://www.sccu.edu/faculty/R_Harris/ evalu8it.htm
- Evaluating the quality of internet information – http://itech.coe.uga.edu/Faculty/ gwilkinson/webeval.html
- Evaluating information found on the internet – http://milton.mse.jhu.edu/ research/education/net.html
- Evaluating information on the internet – http://www.udmercy.edu/htmls/ Academics/library/evaluati
- Ten C's for evaluating internet resources – http://www.uwec.edu/Admin/Library/ 10cs.html
- Guidelines for art, design and media resources – http://adam.ac.uk/adam/ reports/select/sect31.html

Remember, the internet is a wonderful source of information, one that can greatly enrich the research process – but only if it is approached critically.

Keeping up to date via 'current awareness' services

Particularly if you are engaged in research that will extend over a period of years, it is important that you keep up to date with the latest resources and information. As new resources become available you need to consult those relevant to your study in order to ensure that your work and the literature on which it draws is fresh, relevant and up to date. Today, there are electronically-based 'current awareness services' that help you to do this. You can arrange for these services to email you an alert to new print or electronic resources as they are published. Alternatively, you can periodically search relevant webpages in order to check for any new sources or updates. Current awareness services include:

- discussion lists and newsgroups
- funding alerts
- journal alerting
- monitoring webpage changes (particularly important for referencing)
- new publications
- news of forthcoming conferences
- news services with email alerting.

Oral sources of information

Of course, there are also oral sources of information that can feed into the research process, and these can include the following:

- lectures
- seminars
- conference presentations
- professional organisations
- special interest groups (SIGS).

TIP All of these sources of information potentially have a role to play in stimulating thought and generating ideas on your part. However, unless they appear in writing – in the form of conference proceedings, for example – and have been subject to a process of peer review, they should be treated with caution in terms of making any written reference to them. Unless they are soundly documented, they have limited credibility. As such, should you choose to refer to them, it is advisable that you acknowledge their 'insecure' status.

IDENTIFYING AND SELECTING APPROPRIATE INFORMATION

Having identified the types of sources available to you, you will now need to begin a more detailed selection process whereby you sift through the enormous volume of information these sources place at your disposal in order to get at only that information relevant to your own research. This can seem like a daunting task and it can be difficult to know where to begin. However, a few simple strategies can be surprisingly productive.

Know what you are looking for

While this might seem like an obvious piece of advice, it's not unusual for students keen to get their research under way to dive into the process of trying to select material without having considered carefully beforehand what kind of information it is they are looking for in anything other than the broadest of terms. In order to search and select efficiently, you have to constrain or set parameters on your search, and that means clarifying in your own mind which discipline areas, authors, concepts, journals, etc. are relevant to your particular study, as well as knowing how concepts relate to one another. By understanding conceptual relationships, you will be in a better position to identify potentially fruitful links and avenues of inquiry which might otherwise get missed.

Knowing what you are looking for in your search for information and giving time to considering the parameters of your search is the most fundamental information selection strategy in that it underpins all others. This will be evident as we look at the remaining strategies.

Search for titles of books or articles

One obvious place to begin your search and selection of material is to look for the names of books or articles that are known to you and that you recognise as relevant to your research.

Perform an internet search of relevant theories or concepts

There will, of course, be plenty of published materials 'out there' with which you are not familiar but which may be important – even critical – sources of information. One way of identifying such sources is to type into a search engine key words or ideas associated with your area of inquiry. Then, pursue those results that promise to be most productive. Some of the most widely used search engines are listed below:

All the Web	Google	HotBot	Vivisimo
AltaVista	Google Image Search	Mamma	Web Wombat
Anzwers	Google Print	MSN Search	Wisenut
ASK.com	Google Scholar	Scirus	Yahoo!

So-called meta-search engines such as Dogpile, Ixquick and Metacrawler allow you to search a group of search engines at the same time.

Perform a name search of relevant scholars

Similarly, you may wish to use your library's cataloguing system or an online search engine to generate works (books, articles, etc.) produced by individuals you know are associated with your particular area of research interest. Type in the names of scholars recognised in areas related to your research and follow up on those that appear to hold most promise.

Having identified sources that you believe, on a first take, are of potential relevance to your research, you will need to confirm as efficiently as possible whether they are indeed of value to you and worth reading in their entirety. There are a number ways to do this.

Read abstracts

All published articles will begin with an abstract. This is typically a summary of the content of the article and will normally run to no more than about 150 words. The main purpose of the abstract is to give the reader, at a glance, an overview of the article, allowing them to determine whether or not it is relevant to their own interests and something they wish to read in full. An abstract is therefore an important time-saving device that can help you select information quickly and effectively. As journals are increasingly being read online, most electronic journals come with abstracts for all articles that appear in those journals. If, based on its abstract, readers wish to read a complete article, then they can do so, provided they or their institution has subscribed to it.

Read synopses of books

Like an abstract, a synopsis is also a summary statement. However, instead of telling the reader what an article is about, it tells them what a book is about and what it covers. It may also be rather longer than 150 words, although this can vary greatly. There are a number of places you might find a synopsis of a book: on its back cover, in its preface or introduction (if it has one), or on its publisher's or other booksellers' websites. Like an abstract, a synopsis provides a quick way of ascertaining whether or not a particular book is relevant to you and therefore worth reading. There are times when it may indicate to you that while much of the book is irrelevant, certain aspects of it may be of value to your research.

Look through tables of contents

A quick read through of a book's table of contents will often give you a more detailed picture of its content coverage, its perspective and various emphases, and an idea of how much of the book is of potential relevance to you. For most students evaluating a book for the first time, after the title, the table of contents is normally the next logical port of call in the process of determining whether or not to use it.

Once you have identified those sections of the book (if any) that seem most relevant to your purposes, skim read them to get a better sense of their potential value to you, for although they may have appeared useful at first glance, on closer scrutiny they may be less helpful than anticipated. For example, they may be approaching ideas from an unhelpful angle, tell you nothing more than you already know, or perhaps lack adequate depth.

Check indexes

Tables of contents are generally more useful than indexes in determining a book's relevance. While a table of contents will give you a sense of the book's coverage, emphases and the level of detail in which different elements are discussed, an index will normally only tell you if a particular term, idea or author appears somewhere in the book. That appearance may be little more than a passing reference or it may be a complete section. This, however, does not mean that indexes cannot be useful tools in helping you to gauge a book's potential value. For example, a concept that is important for your own research may have little written about it in the literature. As such, while any coverage of it may prove helpful to you, it may well not appear in the table of contents simply because it will not warrant a complete section or sub-section. A quick scan of the index, however, will allow you find out quickly whether the concept is mentioned in the book. If it is, you can flick to the relevant page(s) and get an idea of whether or not the discussion of the concept is substantial and/or interesting enough to deserve your attention. It's also worth remembering that indexes will often indicate not only the particular pages on which ideas appear in the book, but also the page ranges in which those ideas are discussed (e.g. 38–44). Often, a fairly large range suggests that an entire section or sub-section may be devoted to it. Sub-sections, however, are not always presented in the table of contents and consequently the index may be the only way of identifying a relevant sub-section.

Scan books or articles for key terms

Although this can be a tedious, far less efficient way of identifying and selecting information, scanning books for key names, terms or concepts can sometimes be a necessary part of the research process, especially for books that do not have an index, as is sometimes the case with edited volumes. Flicking through a book can also give you a sense of its depth and overall academic quality and integrity – something that a table of contents will not necessarily provide.

Read bibliographies

The bibliographies of articles and books can be a rich source of further information on a particular subject.

Scan library shelves

Although, as we have seen, most searching today can be done electronically, a scan of the relevant sections of library shelves can sometimes throw up unexpected sources that were not in your original 'game plan' and which might not have appeared via an electronic search, simply because you did not input the necessary trigger word or phrase or had not considered an idea or approach that strikes you only as you look through the titles of books or articles that lie before you in hard copy. It may feel a little old-fashioned but wandering up and down university aisles still has its place, so be careful not to dismiss it as outdated and a waste of time!

Read book reviews

While it's important not to take everything you read at face value and to remember that people look for different things in books and will therefore often view them differently, online book reviews – particularly those written by academically credible individuals – can nevertheless give you a helpful glimpse into the areas a book covers, how it covers them and its overall strengths and weaknesses. Although general websites such as Amazon should probably be treated with greater caution in this regard, reviews appearing within respected journals should be given more weight, and, once again, can be accessed either in hard copy or online.

Ask a librarian!

Don't forget, librarians are often very well placed to help you in your search for relevant source material. As we saw ➡ on page 55, librarians today work within discipline-specific areas and therefore have more specialist knowledge than was previously the case. This means that they are better able than ever to help direct your searches and prevent you from wasting time by following unproductive leads. Even when you feel you've exhausted your searches, it's worth consulting a librarian to see whether there are any other avenues of inquiry you've not considered.

A final note

As you work through these strategies in order to identify appropriate source materials, you will feel as though you have embarked on a never-ending process. Just as you feel you may (finally!) have exhausted all possible leads, you come across another set of references . . . that, in turn, direct you to yet more. Hang in there though. Eventually, despite what you might think and the fact that there is always the possibility of further sources cropping up, the process eventually burns itself out. After a while you begin to find that, increasingly, you are referred to materials with which you're already familiar and/or which you may have read. This should be reassuring as it suggests you are nearing the end of your search and confirms that

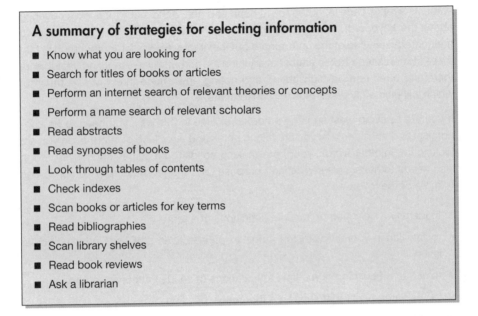

A summary of strategies for selecting information

- Know what you are looking for
- Search for titles of books or articles
- Perform an internet search of relevant theories or concepts
- Perform a name search of relevant scholars
- Read abstracts
- Read synopses of books
- Look through tables of contents
- Check indexes
- Scan books or articles for key terms
- Read bibliographies
- Scan library shelves
- Read book reviews
- Ask a librarian

you've been comprehensive in tracking down relevant material. So, give yourself a gentle pat on the back. Now you can look forward to making notes and organising it all!

NOTE-MAKING

Once you've identified your source materials, you need to embark on the process of extracting and organising only that information you feel is of relevance to you. Particularly in the case of empirical research (as opposed to library-based research), it's important to remember that whether you are writing a dissertation or a thesis, note-making is not typically a neat process that is completed prior to planning, conducting and writing up your research. Although a good deal of reading and note-making will certainly take place early on once you have settled on a topic and before you begin to shape your research project in earnest, it nevertheless tends to be an ongoing process as you continually discover new material that's relevant to your research and which therefore needs to be factored in. This does not mean, however, that you cannot and should not approach this important task systematically. This section will look at some of the ways in which you can make your note-making more efficient and effective.

Directing your note-making

It can be a daunting and unproductive experience to have a pile of books and articles sitting in front of you without a clear plan of attack. Yet a surprisingly large number of students simply wade in, notebook at hand and pen at the ready (or fingers hovering above the keyboard), intent on noting down anything they feel might be useful to their enterprise. One of the unfortunate but inevitable results of this approach is that these students tend to see almost everything as 'potentially relevant and useful' and, therefore, often end up highlighting and noting down huge tracts of text much of which will ultimately be surplus to requirements.

If you are to avoid wasting large amounts of time in this way, you need to be economical and consider why you are taking notes and what kind of information you are looking for. In other words, your note-making needs to be guided and disciplined. It also needs to have a clearly-defined purpose, and that purpose may comprise one or more of the following:

- to identify a definition or multiple definitions of a term
- to familiarise yourself with the range of perspectives that exist on a particular issue
- to get an articulation or multiple articulations of an idea, theory or approach
- to seek arguments that support a theoretical position
- to extract the logic of an argument
- to find contrasting viewpoints on an issue
- to identify a research design/methodology
- to locate research findings associated with a particular area or subject of inquiry
- to get a sense of the issues that bear upon a subject and of which you may not be aware.

Of course, there are times when our note-making isn't quite so directed as the above would suggest. Sometimes we read simply to familiarise ourselves further with an idea or area in general so that we have a comprehensive overview of it and a sense of the various issues that are central to it and which help define it. Yet even in these circumstances some kind of conceptual framework or map is helpful in that it allows you to decide what's important and thus worth noting down, and what's not. Without any kind of constraints or parameters, reading and note-making become too open-ended and inefficient.

In order to acquire such a conceptual map, try to read a complete section, chapter, etc. at least once before starting to take notes on it. Although it may seem an extravagant use of time, it's normally a very worthwhile investment. If you simply start taking notes as you read, you can easily get lost in the detail and lose sight of the main ideas. As a result, you end up noting down too much information. Reading the material in advance allows you to step back a bit and determine what the writer's main points are, what the supporting ideas are, and which of these are most pertinent for your purposes. You can then note these down accordingly.

Making your notes understandable

Clearly, if your notes are to be useful to you then you need to be able to understand them when you come to look at them at a later date. There's no point in being concise in your note-making if, weeks or months later, you're unable to 'reconstruct' the original ideas summarised in your notes. We recommend, therefore, that before you begin making notes you decide on a form of shorthand you're going to use and which will probably be unique to you. As we shall see below, that shorthand can be represented graphically but it can also involve the use of abbreviations and symbols. Having a system of abbreviations and symbols and a scheme of graphical representation of information that indicates the main and supporting ideas and their interrelationships will make you a more efficient note-taker and help ensure that you don't have to waste time revisiting your sources as a result of poor note-taking technique. Furthermore, once you've decided on a system that suits you and feels intuitive, make sure that you're consistent in your application of it.

Examples of symbols and abbreviations

=	equals; is the same as	≠	does not equal/is not the same as
>	is more than/larger than	<	is less than/smaller than
∴	therefore; as a result	∵	because
↑	to increase	↓	to decrease
→	leads to; causes	←	is caused by; depends on
[	includes	]	excludes
+ or &	and; also; plus	...	continues; and so on
$	dollars	%	percent
#	number	~	for example or approximately
Δ	change	k	million
@	at	/	per
#	number	%	percent

You can abbreviate, or shorten, long words and names. For example:

def	= definition	ex or e.g.	= example
co	= company	intl	= international
av	= average	agrs	= agrees
fb	= feedback	diagrs	= disagrees
no.s	= numbers	stats	= statistics
esp	= especially	signif	= significant
fig	= figure	diag	= diagram
w/out	= without	i.e.	= that is; in other words

Activity 3.2 Working with symbols and abbreviations

List below some additional symbols and abbreviations you could use that would improve your note-making.

Symbols   **Abbreviations**

_____ _____ _____   _____ _____ _____

_____ _____ _____   _____ _____ _____

_____ _____ _____   _____ _____ _____

As you read, select and make notes on your source material and consider using some of these other strategies:

- highlighting important information using a highlighter pen
- underlining key words or ideas
- using bullet point lists
- colour coding information as an initial way of organising it
- using mnemonics for efficiency and to aid recall later
- creating numbered lists
- using a distinctive layout that has visual meaning for you.

Some popular ways of graphically representing information include spidergrams, linear notes, time-lines and flow charts.

Spidergrams

In spidergrams, the broader ideas you wish to note down are placed toward the centre of the spidergram. Each of these is then sub-divided into branches, each representing more detailed or supporting information. These sub-branches may, in turn, divide again to provide a further level of detail, and so on. In other words, as you note down more and more information and develop each main strand (or idea), you create a network that presents the information you have read in a structured and informative way, and indicates how the different ideas relate to each other. You may choose to incorporate the related ideas of a number of writers in one spider-gram, provided it is not too complex, or to create a separate spidergram for each source you read, where this seems appropriate. An example spidergram is shown in Figure 3.1.

Linear notes

Linear notes are another way of organising information. They're quite similar to spider-grams in that they also indicate the status of ideas by categorising them and

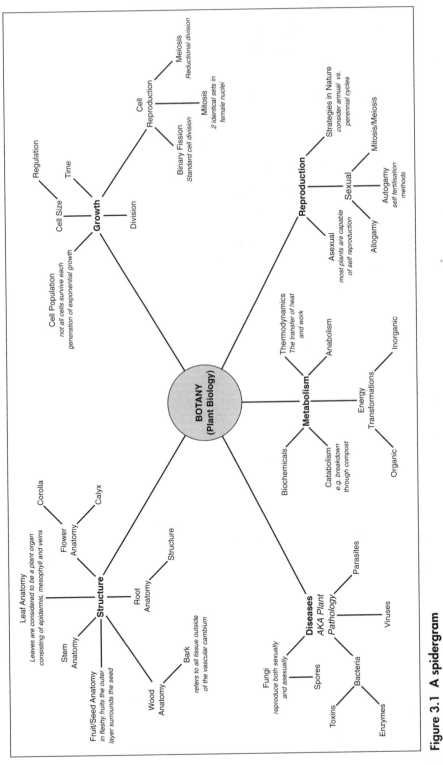

Figure 3.1 A spidergram

MAIN IDEA 1

MAIN IDEA 2

    Supporting Idea 1

    Supporting Idea 2

        Example 1

        Example 2

    Supporting Idea 3

MAIN IDEA 3

MAIN IDEA 4

OR

```
1. _____            I. _____
2. _____            II. _____
   2.1 _____           i. _____
   2.2 _____           ii. _____
      2.2.1 _____          IIia _____
      2.2.2 _____          IIib _____
   2.3 _____           iii. _____
3. _____            III. _____
4. _____            IV. _____
```

Figure 3.2 Linear notes

identifying main ideas and supporting details. A common way of laying out linear notes is to number them using a decimal system and/or stagger them right so that those ideas appearing furthest to the left are the broader, more general ideas and those on the right the more detailed ideas (see Figure 3.2). In other words, as things move rightwards, the level of detail increases. In this way, the status of the different ideas is immediately obvious.

Time-lines

As their name suggests, time-lines lend themselves particularly well to noting down a chronology of events – key events that heralded the emergence of modern medicine, for example, or the coming to power of Benito Mussolini. As you discover more and more about a particular subject or phenomenon from your reading, you can add further detail to your time-line, provided, of course, that your have left yourself space to do so. Look at Figure 3.3 that plots the development of the movement for women's suffrage.

WOMEN'S SUFFRAGE: A TIME-LINE

1792 — Mary Wollstonecraft publishes Vindication of the Rights of Women which raises the issue of women's suffrage

1867 — John Stuart Mill raises issue of women's suffrage in House of Commons

1883 — Women's Co-operative Guild established – it supports women's suffrage

1897 — National Union of Women's Suffrage Societies (NUWSS) formed

1903 — Women's Social and Political Union formed – more militant suffrage

1906 — 300-strong demonstration – largest to date

1907 — First Women's Parliament attempts to force their way into Parliament to present petition to Prime Minister – he refuses to see them

1909 — Suffrage organisations use increasingly violent and drastic measures, such as hunger strikes, to further their cause

1911 — Millicent Garrett Fawcett criticises the passing of the 1857 Matrimonial Causes Act in her book 'Women's Suffrage'

1913 — Emily Davison trampled to death as she throws herself in front of King George V's horse

1913 — Cat and Mouse Act passed - permits release of hunger striking suffragettes from prison when at the point of death, and their re-arrest when partially recovered

1918 — Representation of the People Act gives vote to women over 30 who "occupied premises of a yearly value of not less than £5"

1918 — Christabel Pankhurst stands at Smethwick as the Women's Party candidate - narrowly beaten

1928 — Voting age for women lowered to bring it in line with that of men (21)

Figure 3.3 Women's suffrage: a time-line

Flow charts

Flow charts are a good way of noting down hierarchies, processes, systems or procedures. For example, the process involved in obtaining a PhD degree might be simply illustrated as in Figure 3.4.

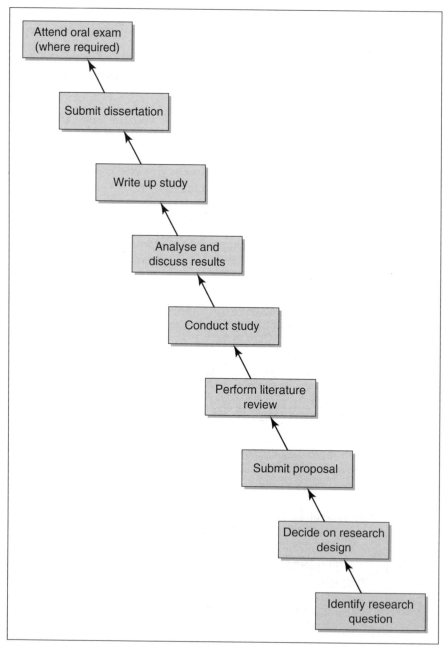

Figure 3.4 A flow chart to obtaining a PhD

➡ See page 133 for an example of a flow chart designed to show the hierarchies of the main civil courts and the criminal courts in the United Kingdom.

Activity 3.3 Practising note-making

Locate an article or a chapter of potential relevance to your research which you have not read. Do the following:

1 Note down why you have selected the article/chapter and what you hope to get out of it (i.e. what's your purpose in reading it?).

2 Skim read the article/chapter in order to ascertain the gist of it and acquire a conceptual map of its content.

3 Make notes on the article/chapter using one of the graphical techniques illustrated above or an alternative technique that works for you.

4 Incorporate abbreviations and symbols into your notes where possible.

5 Try to reconstruct the article/chapter (or relevant parts of it) from your notes.

Recording your sources

Another crucial aspect of being an efficient note-maker is systematically recording your sources. All too often, students get carried away with locating suitable information and getting it down in note form, and they put the crucial business of recording where that information came from on the backburner, to be done at a later time. They then move on to another source and then another, and before they know what has happened they've lost track of where they obtained the ideas they've noted down. They're unable to match the text on their page with its original source. Sometimes this realisation happens quickly and the damage is quite easily repaired. However, it's not uncommon for students to realise only much later – sometimes when they're putting together their bibliography – that they've drawn on a number of ideas that have become integral to their dissertation or thesis but are unable to remember from where those ideas originated because they never did get around to recording their sources. For sure, it's all too easy to get caught up in the moment and to feel that noting down the details of a source is a distraction from the more immediate task of getting through a book, chapter or article, and getting the information down as quickly and painlessly as possible. However, the inconvenience of having to interrupt the flow of your reading and note-making to record details of the source is as nothing compared to that of trying to locate where an idea came from that you may have read weeks or even months before, and the frustration of wasting large amounts of time doing so – time that you realise could be better spent refining your dissertation or thesis.

So that you're not tempted to delay recording a source, make sure you get into the habit of noting down your source before making notes on it. People do this in different ways, some electronically and others more traditionally using filing cards arranged alphabetically in a box. As we shall see, one advantage of doing it electronically is that when you come to constructing your bibliography, there are software packages available that can use your electronic database of sources to create a bibliography for you, thus saving you time.

Whichever method you use, there is certain key information you need to record:

- the author(s) surname(s) and initial(s)
- the full title of the source
- the relevant chapter(s) and page number(s)
- the date and place of publication
- the name of the publisher.

TIP An additional advantage of noting the date of publication of your sources is that as you come across new sources of information, you will be able to 'place' them chronologically. This can be important as it can tell you whether an author failed to acknowledge a particular idea or viewpoint that was already in the public domain at the time of their writing, and whether one idea or research study, say, has been superseded by another. Understanding how ideas develop in relation to one another in time can be crucial to an accurate understanding of a field or area within a field and thus, also the accuracy of your research.

CREATING A PLAN AND ORGANISING YOUR ARGUMENT

Why plan?

So, you've done the necessary 'leg work' and tracked down your sources. You've made notes, added your own commentary and ideas and (in the case of an empirically-based research project – about which more in ➡ Chapter 5) have collected, analysed and discussed your data). There now remains one final but critical process that needs to be gone through before you can begin writing: planning.

The importance of planning your writing cannot be over-emphasised. You may have the best information at your fingertips, a head full of insightful and creative ideas, good data that's the product of a sound methodology and strong analytical skills; however, if you fail to plan your writing, and plan it well, these advantages can very quickly dissipate. On the other hand, get it right and you are well on your way to producing a powerful, credible piece of work that is easy and satisfying to read. For this reason, it's often said that planning is arguably the most important and challenging part of the writing process, and that the writing itself is relatively easy once a good plan has been constructed.

So why is planning so important? Here are a few good reasons:

- Planning is way of helping you to reflect on your material and to clarify in your own mind how the ideas you have collated relate to each other.

- Understanding how ideas relate to each other is essential if you are to organise them logically in preparation for writing.

- Having a blueprint or conceptual map of your writing that helps ensure your ideas are presented in the most logical order will make for a good and powerful argument structure, which in turn will make it easier for your reader to follow your line of thinking.

- Knowing where you are going in your writing allows you to write with confidence and to focus more on the form of your writing than the content and organisation – although these can and should never be entirely sidelined, of course. Because you are able to focus more on form and not having to stop periodically to consider what you want to say and where, you are better able to get into a writing rhythm and produce a better structured, more flowing text.

- Having a plan allows you to locate any point of discussion accurately within the broader context of your work. This means that, among other things, you can refer backwards or forwards with assuredness.

- Planning helps avoid the situation where you suddenly find you don't know where to go next and/or you have taken the wrong direction in your writing. This can lead to frustration, even panic, because it may mean you have to rewrite large sections of your work or even start again from scratch.

- Planning helps avoid a situation where you find you are left with information that you have not taken account of and which you then have to integrate into your discussion retrospectively. This can be difficult to do and result in a forced and unnatural positioning of that idea. Also, in trying to squeeze it in somewhere you can often upset the natural flow of your text.

Laying out your plan

This section will be a fairly brief one. Why? Because the techniques we looked at in relation to laying out your notes ➡ on page 67 apply equally to planning! Although chances are you will opt to use the same technique for your planning as you use for note-making, you may decide to use an alternative or you may use different techniques for different parts of your dissertation or thesis.

Let's imagine you decide to use a spidergram. There are a number of possible ways to proceed and you will need to consider which one(s) suits you best. You may well have the title of your dissertation or thesis in the centre. Then, emanating from there, have three strands: one for your introduction, one for your body and one for your conclusion. In the case of a dissertation or thesis, you may have an additional strand for the literature review (➡ discussed in detail in Chapter 5, p. 158). As with note-making, each of these strands can then sub-divide into a series of 'main idea strands', each of which will further sub-divide into multiple strands reflecting various supporting points. Those 'supporting idea strands' will themselves divide to allow for an even finer level of detail consisting of examples, quotations and references, etc.

Obviously, one characteristic of dissertations and theses is their complexity. This means that it may be difficult to include all the information you wish to incorporate into your plan in one spidergram. In this case, one option is to have a separate spidergram each for the introduction, literature review, body and conclusion. Another is to consider separating the main ideas and constructing a spidergram for each. In other words, you will end up with a series of satellite sub-plans which, when put together, constitute a comprehensive master plan. This, however, has the disadvantage of making it more difficult – though not impossible – to indicate the relationships between the various ideas.

TIP Although it can be difficult, particularly when your plan is complex, where possible try to keep give it an airy feel and avoid cramming in too much information as this can make things feel cluttered and it can become difficult to see the wood from the trees. Furthermore, should you wish to add information later, it's much easier to do so.

Clearly, there are significant benefits to planning your writing. Yet, unfortunately, despite this fact, all too often students see it as unnecessary and something that only serves to delay the business of getting down to what they see as the more important task of getting words on the page. The actual process of writing gives them the sense that they are making real progress, while planning is viewed as a distraction. This is very short-sighted indeed. Planning needs to be seen as a thoroughly sound investment of your time and an essential part of the writing process. Without it, you will almost certainly come unstuck. Remember: the sense of direction and confidence a good plan will give you as you embark on and progress with the writing of your dissertation or thesis, and the ability it will give you to enter into a productive and efficient writing rhythm, will more than compensate for any time spent initially mapping out your work.

In deciding, during the planning phase, how to organise the many elements to be included in your writing, there is a key concept that you will need to guide your decision-making. It's called *coherence*, and we look at it next in our discussion of clarity in writing.

4 ▶ CLEAR AND EFFECTIVE WRITING

This unit looks at presenting relevant source material in an academic style appropriate to dissertations and theses, while also conforming to the rules and regulations concerning punctuation.

The chapter will cover:

- the style of academic writing
- the mechanics of academic writing.

USING THIS CHAPTER

THE STYLE OF ACADEMIC WRITING

Clarity

The key to achieving clarity in your writing is to keep your reader in mind constantly and to try and be as objective and honest with yourself as possible when reading and evaluating your writing. You need to keep asking yourself questions such as:

- Is this going to be clear to my reader?

- Is this idea really going to be transparent to someone who doesn't have direct access to the ideas in my head in the way that I do?

- Is this reference or connection going to be evident to the reader or am I assuming too much?

- Is the reader going to be able to infer my meaning here?

- Is this idea going to be sufficiently clear to somebody who doesn't have an in-depth understanding of this topic or field?

- Will the reader have to work too hard to understand where I'm coming from and what I mean?

Be sure your writing is coherent

Coherence is probably the most important element in achieving clarity in writing. Coherence is that quality that makes text stick together and gives it a sense of flow and unity. It's what links ideas together in such a way that there's a logical progression from one idea to the next. If a text has been carefully planned and is coherent as a result, then the reader will be able to follow its writer's train of thought and will sometimes even be able to anticipate where the discussion will go next. If, on the other hand, a text is incoherent, then it will be difficult to follow the writer's train of thought and therefore to identify any argument structure. Consequently, what the reader will be left with is merely a series of apparently random ideas stitched together in no particular order and to no obvious end.

In order to achieve coherence in your writing you:

- Need to have a very clear sense of direction. Ask yourself, "What is it I want to say? What is my purpose in writing? What do I want to achieve?"

- Need to decide which ideas and what organisational structure will best achieve your purpose.

- Need to ensure that the ideas you employ are clear in your own mind. If they are not clearly defined or fully-formed in your mind, how can you expect others to understand them? Furthermore, it's difficult to fully understand and therefore articulate relationships between ideas that are poorly defined. This in turn means that organising those ideas logically in your writing becomes virtually impossible.

■ Need to keep in mind, during the planning phase, the readability and impact of your writing. Consider how to arrange your ideas so that (a) your purpose unfolds clearly and easily for the reader, and (b) you achieve maximum impact through being methodical and logical in the way you construct and present your discussion.

Assume little or nothing on the part of your reader

One way of achieving clarity for your reader is to minimise the work they have to do in order to understand your meaning. One way to do this is to spell out almost everything that is not self-evident. One mistake students often make in their writing is to assume that their reader is already privy to certain information and that, consequently, that information does not need to be stated explicitly. Don't forget that as a writer with direct access to the ideas in your own head, you almost automatically fill in any gaps in your writing as you write and later read your writing. Remember, your reader doesn't have such privileged access. What may be evident to you may not be so to them!

Another advantage to spelling everything out explicitly is that it makes more evident the links between your ideas. Even if the reader is able to fill in any gaps through a combination of their own knowledge and good inferencing skills, your writing loses some of its natural flow when those links are not made explicit.

Don't be vague

We have seen how important it is for you as a writer to have ideas clear in your own mind before you set them down in writing, and to provide your reader with ample information so that the onus is *not* on them having to work out what you mean and what the exact nature of the connections is between the ideas you've expressed. Failure to do these things tends to show itself in vague, imprecise and waffly language, characteristics that are penalised heavily by lecturers and examiners. Be sure to check your work carefully for vagueness by defining your terms clearly, being accurate in your use of language, making relationships between ideas amply clear, adding further detail to ideas and descriptions where necessary, and using plenty of examples.

Be concise

Increasingly in academic circles – and indeed in other walks of life – there is a move towards plain English. Today, university students are constantly told to be concise and to the point. Keep your sentences short and don't let verbosity and unnecessary terminology get in the way of your message. The more verbal padding there is the more difficult it becomes to see the wood from the trees. Being concise is not easy: you have to cut to the chase, know precisely what you want to say, and have a facility with the language that enables you to be economical while remaining eloquent in your use of it.

Keep a look out for ambiguity

When writing and checking your work, try to be sensitive to words or ideas that can be read in a way different from what you intend. Confusion can result when a reader identifies two or three meanings each of which is a possible interpretation of what is written.

Beware of jargon

Increasingly, the use of jargon in academic writing is being discouraged. This is very much in keeping with the trend towards plain English discussed earlier, for jargon often serves only to obscure meaning and thus easy accessibility by the reader. Minimise your use of it as far as possible.

Eliminate repetition

As you write and edit your work, keep a careful eye out for instances of repetition. Although, to some extent, careful planning and an effort to be concise can help you avoid this problem, nevertheless, when you become very involved in getting your ideas down on the page, it can be all too easy not to notice when you've repeated yourself. This makes the editing process all the more important. Although there is sometimes a case for repeating information – in a summary, for example – it generally looks careless and can be irritating for a reader.

> **TIP** In order to test how effectively you have met the condition of clarity in your writing, ask a friend or colleague to read your work and give you feedback on those areas they felt were insufficiently clear or confusing.

Level of formality

Although, as we've seen, there has been a move towards plain, concise language in academic writing in recent years, this is not the same thing as casual language. While there exists a certain amount of variation in what different disciplines and departments require and will accept in terms of writing style, most still expect academic work to be written in a more formal register and tend to look unfavourably on language that is too casual. Equally, they do not welcome unnecessarily pompous language for its own sake.

So, how can you achieve the correct tone in your writing? Here are a few tips.

Never use unconventional spellings

Although they're becoming increasingly common in many non-academic contexts such as text messaging, email exchanges and personal letter writing, unconventional spellings should never be used in academic writing. This includes forms such as *wanna* (want to) and *thinkin'* (thinking).

Avoid casual fonts

Fonts *like this one* give your writing an informal, unprofessional feel. Stick to plain, more traditional fonts such as Times New Roman or Arial.

Avoid overly ornate titles

Although they may show your creativity and word-processing skills, they can also make your work look unprofessional and have the effect of detracting from the seriousness of the content.

Minimise the use of colour

Similarly, the use of multiple colours, while striking, can also make your work look trivial and playful rather than a serious piece of academic discourse. While the use of colour can have a place – for example, by helping distinguish the various sectors of a chart – it needs to be used discerningly. Furthermore, avoid exotic or overly bright colours.

Avoid shortened forms

Contracted forms such as 'it's', 'there's' and 'hasn't' are generally discouraged in academic writing. Write out their full forms: 'it is', 'there is', 'has not'.

Don't use a 'jokey' tone or try to be comical

Writing a dissertation or thesis is a serious business and your supervisor and/or examiners will not take kindly to you adopting a tone that is inappropriate and which trivialises your work. While your writing does not necessarily have to be dry, it does have to be business-like.

Avoid emotive language

As soon as you use emotive language, the sense of objectivity so important to academic inquiry is compromised. You begin to sound 'un-academic' and amateurish, and your credibility and that of your work will suffer as a result.

Avoid biased or stereotypical language

Like emotive language, biased or stereotypical language also undermines your objectivity as writer. Bias and stereotyping can show themselves in the way in which you acknowledge and deal with ideas of other scholars that may be different from your own (➡ see p. 103), as well as the way in which you deal with issues such as gender, sexual orientation, ethnicity or race. Look at the examples in the box.

Examples

Because they were Asian, they found it difficult to be direct in expressing their opinions.

This wrongly stereotypes all Asians as being reticent to express their opinions directly.

'The Homosexual Agenda'

The word 'homosexual' is rarely used anymore by gay rights advocates; it is almost exclusively used by opponents of gay rights and lifestyles, particularly by people and organisations in the 'religious right'. Given the usage of 'homosexual', and the fact that the headline appears in a journal of conservative political commentary, the word 'agenda' connotes 'underhanded scheme' rather than 'harmless plan'. Further, the use of 'The' rather than 'A' reinforces the notion of a master plan or a united group – them against us.

Friends of Rexmont Dam is a grass roots organisation dedicated to conserving these historic natural resources for the community.

Grass roots organisations are widely admired, as they connote 'of the people, by the people, for the people'. Who could be against 'conserving', particularly the conservation of 'historic natural resources?' Yet it seems unlikely the dam is 'natural', and the extent

---

➡

to which it is or is not a 'resource' is precisely what's under debate. 'Community' has to be one of the most popular words in politics today; no reasonable person would be against anything that was done for the sake of 'community'.

> Anti-flag-burning sentiments are another manifestation of an old spectre of scientific history: the prioritisation of sensibilities over the expression of opinion or fact.

This writer is trying to hide behind syllables and in doing so attempting to sound more educated than the reader, thereby putting the reader in their place – a more subtle form of bias.

> The United States is a great achievement in human rights, economics, science and health. The protocol for this success depends heavily on the Constitution and the Bill of Rights, and there is a faction of people that equates these principles with the flag.

'Faction' is an overtly political term that denotes minority status and connotes splinter or even extreme politics. In this context, the term can come off as patronising, even though the passage surrounding it seems to be making every effort to fairly explain the position of people who are against flag burning. While many disagree with that position on first-amendment grounds, those taking that position are hardly extreme or in the minority.

(Adapted from http://wps.ablongman.com/long_hult_nch_3/0,9398,1483997-,00.html – the website accompanying *The New Century Handbook*, 3rd ed., Pearson Education (Hult, C.A. and Huckin, T.N. 2005) Copyright Pearson Education 2005. Reprinted by permission.)

Avoid using rhetorical questions

Although you may occasionally see a rhetorical question such as 'So, what is the point?' or 'So, what is the alternative?' in a journal article or textbook, as a general rule it's preferable not to use them in the writing of a dissertation or thesis.

Minimise the use of abbreviations

Abbreviations such as *e.g.* and *i.e.* frequently crop up in students' writing. It is preferable to use full forms in academic writing. *Etc*, in particular, is often seen as a way of being vague or avoiding the trouble of having to spell out additional information for the reader! Either provide the additional information in full or use a phase like 'such as . . .' that makes it clear to the reader that other information exists beyond that which you are supplying.

Example

Instead of:

> Shells, cattle, gold, coins, etc. are some of the forms money has taken.

write either:

> Money has taken a number of forms such as shells, cattle, gold and coins.

or:

> Shells, cattle, gold, coins, banknotes, credit cards and e-money are forms money has taken.

Avoid using slang and other casual forms of language

Words such as *totally*, *really* or *dead* (meaning *very*), *pretty* (meaning *quite*) and *okay* are not considered appropriate in the context of university writing.

The use of 'I': a special note

The question of whether or not to use the first person singular ('I') in academic writing can be a cause of some anxiety for students, often because they get conflicting messages on its acceptability. The truth of the matter is that, traditionally, 'I' was not considered acceptable in academic discourse, perhaps because it called into question the writer's objectivity as well as their right to presume that their opinion mattered or had any authority. There's no doubt, however, that attitudes toward 'I' are changing and it's becoming more widely accepted in the academic community. This is the case more in certain disciplines and types of research activity/reporting than others. There can even be variation between individual departments of the same institution.

Our recommendation is that, in the first instance, you take advice from your supervisor on whether it's considered acceptable within your particular discipline area and given the nature of your own research project. If you're still in doubt, play safe and avoid using 'I'. Needless to say, this is something you need to be clear about before you begin writing. If you wait until later, you'll have to spend a significant amount of time reworking your sentences in order to substitute alternative forms of expression.

In the box below are examples of how to avoid the use of 'I' by de-personalising your language.

Examples of how to de-personalise your language

I	The author(s)/This writer(s)
I observed that	It was observed that
I interviewed ten subjects	Ten subjects were interviewed
I decided to employ a qualitative approach	The decision was taken to employ a qualitative approach
I considered it unethical to ask . . .	It was considered unethical to ask . . .
I found the results surprising because . . .	The results were surprising in that . . .
I believe that . . .	It can be argued that . . . /There is reason to suppose/believe that . . .
I take this to mean that . . .	This can be taken to mean that/This suggests that . . . /This can be interpreted as meaning that . . .
I was intrigued to find that . . .	The finding that . . . was intriguing.

> **TIP** Notice how, in de-personalising statements in this way, the active voice changes to passive voice (i.e. the past tense of the verb *to be* + the past participle of the following verb). In other words, one good strategy for avoiding the use of 'I' is to try and restructure your sentence so that you use the passive voice.

Example of active to passive voice

I observed that . . . → It was observed that . . .

(past tense of verb *to be*) + (past participle of verb)

Consider more academic words and phrases

While your writing needs to be concise and to the point, it also needs to have a modicum of eloquence or sophistication that may, for example, be absent in a letter to a friend and other more casual forms of writing. This doesn't mean that it needs to be stodgy, packed with long and 'difficult' words, and hard work to read. It does mean, however, that on occasion you may wish to select certain words rather than others in the course of your writing. Look at the boxed examples.

Casual words/phrases . . . and their more 'academic' counterparts

Consider using . . .	instead of . . .
highly, considerably, exceptionally	very
frequently	often
particularly	especially
observed	saw, noticed
illustrates, indicates, demonstrates	shows
eliminated	got rid of
conducted, carried out	did
therefore, consequently	so
discovered	saw, found
however, nevertheless, although	but
subjects	people
large, considerable, substantial	big
significant	important
extensive, extended	long
appears	seems
distinct, distinguishable from	different from
widely, extensively	a lot
examined, investigated	looked at/into
verified	checked
identified	found, noticed, recognised

While most examiners of dissertations or theses will not welcome a report the reading of which feels like wading through mud, they will certainly appreciate fine writing that shows the sort of varied, careful and considered use of language appropriate to an academic context and to this level of study.

Avoiding clichés

Clichéd phrases and expressions are those that are overused and which therefore lose their power to affect the reader. Try to avoid them in your writing. Some examples of clichés that frequently appear in students' work include the following:

fall on deaf ears	stick out like a sore thumb	nipped in the bud
march of history	in the same boat	leave no stone unturned
the end of the line	leaps and bounds	the powers that be
see their way clear	hit the nail on the head	at this point in time
in this day and age	at the end of the day	at the heart of the matter
the powers that be	trials and tribulations	the bottom line

Activity 4.1 Avoiding clichés and using alternatives

Look at the sentences below. Rewrite each sentence without using the italicised cliché.

1 *The winds of change* were all too evident following the fall of the Berlin Wall and the historic meetings between Gorbachev, Reagan and Thatcher.

Alternative: _____

_____

2 With the advantage of hindsight, the years immediately following Armistice Day could be characterised as *the calm before the storm*.

Alternative: _____

_____

3 In the initial weeks following the Watergate scandal, some constitutional experts were confident that the *writing* was *on the wall* for President Richard Nixon.

Alternative: _____

_____

4 Research has shown that people *from all walks of life* share similar attitudes to violent crime.

Alternative: _____

_____

➡

5 *From time immemorial*, man has sought to explain his world and give meaning to his existence.

Alternative: _____

_____

6 One common perception was that honest politicians are *few and far between*, with the vast majority being seen as self-serving.

Alternative: _____

_____

Keeping your writing gender-neutral

In an age where the issue of sexual equality is very much on the social agenda, it's not surprising that, in academia, the use of *he*, *his*, *she* and *her* in written work is increasingly discouraged, unless of course reference is being made to an actual person (a particular subject in a study, for example) or a gender-based study is the focus of a discussion. The need to avoid these words can present students with a challenge as they struggle to find alternative means of expression. So what are the options? There are really only two: either you completely rework your sentence in such a way that you simply do not have to refer to individuals and therefore do not need to employ one or other of these words, or you generalise or 'open up' the statement and use the word *they* instead, as we have done in this book. In many cases, the second option will be the only one available to you.

Examples

Gender-specific

> An individual who ultimately makes the decision to take his own life clearly believes there are no other options available to him.

Gender-neutral

> Individuals who ultimately make the decision to take their own lives clearly believe there are no other options available to them.

or

> The option to take one's own life is only exercised if it is believed there are no other options available.

Supporting your statements

One of the golden rules of academic writing is that all statements need to be supported. Statements that are made in the absence of any supporting information are little more than conjecture or personal opinion. As such they not only carry no weight but are also regarded as naïve and irresponsible. A reader who is presented with a series of unsupported statements has every right to ask the question, 'On what basis is this person saying that? Why should I believe them?'

There are a number of ways in which you can support your statements and therefore lend credibility and rigour to what you say:

- *Quoting data/statistics* that are generated by your own research or from empirical studies, both quantitative and qualitative, undertaken by others and reported in peer-refereed journal articles or textbooks.

- *Citing authorities* who, by definition, are known and respected in the field by virtue of having presented and published in well-regarded publications.

TIP It may be that you wish to cite a relative newcomer to the field who has published only one major article. Nevertheless, provided that article appeared in a refereed journal or book, then it may be regarded as authoritative. Conversely, it is not advisable to quote a widely published, highly regarded academic based on something they said at a conference or other event but which has not appeared in writing. In other words, hearsay – or indeed anecdotes – are generally not considered very credible sources with which to support statements.

- *Rational exposition* which convinces the reader of the soundness of any statements you make by showing, through the careful development of a good overall argument structure, a sound logical relationship between them such that each can be seen to follow necessarily ('a priori') from those that precede it. This ability to illustrate the integrity of statements you make through reason or logic is an immensely powerful weapon in your armoury as a researcher and it's one you'll be required to draw on constantly if your work is to be credible and persuasive.

TIP The need to ensure that there's a sound rationale for everything you say is a good way of keeping you on the straight and narrow as a researcher. By being very rigorous in this regard there's less likelihood that you'll develop arguments that have flawed foundations. Remember: it's perfectly possible for an entire dissertation or thesis to be fatally undermined by a rationale that's underpinned by unwarranted assumptions – a sobering thought!

Avoiding plagiarism

Plagiarism is the act of using someone else's work and passing it off as your own. In other words, when you plagiarise you fail to acknowledge the sources of those ideas that are not your own. This is one of the most serious offences you can commit as an academic and the punishment can consequently be severe. If your examiners feel you have a case to answer, you will probably be asked to explain yourself formally to a committee and you may be downgraded or even fail your dissertation or thesis should the committee determine that you are guilty of plagiarism.

What is particularly sad about many plagiarism cases is that they are, in fact, unintentional. Either because they come from an educational culture with different academic writing conventions and/or a different perspective on the citing of others' work, or because they simply forget to acknowledge a source, students often submit their work unaware of what they've done and the reaction it will provoke. Another problem is that some find it difficult to know when an idea is somebody else's and when it's their own. This tends to happen when they've taken another scholar's idea and either developed it in some way or applied it in a completely different context to that in which it was originally proposed. Unfortunately, whatever the reason, a plagiarism committee will not be interested in it; they will consider it a case of plagiarism regardless of whether it was deliberate or not. So beware!

The main way to avoid accusations of plagiarism is to be attentive to the origins of your ideas, meticulous in the way you record your sources (➡ see p. 75) and comprehensive with your in-text referencing, the focus of our next sub-section.

Referencing and quotations

As we saw earlier, if we are to add credibility to our ideas while also avoiding accusations of plagiarism, one key way in which we do this is by citing other reputable sources. Sometimes we may simply mention another scholar's theory of the idea and/or paraphrase it, and sometimes we may wish to quote that scholar. In both cases, a reference needs to be provided, and it needs to be correctly formatted.

Why is it so important to provide references and to format them correctly? Because it enables the reader to (a) understand the provenance of the ideas you are borrowing, and (b) to locate and read them, should they wish to do so. The reader's ability to locate and read any sources you cite is important, not only because it gives them the opportunity to understand more fully those ideas and the context in which they originally appeared, but because it allows them to determine whether or not you have represented them accurately. In-text references should therefore have the author's surname, the year of publication of the work being cited, and the relevant page numbers on which the quotation appears.

There are number of different referencing styles used in academic writing, including the Vancouver, Chicago and Modern Languages Association (MLA) styles. In this sub-section (and that on writing a bibliography, ➡ see p. 135) we will focus on the Harvard Style, as this is by far the most widely used, particularly in the Humanities and Social Sciences. However, what is considered acceptable can vary according to discipline, department and even lecturer/supervisor. We would recommend, therefore, that you consult carefully before adopting a particular style. Once you have established which style is appropriate for you, the following links will provide helpful information on referencing conventions other than Harvard, should you need to adopt one of these alternative styles.

Citation styles

HUMANITIES

Chicago

- Writer's Handbook: Chicago Style Documentation
  http://www.wisc.edu/writing/Handbook/DocChicago.html
- Quick Reference Guide to the Chicago Style
  http://www.library.wwu.edu/ref/Refhome/chicago.html
- Excellent FAQ on Usage in the Chicago Style
  http://www.press.uchicago.edu/Misc/Chicago/cmosfaq/
- Online! Guide to Chicago Style
  http://www.bedfordstmartins.com/online/cite7.html

MLA (Modern Language Association)

- Writer's Handbook: MLA Style Documentation
  http://www.wisc.edu/writing/Handbook/DocMLA.html
- The Documentation Style of the Modern Language Association
  http://www.newark.ohio-state.edu/~osuwrite/mla.htm
- MLA Citation Style
  http://campusgw.library.cornell.edu/newhelp/res_strategy/citing/mla.html
- Online! Guide to MLA Style
  http://www.bedfordstmartins.com/online/cite5.html
- Useful Guide to Parenthetical Documentation
  http://www.geocities.com/Athens/Acropolis/1623/document.html

Turabian (an academic style that works in other disciplines as well)

- Turabian bibliography samples (Ithaca College Library): based on the 6th edition of Turabian's *Manual*
- Turabian Style: Sample Footnotes and Bibliographic Entries (6th edition) (Bridgewater State College)

➡

- Turabian style guide (University of Southern Mississippi Libraries)
- Turabian Citation Style Examples (Northwest Missouri State University)

SCIENCES

ACS (American Chemical Society)

- ACS Style Sheet
  http://www.lehigh.edu/~inhelp/footnote/acs.html
- ACS Books Reference Style Guidelines
  http://pubs.acs.org/books/references.shtml

AMA (American Medical Society)

- AMA Style Guide
  http://healthlinks.washington.edu/hsl/styleguides/ama.html
- AMA Documentation Style
  http://rx.stlcop.edu/wcenter/AMA.htm
- AMA Citation Style
  http://www.liu.edu/cwis/cwp/library/workshop/citama.htm

CBE (Council of Biology Editors)

- Writer's Handbook: CBE Style Documentation
  http://www.wisc.edu/writetest/Handbook/DocCBE6.html
- Online! Guide to CBE Style
  http://www.bedfordstmartins.com/online/cite8.html
- CBE Style Form Guide
  http://www.lib.ohio-state.edu/guides/cbegd.html

IEEE (Institute of Electrical and Electronics Engineers)

- Handbook: Documentation IEEE Style
  http://www.ecf.utoronto.ca/~writing/handbook-docum1b.html
- Sample IEEE Documentation Style for References
  http://www.carleton.ca/~nartemev/IEEE_style.html
- Electrical Engineering Citation Style
  http://www.lehigh.edu/~inhelp/footnote/footee.html

NLM (National Library of Medicine)

- NLM Style Guide
  http://healthlinks.washington.edu/hsl/styleguides/nlm.html
- Citing the Internet: A Brief Guide
  http://nnlm.gov/pnr/news/200107/netcite.html
- National Library of Medicine Recommended Formats for Bibliographic Citation (PDF format)
  http://www.nlm.nih.gov/pubs/formats/internet.pdf

Vancouver (Biological Sciences)

- Introduction to the Vancouver Style
  http://www.lib.monash.edu.au/vl/cite/citeprvr.htm
- Vancouver Style References
  http://www.library.uq.edu.au/training/citation/vancouv.html
- Detailed Explanation of the Vancouver style
  http://www.acponline.org/journals/annals/01jan97/unifreqr.htm

SOCIAL SCIENCES

AAA (American Anthropological Association)

- Citations and Bibliographic Style for Anthropology Papers
  http://www.usd.edu/anth/handbook/bib.htm
- AAA Style Handbook (PDF format)
  http://www.aaanet.org/pubs/style_guide.pdf

APA (American Psychological Association)

- Writer's Handbook: APA Style Documentation
  http://www.wisc.edu/writing/Handbook/DocAPA.html
- APA Style Guide
  http://www.lib.usm.edu/~instruct/guides/apa.html
- Bibliography Style Handbook (APA)
  http://www.english.uiuc.edu/cws/wworkshop/bibliography_style_
  handbookapa.htm
- APA Style Electronic Format
  http://www.westwords.com/guffey/apa.html
- Online! Guide to APA Style
  http://www.bedfordstmartins.com/online/cite6.html
- APA Style.org
  http://www.apastyle.org/elecref.html

APSA (American Political Science Association)

- Writer's Handbook: APSA Documentation
  http://www.wisc.edu/writing/Handbook/DocAPSA.html

Legal style

- Cornell University's Introduction to Basic Legal Citation
  http://www.law.cornell.edu/citation/citation.table.html
- Legal Citation: Using and Understanding Legal Abbreviations
  http://qsilver.queensu.ca/law/legalcit.htm
- Legal Research and Citation Style in the USA
  http://www.rbs0.com/lawcite.htm

➡

OTHER

- General information on citing web documents
  http://www.lib.berkeley.edu/TeachingLib/Guides/Internet/Style.html
- Recommended Multi-Style Links
  http://www.aresearchguide.com/styleguides.html
  http://www.dianahacker.com/resdoc/

(Source: provided by Turnitin.com and Research Resources. Turnitin allows free distribution and non-profit use of this document in educational settings.)

TIP Even within a particular style there can be some minor variation in the use of capitalisation and punctuation. What is essential, however, is that you are consistent in how you present your references.

Quoting extended extracts

A quotation that is longer than two or three lines and/or which comprises more than one sentence is normally set off from the rest of the paragraph by:

- a blank line before and after it, and
- indenting it slightly left.

Look at these examples.

Example 1

Despite many reforms, by the far the most blatant example of sexist language is still the use of 'man' as the generic form for 'people' or 'humanity', and along with this goes the frequent use of the personal pronoun 'his' – especially in expository writing – as though women were pretty much an afterthought. One critic writing on gender formulates the problem this way:

> The abstract form, the general, the universal, this is what the so-called masculine gender means, for the class of men have appropriated the universal for themselves. One must understand that men are not born with a faculty for the universal and that women are not reduced at birth to the particular. The universe has been, and is, continually, at every moment, appropriated by men.   (Wittig, 1986: 66)

The implication that men are the more important members of the human race can be changed in many ways. For example . . .

(Source: Tubbs and Moss, 2000: 89)

Example 2

The notion of self-concept has been discussed extensively in the psychology and communication literature and is generally seen as being composed of two parts: self-image and self-esteem. Pearson and Nelson describe self-image as

> the picture you have of yourself, the sort of person you believe you are. Included in your self image are the categories in which you place yourself, the roles you play, and other similar descriptors you use to identify yourself. (Pearson and Nelson, 2000: 42)

As the authors go on to point out, self-image goes beyond simply the way in which an individual pictures themselves; it also involves how others see them. (Source: Adapted from Pearson and Nelson, 2000: 42)

Example 3

According to Tannen, it is these differences in style that account for so many misunderstandings. She gives a striking example:

> Though both men and women complain about being interrupted by each other, the behaviors they are complaining about are different.
>
> In many of the comments I heard from people I interviewed, men felt interrupted by women who overlapped with words of agreement and support and anticipation of how their sentences and thoughts would end. If a woman supported a man's story by elaborating on a point different from the one he had intended, he felt his right to tell his own story had been violated. (p. 210)

Feminist critic Deborah Cameron identifies two current approaches to the language styles of men and women . . . (Source: Tubbs and Moss, 2000: 91)

Notice how, in example 3, the writer does not provide a full in-text reference at the end of the quotation. This is because the author of the quotation, Deborah Tannen, and the book from which is was taken, were mentioned previously, two paragraphs earlier. It is therefore assumed that the writer can infer that this quotation is from that same book. Had there been other Tannen publications mentioned earlier and in close proximity, then it would have become necessary to provide a full reference at the end of the quotation in order to make it absolutely clear from which of those publications it was taken. Writers will often use the Latin abbreviation ibid. to indicate this; thus, 'Janiker, ibid. p. 134' literally means 'page 134 from the same Janiker book/article'. (See p. 128 for a list of Latin and English abbreviations commonly used in academic writing.)

Activity 4.2 Integrating and formatting long quotations

Look at the following long quotation that discusses some limitations of law in the context of social work. The quotation is taken from page 191 of a 2008 publication entitled *Social Work: An Introduction to Contemporary Practice*, written by Kate Wilson, Gillian Ruch, Mark Lymbery and Andrew Cooper. Try to frame the quotation with a relevant one- or two-sentence introduction, as in the above examples. Then include the long quotation, formatting it correctly and providing full reference details. Ignore our source reference at the end!

To practice social work effectively it is necessary to have a critical under-standing of law and to recognise its limitations alongside its strengths. A common misconception about law is that it is clear-cut and provides unambiguous answers or solutions. In fact some provisions of the law lack that clarity and may be open to interpretation. When new legislation is introduced it is some-times necessary to wait for clarification on meaning of certain provisions from the courts. In other situations law may appear to lack clear direction because it allows discretion for practice within broad boundaries.

(Source: Adapted from Wilson *et al.*, 2008: 191)

Quoting short extracts

A short quotation is one that is no longer than a few words or that constitutes a sentence spanning two or three lines at most. As such, it can be integrated within the main text of the paragraph and, unlike a longer quotation, does not need to be set off by a blank line and a left indent. However, you do need to provide exactly the same reference information. Look at these examples:

Example 1

Drefuss states quite categorically that 'were it not for the personality, common touch and vision of Tony Blair, New Labour would not even have come close to achieving what it has' (2007: 56).

Example 2

Drefuss (2007: 56) states quite categorically that 'were it not for the personality, common touch and vision of Tony Blair, New Labour would not even have come close to achieving what it has'.

Note how, in the following example and in contrast to the two examples above, the name of the author quoted appears in parentheses, along with the year of publication and page number. This is because it does not feature in the sentence surrounding the quotation:

Example 3

Verbal elaboration has been described as 'a cognitive strategy that involves the individual talking in a meaningful way about information they are trying to remember' (Vachek, 2001: 92).

Activity 4.3 Integrating and formatting short quotations

Look at the three texts below. For each text, create a suitable short paragraph in which you quote part of the text. Remember to use only a short quotation that can be incorporated within the main text of the paragraph and that does not need to be set off in the same way as a long quotation. Ensure you format and reference the quotation correctly.

Text 1

The study of consumer behaviour does not end with a purchase. What makes people satisfied or dissatisfied? Increasingly, marketers are drawing on anthropology to understand how we relate to products. We need to know how they are used. Gift purchases are very different from products purchased for self use. Companies want to know how to establish long-lasting relationships with consumers. This interest in the period after a purchase makes the study of consumers a circular rather than linear activity. People's attitudes and lifestyles are influenced by past purchases, and each passage through awareness interest, desire and action influences all other purchase decisions.

(Kotler *et al.*, 1996: 44)

Text 2

Gender underachievement is easier for schools to combat than underachievement that is caused by poverty or ethnicity that rely on national strategies. Many strategies that are working to reduce attainment gaps are reliant on government funding and initiatives, and rely on a national vision and drive to counteract disadvantage and deprivation . . . Resources should be targeted at those most at risk and children with poorly educated mothers could need extra support. To do this schools will have to work with and through the community to bring about improvement.   (Adapted from Davies, 2006: 55)

> **Text 3**
>
> Good teachers realise that within any class whether it is banded, streamed or set there will be a range of pupils with different strengths and weaknesses. There will also be pupils who learn in different ways depending on the individual preferred learning style of the pupil. The best teacher will ensure that their lesson is differentiated so that pupils who are finding the topic easy will be able to develop and enrich their learning and not be held back. Those who find the topic or area of work more challenging will be supported so that they will in time get to a competent level of understanding. (Davies, 2006: 19)

Deliberately omitting information from a quotation

Sometimes you may wish to omit part of a quotation, if, for example, you feel it's providing information that's peripheral to the main idea captured in the quotation and therefore something of a distraction. In this case, it's important that you alert your reader to the omission by substituting the missing information with three dots (the technical term is ellipses) as follows:

> **Example 1**
>
> In their discussion of non-verbal communication, Hybels and Weaver suggest that "The higher your status, the more control you have over your time . . . Professionals in our society often make others wait for them" (2001: 151).
>
> **Example 2**
>
> Davies discusses this natural change in aptitude in the following terms:
>
> > Those who argue for a critical period in language learning believe that around puberty, the ability to learn language atrophies . . . and that our ability to 'pick up' language from our environment with minimal effort diminishes as a result of changes in the brain. (Davies, 1999: 59)
>
> She goes on to point out while there is compelling evidence for the existence of a critical period, there are people who nevertheless appear to develop native or near-native speaker proficiency levels in language despite commencing learning late in life.

TIP If you choose to omit part of a quotation, you need to make absolutely certain that you have not changed the meaning of the original in any way; otherwise, you could be accused of taking the quotation out of its original context in order to suit your own theoretical agenda and/or mislead the reader.

The use of *et al.*

When citing or quoting work written by more than two authors, it's common practice to use the name of the first author followed by *et al.* in your in-text reference. '*Et al.*' means 'and others', and using it makes writing and reading multi-authored references far less tedious. Here are two examples:

Example 1

Franklin *et al.* (1988) have perhaps provided the strongest case yet for the need to reduce greenhouse gases.

Example 2

Alliance Theory, seen by many anthropologists as one of the main benefits of the institution of marriage, has been described in the following terms:

> marriage increases social cooperation through the relations that develop between people and their in-laws. And this kind of human network is, in turn, good for society as a whole.　　　　　(Matlock *et al.*, 2008)

Et al. should only be used for in-text referencing and should not be used in your bibliography. When writing your bibliography (➡ see p. 135), all authors should be listed in full, along with all other publication details.

Dealing with multiple sources written by the same author in the same year

Sometimes may you find that you want to use two or more titles written by the same author and with the same year of publication. In order to distinguish between the titles in both your in-text and bibliographical referencing, you will need to place lower-case letters – a, b, c, etc. – immediately after the year in the text citation, as follows:

> Although Carrera (1979a: 42) states categorically that 'the only . . .', he later appears to backtrack in his claim that 'It would be best . . .' (1979b: 187).

Single vs double inverted commas

Increasingly, the use of double inverted commas (". . .") to indicate a quotation is becoming the norm in academic writing, although single inverted commas ('. . .') are still widespread. The fact that a single inverted comma can be mistaken for an apostrophe and therefore cause momentary confusion or the misreading of a text is one of the frequently cited advantages of using double inverted commas. Once again, it's a good idea to check with your particular discipline and/or department whether they have a preference. If not, you should feel free to use whichever system you prefer. Whatever you decide, it's worth remembering that both have a place in your writing, specifically when you are quoting a source who in turn quotes somebody else. In this case, whichever system you use for the main quotation, you will need to use the other system for the embedded quotation.

If you have decided to use a system of double inverted commas for main quotations, then you would deal with an embedded quotation in the following way:

> Greeves argues that 'despite Elder's claims that 'the scandal was the single most damaging event of his prime ministership', the events that unfolded in the weeks immediately following its emergence were to have a far more profound effect not only on the leader and his government but on the country at large' (2003: 69).

If, on the other hand, you have decided to use a system of single inverted commas for main quotations, then you would deal with an embedded quotation in the following way:

> Greeves argues that 'despite Elder's claims that "the scandal was the single most damaging event of his prime ministership", the events that unfolded in the weeks immediately following its emergence were to have a far more profound effect not only on the leader and his government but on the country at large' (2003: 69).

Whichever option you use, make sure you apply it consistently.

Paraphrasing

Sometimes, instead of quoting a scholar directly, you may wish to report what they've said in your own words. Restating someone else's ideas in your own words is called paraphrasing, and, as with direct quotations, you are still required to acknowledge the original author of those ideas by providing a reference – after all, just because you've restated their ideas doesn't mean you've taken ownership of them! This crucial fact emphasises one key characteristic of a good paraphrase: the restatement of information in such a way that it does not change the meaning of the original.

The five stages of effective paraphrasing

1 Read and make sure you understand the original text.

2 Make notes on the original text that can serve as cues during the rewriting of it. We recommend doing this without referring to the original text as this keeps distance between your version and the original – an important consideration seeing as you are not quoting it directly.

3 Rewrite the original text from your notes. This will involve some restructuring, rephrasing and perhaps the use of synonyms.

4 Ensure that the new text flows smoothly.

5 Check that your text is an accurate reflection of the original and does not misrepresent it. Remember that taking an idea and placing it in a new context can sometimes change the way in which that idea is understood.

Ways of introducing quotations and paraphrases

Whether you are introducing a direct quotation or paraphrasing another writer, you will need to introduce their views. The expressions in the box opposite are commonly used for this purpose.

Introducing quotations and paraphrases: useful expressions

X claims that . . .	X contends that . . .	X demonstrates that . . .
X suggests that . . .	X warns that . . .	X declares that . . .
X explains that . . .	X argues that . . .	X takes the view/position that . . .
X states that . . .	X notes that . . .	X judges that . . .
X found that . . .	X discovered that . . .	X considers that . . .
X alleges that . . .	X shows that . . .	X asserts that . . .
X reports that . . .	X determines that . . .	X believes that . . .
According to X . . .		

Of course the formula 'X _____ that . . .' is not always employed! To avoid tedium, there are variations that can be used such as:

As Mitchell and Francis note, . . .
Yousefpour, however, claims it was never . . .

Then there are expressions such as:

According to Qiang (1989), . . .
As Scupper explains/asserts/reports, . . .

Sometimes, with direct quotations, a simple colon can be used as follows:

As Chomsky so famously remarked: 'States are not moral agents, people are, and can impose moral standards on powerful institutions.'

or

In his discussion of faith, Dawkins states:

Faith is powerful enough to immunize people against all appeals to pity, to forgiveness, to decent human feelings. It even immunizes them against fear, if they honestly believe that a martyr's death will send them straight to heaven . . .

Activity 4.4 Paraphrasing a text

Look at the two quotations below. Paraphrase them and provide references.

The teacher's dilemma in the selection of instructional techniques is also not likely to be resolved by the discovery of a new and ideal method for teaching all children. From the huge expenditures of commercial enterprises and government agencies in pursuit of a technology of reading instruction that will prove infallible, and preferably 'teacher-proof', the only conclusion that can safely be drawn is that nothing could possibly be invented that is significantly better than or even different from the methods and materials we have always had available, even if they are dressed up for use with computers.   (Smith, 1988: 4)

> The reasons why closed questions nevertheless remain a popular and valued means of gathering data is because they provide answers that are easier to process and score for. Closed questions make possible a range of formats for tallying and comparing responses.
>
> (Wray et al., 1998: 174)

Quoting electronic sources

We emphasised, in an earlier section (➡ see p. 60), the need to be cautious when using electronic sources. However, with so much information now available online and the resulting trend toward electronic modes of research, the likelihood is that you will wish to cite electronic sources in your dissertation or thesis. Here, the main thing to remember is that you need to provide the same information as you would with any other type of source, namely the author's name, the year of publication, and the page number(s) where relevant. This is true regardless of whether the source is a journal article from an electronic database, an internet website, an e-book, an internet blog, electronic conference proceedings or an email.

Example

Richards argues cogently that, despite numerous claims to the contrary, second language acquisition research has, in reality, impacted only minimally on second language pedagogy (Richards, 2003).

As we shall see ➡ on pages 135–8, the way in which electronic sources are dealt with in your bibliography is far more particular and needs to be given careful attention.

Quoting primary vs secondary sources

Quoting a primary source means going to the work (book, article, etc.) in which an idea was *originally* proposed and quoting directly from that source. In contrast, quoting a secondary source means quoting a writer who has, in turn, quoted, paraphrased and interpreted an idea originally proposed by somebody else. Although in some disciplines it's difficult to avoid drawing on secondary sources in research, as a rule, it's best to avoid quoting secondary sources if at all possible because their integrity can usually be called into question. Once ideas are taken out of their original context and introduced into a new context their meaning can change, often subtly but significantly. As we've seen in our discussion of paraphrasing, either deliberately or otherwise, ideas can be re-presented by writers in such a way that they misrepresent the original.

TIP Where possible, always to try to quote primary sources rather than 'second-hand' versions of others' ideas. If you wish to quote someone who is commenting on the idea of another writer, try to sight the original work yourself.

If you need to quote a secondary source, here's an example of how it's done:

> It has been argued that this was the unstated rationale behind the government's machinations (Entwistle 1999, cited in Whittle 2001).

or

> Davies (cited in Haggard 1995) reports that there is absolutely no correlation between social class and ultimate level of success in this regard.

Activity 4.5 Quoting secondary sources

Read the following quotation from page 393 of a book entitled *English Legal System*, published in 2007 and written by Catherine Elliott and Frances Quinn. Create a brief text in which you cite Vennard – a secondary source (from Elliott and Quinn). Use the correct referencing conventions as illustrated above.

> Many defendants believe they stand a better chance of acquittal in the Crown Court. A study by Vennard in 1985 (*The Outcome of Contested Trials*) suggests that they may be right: acquittal rates were significantly higher in the Crown Court (57 per cent) than in magistrates' courts (30 per cent). However, most of those who choose to be tried in the Crown Court then proceed to plead guilty.
>
> (Adapted from Elliott and Quinn 2008: 377)

Finally, never cite an article solely on the basis of its abstract. With many journal articles now available online it's commonplace for publishers to make only abstracts available to visitors to their websites. To view complete articles, you or your institution will need to have subscribed to the journal(s) in question. For cost reasons, or to save time, it can sometimes be all too tempting not to read articles in their entirety!

Acknowledging alternative perspectives

As we have seen, sound academic inquiry must be objective. The moment your reader senses that you've lost objectivity, they lose faith in what you are writing. They believe you are not providing a full picture, either because you have tunnel vision and are unable to see beyond your own ideas or because you are deliberately skewing information or being selective about what you choose to present in order to promote your own agenda or perhaps camouflage weaknesses in your work. In order to pre-empt any such criticism, it's important that you survey the literature thoroughly in order to familiarise yourself with all arguments and perspectives voiced on the issues you discuss in your work. You must then make your reader aware that you've done so by explicitly acknowledging them and, where necessary, countering them. Only by your doing this will you satisfy the reader that your own views are well-informed and that you are offering an honest and balanced commentary and analysis.

Just as acknowledging alternative perspectives reassures the reader of your integrity, so does the kind of language you use. In the same way that emotive language undermines the sense of objectivity you should be trying to achieve in your writing, biased language which, for example, offhandedly dismisses views contrary to your own, can seriously damage the credibility and impact of your work.

Introductions

Introductions are an essential part of academic writing, yet students often find the writing of a good introduction quite a challenging task; the whole business of 'getting started' is a painful struggle and a lot of time can be lost fumbling around looking for a good 'way in'. Often, what eventually gets onto the page feels less than satisfactory both to the writer and to the reader. This is actually unsurprising seeing as the writing of an introduction is more complex than many people realise and involves achieving a number of aims. Let's look at each of these in turn.

Providing a contextual frame for your discussion

Whether you are writing an introduction for a single chapter of your dissertation or thesis or for the entire work (➡ see Chapter 5, p. 146), its most important function is to make it clear to the reader why what you are about to discuss is important and therefore worth reading. It does this by placing your discussion within a broader theoretical context in order to demonstrate how it fits in and is relevant. In academia, any discipline has developed over time as the product of a cumulative process of research and debate in which each piece of the jigsaw that has come to make up that discipline has been motivated by or built upon those that preceded it. Without this continuity of thought and inquiry, any discipline would consist merely of a collection of random ideas and as such its progress would be severely retarded, if not halted altogether. Indeed, one could legitimately question whether a collection of random ideas has any right to be called 'a discipline'.

An introduction, then, needs to anchor your discussion by providing relevant background information that shows the reader the relevance and significance of your contribution. For example, if you intend to discuss the pros and cons of access/ equity programmes into higher education, as an entrée into your discussion you may wish to begin by (a) discussing what equity programmes are, (b) highlighting the fact that the notions of opportunity for all, social justice and an educated workforce are currently high on political, social and educational agendas, and (c) provide an indication of the extent to which financial and human resources have been invested in such programmes. After all, before a reader can appreciate the importance of an evaluation of such programmes, they need to understand what these programmes are, what commitment has been made to them, and the nature of the discourse surrounding them.

Activity 4.6 Writing an introduction 1

Imagine that you need to write an introduction to a dissertation or perhaps a chapter or section of a dissertation the focus of which is the importance of intercultural communication skills in the workplace. On a separate sheet of paper, list some of the ideas you might include in your introduction in order to frame your discussion in the way described above. One idea has been included to help get you started. You should aim for at least six.

■ *Advances in technology – flight and information technology in particular – have created a 'smaller', more inter-dependent and more homogeneous world.*

Engaging the reader

Another important function of an introduction is to whet the reader's appetite in such a way that they want to read on and see 'how the story unfolds'. Providing background information of the kind described in the previous section in order to contextualise your discussion is clearly one way to do this; however, there are at least two other strategies. The first is to use language that engages readers, is clear, easy to read and understand, and not dense or pompous; language that inspires them and stimulates their interest. The second is to build interest and anticipation through careful structuring of your introduction. One important part of this strategy involves the positioning of the thesis statement, the focus of the following text.

The thesis statement

Put simply, a thesis statement is a statement of intent. It tells your reader, often in a single sentence, what you are going to be discussing in the chapter, article, essay, etc. that follows. It is an essential part of any introduction and, in theory at least, can appear at the beginning of the introduction, in the middle or at the end. In practice, however, most thesis statements usually appear either at the beginning or at the end, mainly because this is where they tend to have the greatest impact on the reader.

Thesis statements at the start vs thesis statements at the end of the introduction

When deciding where to place your thesis statement, it can be helpful to understand the different effects that are achieved by placing it at the start and at the end of the introduction respectively. By placing it at the start, the reader knows from the outset what the main focus of the discussion will be; the background information which follows and constitutes the remainder of the introduction will then be read in light of that knowledge. In contrast, by placing the thesis statement at the end of the introduction, the reader is first presented with the background information and only later learns what the focus of the discussion is to be. The advantage with this approach is that it builds a sense of anticipation or expectation in the reader that is arguably more engaging and that helps create reader momentum.

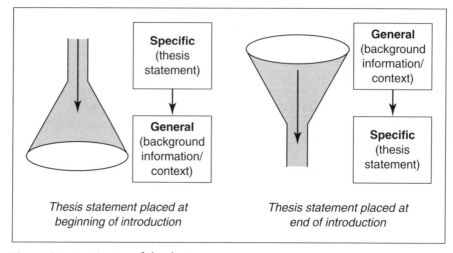

Figure 4.1 Positioning of the thesis statement

The difference between these two approaches can be represented in terms of a funnel (see Figure 4.1). When the thesis statement appears at the beginning of the introduction, there is a move from specific (the statement itself) to more general (the contextual backdrop); when it appears at the end, there is a move from general (the contextual backdrop) to more specific (the thesis statement).

In the case of the second option, if your introduction has been well constructed you should begin with the more general information and gradually narrow your focus in such a way that the reader may well be able to predict the thesis statement. In other words, your thesis statement should naturally emerge or 'drop out of' the contextual discussion that precedes it.

Look at these two examples, one of which places the thesis statement at the beginning of the introduction, and the other which places it at the end.

Example 1: at the beginning

This study critically evaluates that body of evidence frequently cited in support of the idea that the prolonged use of mobile phones is harmful to health.

Ever since analogue mobile phones appeared in the 1980s, there has been a debate over the health risks associated with their use. Some claim that the radio-frequency radiation that handsets emit enters the head injuring living tissue and possibly triggering a brain tumour or other disease. However, while their use does appear to produce changes in brain temperature and activity as well as blood pressure changes, many dispute findings as inconsistent and unreliable.

Given that nearly 2 billion people use a mobile phone, the question over their safety is an important one. It is also divisive. Just as there is no agreement within the academic research community, so too there is none among the wider population many of whom express scepticism and mistrust over the claims of researchers and mobile phone manufacturers respectively. What many call for, however, is an honest presentation of the facts and an objective evaluation of the evidence presented to date.

Example 2: at the end

Both in the United Kingdom and elsewhere (Australia and the United States), enabling education today occupies an increasingly prominent place on social, political and educational agendas, driven as it is by notions of a better educated, more fulfilled society, and a more competent and productive workforce that is able to respond to the changing needs of a dynamic labour market.

University foundation programmes constitute one important vehicle through which to provide those individuals who, for a variety of reasons (economic, family, health, etc.) were unable or disinclined to pursue their education at an earlier stage in their careers, with the opportunity to develop themselves through the completion of a course of study designed to prepare them for life as undergraduates and ultimately as fulfilled members of society.

In establishing these programmes, universities are seen as being responsive to the current climate of social justice and opportunity for all. However, their increasing popularity has meant a substantial investment of human and financial resources on the understanding that they do indeed benefit the individual and society at large. With this in mind, this paper investigates the perceived and actual benefits of such programmes from the points of view of students in pre-tertiary enabling education, and the academic staff who encounter them in subsequent undergraduate courses.

Activity 4.7 Constructing and positioning thesis statements

Write the introduction to a chapter on the causes of teenage depression. Using the information listed below as a series of bullet points, write two versions of the introduction, one with the thesis statement at the beginning and the other with it at the end. Feel free to rearrange the information or to add additional information, if you wish, but try to keep the introduction brief.

- Research shows that in the past 10 years the incidence of teenage depression has increased markedly.
- Counsellors, GPs, psychiatrists and psychologists are seeing a general increase in the proportion of young people requiring treatment for the disorder.
- Teenage depression is far more of an issue in the developed world.
- Teenage girls are more susceptible to depression than teenage boys.
- Depression in children can take an enormous psychological toll on the parents of those who suffer.

Explicit vs implicit thesis statements

Another decision you may want to make about your thesis statement is whether to make it an explicit or implicit statement. Explicit thesis statements state directly what issue the upcoming discussion will address. Both thesis statements in the two examples above do this:

> ...this paper investigates the perceived and actual benefits of such programmes from the points of view of students in pre-tertiary enabling education, and the academic staff who encounter them in subsequent undergraduate courses.

> This paper critically evaluates that body of evidence frequently cited in support of the idea that the prolonged use of mobile phones is harmful to health.

In contrast, implicit thesis statements state indirectly the issue that will be addressed in the upcoming discussion. In other words, the reader is left to infer what the main focus of that discussion will be. Look at the example below in which Example 1 above has been rewritten using an implicit thesis statement.

In establishing these programmes, universities are seen as being responsive to the current climate of social justice and opportunity for all. However, their increasing popularity and the substantial investment of human and financial resources that they represent begs the question of what the perceived and actual benefits of such programmes are from the points of view of students in pre-tertiary enabling education, and the academic staff who encounter them in subsequent undergraduate courses.

Here's another example of an implicit thesis statement that appeared at the end of an introduction to a piece of writing that discussed the ways in which schools and parents need to co-operate in the moral education of children.

If children are to feel secure in this way and acquire a clear, unambiguous sense of right and wrong, it is imperative that they not receive mixed messages about what is and is not acceptable behaviour. Consistency and reinforcement are everything and as such there is a series of measures currently under discussion which seeks to ensure an ongoing dialogue between schools and parents and revolving around children's moral education.

If the introduction has been carefully constructed, an implicit thesis statement – despite being indirect – should leave the reader in little or no doubt what the main focus is of the subsequent discussion. However, for it to work, there will normally need to be enough contextual or 'lead-up' information preceding it (see the right-hand funnel in Figure 4.1). This means that implicit thesis statements almost always occur at or toward the end of an introduction.

Occasionally a question might serve as an implicit thesis statement, as in the following example:

> In establishing these programmes, universities are seen as being responsive to the current climate of social justice and opportunity for all. However, their increasing popularity has meant a substantial investment of human and financial resources. What then, it might reasonably be asked, are the perceived and actual benefits of such programmes from the points of view of students in pre-tertiary enabling education, and the academic staff who encounter them in subsequent undergraduate courses?

As a rule, however, we suggest that you avoid the use of questions as thesis statements in a dissertation or thesis. While they may occasionally be used discriminatingly in a chapter introduction, they should certainly not be used in the main introduction to the work (➡ see Chapter 5, p. 146).

Activity 4.8 Writing an introduction 2

Look again at the introduction you created in Activity 4.6, earlier in this section. Think of two implicit thesis statements either of which could replace the original thesis statement you constructed for that exercise and which appeared at the end of the introduction. Write your two implicit thesis statements below:

1 _____

_____

2 _____

_____

Introductions: useful expressions

This chapter/section/article seeks to address (the question of) . . .

In the pages that follow, . . .

This chapter/section/article will look at/consider/present/discuss/assess/evaluate . . .

This chapter will argue that . . .

In this section/chapter, evidence will be presented in support of the idea that . . .

This raises the question of whether and to what extent . . .

Providing an overview

Another way to build reader interest is to give them an overview of what is to come in your discussion. This (hopefully) not only motivates them to read on, but also serves as a navigational tool that helps orientate them as they read through your work. Knowing in advance in what direction a discussion is going can be reassuring for a reader, not least because it can help them better understand and appreciate the significance of what they are reading at any particular point.

One common student misconception is that an introduction should consist of one paragraph. Not so! It can consist of any number of paragraphs. The rule for beginning a new paragraph applies in introductions in exactly the same way as it does elsewhere in your writing: whenever you begin a new idea with its own clearly-identifiable topic sentence, start a new paragraph. An introduction may well contain a number of such ideas and will therefore warrant a series of paragraphs. The same is true of conclusions, discussed below.

Activity 4.9 Writing an introduction 3

Look at the ideas you listed in Activity 4.6, earlier in this section. On a separate piece of paper, write a short introduction to a chapter designed to focus on the importance of intercultural communication skills in the workplace.

Think carefully about these things:

- how you will engage your reader
- where you are going to put your thesis statement
- how you are going to organise the information to create a good flow
- how you will indicate the structure/direction of the chapter.

Summarising and concluding individual chapters

Conclusions, like introductions, can often present students with difficulties. Just as they find it difficult to open up their discussion, they also tend to have problems 'rounding it off' in such a way that it comes to a natural close.

One of the main weaknesses with students' conclusions is that, frequently, they actually conclude nothing but merely repeat what they've already said. In other words, they summarise and in doing so appear to consider summaries and conclusions to be one and the same thing. They are not! Let's look at each in turn, starting with summaries.

Summaries

Summarising means taking information you've already discussed and restating it in a more condensed form. Sometimes it may be in the form of full prose, at others it may consist of a series of bullet points. The contents of a 15-page dissertation chapter, for example, might be reduced down to two-thirds of a page or a series of eight bullet points. The main purpose of summarising is to give the reader an at-a-glance overview of the main points of a chapter (or part of a chapter), and this in turn has a number of benefits:

- It helps the reader see the wood from the trees. Particularly if a chapter or journal article is long, complex and information-rich, the reader can become disorientated and lose their sense of its structure, how the various sections and sub-sections relate to each other, and where exactly they, the reader, are currently located in the chapter. This can happen despite the fact that the introduction may have mapped out the direction of the article or chapter.

- It serves as a reminder of the main points discussed.

- It can help link what has been discussed to what is about to be discussed. In other words, it can help smooth the transition between two consecutive parts of a chapter or article, or between two chapters.

Although they are often encouraged, particularly within the context of dissertations and theses where chapters tend to be long and complex, whether or not to include a summary is very much down to the judgement of the individual writer/researcher. Once again, accessibility and comprehensibility must be paramount and each writer has to put themselves in their reader's shoes and ask whether, in the absence of a summary, their work remains clear and easy to process. Conversely, they may wish to ask themselves, 'Would a summary make the reader's life easier here?'

If it is considered necessary, a summary will often form the initial part of a conclusion but it does not need to. It may stand alone as a 'Summary' or be incorporated within the main text of the body of the chapter or article. There may, in fact, be a number of short summaries within a single chapter, particularly if it's a long and complex chapter with a number of foci. The summary may be presented as a series of bullet points or as normal prose.

Summaries: useful expressions

This chapter/section has discussed the following: . . .

This chapter/section has sought to . . .

This chapter/section has . . .

This chapter has looked at/addressed a number of . . . First, . . .

The key points discussed so far are: . . .

Five main ideas have been critically appraised in this chapter. To begin with . . .

In summary, . . .

To summarise, . . .

The main points discussed in this chapter can be summarised as follows: . . .

In summary, the argument/position is as follows: . . .

We might summarise the main points thus: . . .

Now look at the examples of chapter summaries.

Examples of chapter summaries

This chapter has examined communication strategies used by second language learners (and native speakers) when they are faced with a production problem. They consist of substitute plans and are potentially conscious. A typology of communication strategies distinguishes reduction strategies, which are used to avoid the problem altogether, and achievement strategies, which are used to overcome the problem. The latter can be further subdivided into compensatory strategies (including both first language and second language based strategies) and retrieval strategies. There has been only limited empirical study of communication strategies, but there is evidence to suggest that their use is influenced by the learner's proficiency level, the nature of the problem-source, the learner's personality, and the learning situation. It is not yet clear what effect, if any, communicative strategies have on linguistic development.

(Adapted from Ellis, 1985: 188)

This chapter has sought to show that since the 1990s there has been more television news produced for the UK audience than ever before, and that despite the concerns of some within the industry, the traditional public service commitment to high-quality news remains written into the broadcasting legislation. Furthermore, the statistics suggest that commercial television is similarly committed to quality journalism at peak-time. News, it seems, is popular and therefore justifiable on purely commercial grounds. The prospects for current affairs broadcasting, particularly on Channel 3, are less certain because financial pressures may lead to cuts in the number of programmes broadcast as well as changes to scheduling. (Adapted from McNair, 1994: 121–2)

Activity 4.10 Summarising a text

Look at the text below. Although it's considerably shorter than a chapter in a dissertation or thesis, write a summary of the information it contains using the guidelines above.

Both Burma and Iran are repressive authoritarian regimes: the former a military regime, the latter a theocratic state. Of the two, Iran seems to exhibit a greater tendency to totalitarianism, although in an incomplete form. Nevertheless, the near total control of all levers of power by Iran's conservative clergy since 2005 indicates that there may be further movement in this direction (Linz, 2000: 36; Kaboli, 2006b). Regardless of definitional debates about regime types there can be no question that the opportunities for genuine green dissent in these countries are severely constrained, but also constrained differently. In Iran, green issues have been largely coopted by the state, with state-sanctioned NGOs the dominant voice – dissenting groups exist, but with little public

---

presence. In Burma, green issues are linked inextricably with human rights, particularly those of ethnic minorities, and this nexus has led to the development of the new discourse of earth rights. The only options for dissent here are military insurgency or the voicing of grievances in international fora.

In Iran, the state-sanctioned green sector is encouraged by the regime as a safe form of participation. Opposition is even more limited than in the 1990s because many Iranians understandably fear foreign invasion or attacks. The military forces of the United States are at both the Afghanistan and Iraqi borders with Iran, and concerns about foreign military action including nuclear strikes are not without foundation (Hersh, 2006). Thus, the emergence of a tightly controlled green politics in Iran may further perpetuate oligarchic control by the theocracy, rather than being a harbinger of change, as it was in Hungary (see Kerenyi and Szabo, this issue). Contrarily, the most exciting thing about green politics in Iran is that it gives a voice for young women, a voice sadly missing since 1979.

So the transnational messages of environmentalism emanating from the West have managed to cross the borders of these two non-democratic regimes, but not in a form recognisable as western environmentalism, as these state boundaries are not mere speed bumps. Although limited in their power and very different in character in each country there are green elements at work that may provide the foundation for profound societal change in the future. This is by no means guaranteed, however, and it may be that the prospects are greatest in Burma, where environment and human rights have been linked more strongly in struggles for survival. As the Burmese regime fights to maximise its exploitation of energy supplies it is provoking a broader opposition. In Iran the coopted elements of the green movement may actually contribute to sustaining authoritarian or totalitarian rule by offering a narrow, post-materialist version of environmentalism, alongside a callow and tepid version of civil society.   (Adapted from Doyle and Simpson, 2006: 763–4)

Conclusions

A conclusion is a way to round off a discussion; it may be a discussion that has taken place in an essay, a chapter of a book, thesis or dissertation, or the entire work (➡ see Chapter 5, p. 182). Either way, the purpose of a conclusion is always the same: to draw together all strands of the discussion up to that point and provide a resolution of some kind.

What is a 'resolution'? It is a statement that may span a single paragraph, a series of paragraphs or a whole document, and which will comment in general terms on information presented in the foregoing discussion. It is statement, based on observation and reason, of what can be said *in the light of that* discussion, and as such will offer new information or insights that emerge from it. This providing of *new* information is a key characteristic of a conclusion and one that distinguishes it from the mere restatement of information that constitutes a summary. The information itself and its significance can only be fully understood and appreciated within the context of the foregoing discussion.

As we have seen, a summary can be a useful reminder of that foregoing discussion and therefore help to ensure that the reader is able to see the relationship between the ideas expressed in the body of the chapter or article, and those that the author claims follow from them and that constitute the conclusion.

Below are some of the expressions commonly used to introduce conclusions. Notice how they signal this necessarily close relationship between the preceding discussion and the conclusion itself.

Conclusions: useful expressions

In conclusion, . . .

Together, this evidence suggests that . . .

From the foregoing discussion we can say that . . .

A number of things can be gleaned from this . . .

Based on these findings we can say that/it is apparent that . . .

To return to our original question, . . .

This chapter began with . . .

This chapter sought to/set out to . . .

Example: conclusion 1

This chapter has surveyed a number of methods and approaches to the teaching of foreign languages, along with research that has sought to measure their respective levels of efficacy. The picture that emerges is that learners have learnt and continue to learn languages, often to the highest levels of proficiency, having been taught by each of these methods and approaches. It seems, therefore, that there may well be no such thing as the 'ideal' or 'perfect' method or approach, and that there are other more important factors that determine learners' success in acquiring foreign languages.

Example: conclusion 2

As the preceding section makes clear, it is important to place great value on the knowledge and experience of service users and to incorporate this into policy, practice and education. The direct experience of service users does provide a source of knowledge that has long been undervalued in social work, even though the occupation has taken more steps in this direction than many others (Beresford, 2000). However, social workers have to balance these against other sources of knowledge that lie outside of the direct experience of service users, as we have noted earlier. As the case studies have demonstrated, there are also numerous practical difficulties that can complicate a social worker's intention to work alongside service users, acting as far as possible in accordance with their wishes.

There is no single way if managing service user engagement, a message that is made clear from a variety of different pieces of research. There will be numerous sets of circumstances where the actions one takes as a social worker will contradict an individual's expressed desires, or will not balance the competing preferences of users and carers, or when the evidence from other forms of knowledge would strongly suggest a course of action that a service user does not welcome. In such circumstances, the challenge will be to reach a solution that respects the desires of each individual even if it does not equate with that person's wishes (Beresford *et al.*, 2007).   (Adapted from Wilson *et al.*, 2008: 428)

Example: conclusion 3

In terms of pronunciation, what the discussion in this chapter indicates is the need for some sort of international core for phonological intelligibility: a set of unifying features which, at the very least, has the potential to guarantee that pronunciation will not impede successful communication in EIL [English as an International Language] settings. This core will be contrived to the extent that its features are not identical with those of any L1 or L2 variety of English. As we will see in Chapter 6, a phonological core of this kind already exists among all L1 speakers of English, whatever their variety. A core of sorts also exists among L2 speakers, insofar as speakers of all languages share certain phonological features and processes. However, this shared element is limited. Thus, while we can build on what L2 speakers already have in common phonologically, we must take the argument one very large step further by identifying what they need to have in common and contriving a pedagogic core that focuses on this need. However, such a core, while necessary, will not alone be sufficient to achieve the goal of preventing pronunciation from impeding communication. Mamgbose makes the obvious yet frequently missed point that 'it is people, not language codes, that understand one another' (1998: 11). Participants in EIL will also need to be able to tune into each other's accents and adjust both their own phonological output and their respective expectations accordingly.

In Chapters 6 and 7 we will look more closely at these two approaches to EIL communication and consider their pedagogic implications. Chapter 6 is both a discussion of the complex issues involved in the establishing of a core of phonological intelligibility for EIL, and a presentation of the core being proposed here. Then, in Chapter 7, we move on to a consideration of how best to both promote learners' productive and receptive use of this core, and to encourage the development of speaker/listener accommodative processes which will facilitate mutual intelligibility in EIL. But first, in the following chapter, we will consider in detail the relationship between L1 phonological transfer and EIL intelligibility.   (Adapted from Jenkins, 2000: 95–6)

> **TIP** Sometimes, the conclusion of one chapter ends with an indication of what will be discussed in the next chapter. The writer of the text in the conclusion 3 example could, for instance, have added an additional sentence such as:
>
> 'Chapter 5 will look at a number of these factors as they have been articulated in the literature, in particular that of individual learner differences.'

Finally, a conclusion will frequently echo the introduction to the particular chapter that it's concluding, often by answering a question raised in the introduction, either explicitly or implicitly. This notion again evokes the idea of resolution as by doing so the conclusion brings the discussion full circle. Consider this example:

> This chapter set out to evaluate a relationship-based and reflective model of social work practice in terms of its ability to address contemporary challenges. On the basis of the evidence presented, it would seem that the model has considerable potential in this regard and that there is, therefore, a strong argument for promoting it in professional practice.

THE MECHANICS OF ACADEMIC WRITING

Capitalisation and punctuation

Most students, both native speakers of English and non-native speakers, have some difficulty with certain aspects of capitalisation and/or punctuation. Although it's certainly not intended as a comprehensive guide – that would take a book in itself – this section has been written to provide you with an easy-reference guide to some of the main rules governing the use of capitals and punctuation in English.

Punctuation is not an exact science and two people may well punctuate exactly the same text slightly differently. The key to using punctuation well is, first, knowing the basic rules of punctuation, and secondly, always having your reader's comprehension in mind. Punctuation exists to make what you write clear to your reader; so always try to ask yourself the question, 'Can I make this clearer to my reader by punctuating it differently?'

Using capital letters

There are three main situations in which capital letters are required:

1 **After a full stop and at the start of new sentence.**

> Just as tribes are mobile in different ways, so are we. Our kinds of mobility are vastly various. The upward and outward movement of the young executive who leaves his local suburb and travels in ever-widening circles on international airlines is utterly different from the rootless and unattached mobility of the urban proletariat. (Douglas, 1975: 80)

Context is essential to understanding meaning. Malinowski recognised this early in the twentieth century when he observed that only by looking at language in its 'context of situation' could we understand the functions served by particular grammatical structures.

2 **At the beginning of all words that are proper nouns (or names), as well as their abbreviated forms.**

Proper nouns may refer to individuals, institutions and organisations, places, titles of books, articles or films, names of theories, international treaties, governmental bills, competitions, etc.

the United States of America
   (or the USA)

the Golden Gate Bridge

the Houses of Parliament

Professor Hilda Flissert

the British Government

the British Broadcasting
   Association (or the BBC)

The *Origin of Species*

the Terrorism Act

Clare College Cambridge

Harvard University

The Cooperative Principle

Abraham Maslow

The Warsaw Pact

The Kyoto Protocol

The World Cup

Social Comparison Theory

the Treaty of Versailles

Operation Barbarossa

> **TIP** Words such as *government*, *bridge*, *university* and *treaty* do not need to be capitalised if they are referring to governments, bridges, universities or treaties in general (i.e. generically), rather than specific ones. Look at the following examples:
>
> The primary job of a university is to educate, not to make profit.
>
> It should be mandatory for all governments to fulfil their pledge.
>
> A new bridge has been proposed that will span the River Avon.
>
> It is expected that the talks will result in the signing of a treaty.

3 **At the beginning of content words in titles.**

An Investigation into Gender Differences in Management Style within Multinational Organisations

Pragmatics, Awareness-Raising and the Cooperative Principle

A Brief History of Time

A Tale of Two Cities

> **TIP** Content words are usually keywords and consist mainly of nouns and adjectives. Articles (*a*, *an*, *the*), conjunctions (*and*, *but*, etc.) and prepositions (*in*, *of*, *by*, *for*, *into*, *within*, etc.) are not normally capitalised in titles.

Using commas

Use a comma to separate a series of items that exceeds two in number:

> Each subject was required to maintain a diary, complete a questionnaire, and take part in a 15-minute interview.

> A dissertation should include an abstract, an introduction, a literature review, a methodology section, a results section, a discussion section and a conclusion.

TIP Traditionally, a comma was seen as unnecessary before the 'and' that precedes the final item of the series (the technical term is a serial comma). However, the absence of a comma can mean that the two last items in the series get 'lumped' together and this can be confusing for the reader, particularly in long, more complex lists. So use your commonsense to decide if it is needed. (You will always see the serial comma used in US-style texts.)

Use a comma and a co-ordinating conjunction (*and, but, or, nor, for, yet, so*) to separate two independent clauses. An *independent clause* is a clause that can stand by itself as a separate sentence:

> Many people believe in the death penalty, but the government is adamant in its refusal to pass legislation that will permit its implementation.

The second sentence could be written as two independent clauses:

(1) Many people believe in the death penalty.

(2) The government is adamant in its refusal to pass legislation that will permit its implementation.

Here are two further examples:

> He knew that Operation Barbarossa would mean a war on two fronts, yet Hitler went ahead and ordered the invasion of Russia regardless.

> The party would not elect a new leader, nor would it change its policy on what would become a key electoral issue and one of critical national importance.

TIP If the two independent clauses are both short and make for a fairly simple sentence, then the comma can be omitted, for example:

> He liked the idea but chose not to adopt it.

However, the safest option is to always include a comma.

Use a comma to separate, or 'set off' introductory information. That information may 'frame' what follows it in the sentence and/or it may help link the current sentence to the preceding one:

> Although the majority of citizens support the idea of surveillance as a means of increasing their personal security, civil liberties organisations are increasingly concerned that it is whittling away the individual's right to privacy.

Despite these efforts, millions died of starvation.

In 2008, the Bush presidency finally came to an end.

Much to the dismay of the environmental lobby, Gore was beaten to the presidency in highly controversial circumstances.

Seeing as pragmatics is inextricably linked to context, that is where our discussion will begin.

> **TIP** The kind of 'introductory information' that appears in these examples is sometimes technically referred to as a *subordinate clause*. Some of the words and phrases that introduce subordinate clauses and therefore help identify them are: *because, although, providing, despite, unless, since, before, while, when, after, if* and *whenever*.

Use a comma to separate neighbouring adjectives:

The delicate, orange, miniature species tends to live longer, despite looking more fragile.

The subjects selected were fair, male and Caucasian.

Use a comma to highlight contrast or reservation:

It was for financial reasons that they chose not to pursue their studies, not academic ones.

The results were comprehensive, but disappointing.

The majority of subjects expressed pleasure and surprise, not disappointment, when they viewed their reactions on videotape.

Use a comma between cities and countries, counties or states and countries, a date and the year, and a name and a title:

He began his career in Oxford, England.

Constable's most famous works were painted in Suffolk, England.

Her first play first showed in London's Drury Lane on October 5, 1953.

Gavin Hessler, Professor of Economics, gave his seminal paper later that year.

Freda Walker, Assistant Director of the Research Centre, voted against the move to merge the two Schools.

> **TIP** Where the title comes first, as in the following sentence, commas are unnecessary:
>
> Professor Gavin Hessler gave his seminal paper later that year.

119

Use a comma to set off parenthetical (added) information:

The housing market, which had been buoyant for ten years, was about to collapse.

Mount Etna, an active volcano on the Eastern coast of Sicily, last erupted in May 2007.

Roosevelt, a cripple confined to a wheelchair, successfully hid his disability from view during his political career.

Jackson, a merchant banker by trade, was to become a figure of disgrace.

There are, needless to say, other perspectives on the issue.

There is little evidence to support the claim, in Grappler's view.

Notice how, in the above examples, the added information can be omitted without changing its basic meaning or making it ungrammatical – just like in this sentence! Also notice how the added information often describes a noun that precedes it.

Use a comma after connectives such as *however, nevertheless, moreover, furthermore, consequently, for this reason, as a result, on the contrary*.

Numerous studies have sought to shed light on this issue; however, it is generally accepted that the majority of them are methodologically flawed.

Climate change is melting the Arctic ice shelf; as a result, polar bears are sometimes having to swim up to sixty miles across open sea to find food, and many drown in the process.

Unless it appears at the beginning of a clause or sentence, *for example* is also set between commas:

Man's destruction of wildlife habitats that sustain different species has led to an increased incidence of contact between certain of those species and human settlements. Bears, for example, can frequently be found scavenging in certain towns in Alaska.

Using colons

Colons normally precede a list or an explanation (development or amplification). They also follow a clause that can exist grammatically by itself:

Inequality can occur in a variety of areas:

– physical and mental characteristics – this is a basic fact of human existence;
– social status and prestige;
– wealth;
– power;
– laws, rights and rules – 'privileges' are private laws.

Inequality in these areas need not go together: social inequality is multidimensional (Runciman, 1969).   (Adapted from Hofstede, 1984: 67)

A good way to think about the colon is as an invitation to go on. The part after the colon often indicates a step forward, for example, from cause to effect. If you put a colon into words, it would mean something like 'And here it is . . .', 'as follows', 'Let me explain', or 'Here's what I mean'. Here are some further examples:

The results showed a distinct gender difference: while men cited work reasons for their decisions, women tended to cite family responsibilities.

An 'activity' is a segment of classroom life that can be separated from others in terms of four features: temporal boundaries, physical milieux, program of action, and content (Burnett, 1973).
(Crookes, 2003: 144)

According to Millward, Brown, Optimar, in 2007 Google was the highest valued world brand: $66,434 m.
(Adapted from McLaney and Atrill, 1999: 59)

The definition of a child in need is:

(a) he is unlikely to achieve or maintain, or have the opportunity of achieving or maintaining, a reasonable standard of health or development without appropriate provision for him of services by a local authority under this Part;

(b) his health or development is likely to be significantly impaired, without the provision for him or her of services by a local authority under this Part; or

(c) he is disabled.
(Adapted from Wilson et al., 2008: 227)

He suggested that these receptors were sensitive to three of the colours that people perceive as 'pure': blue, green and red.

(Martin et al., 2000: 187)

Sometimes a colon is used with words and phrases such as *thus* and *as follows*, rather than simply substituting for them:

Based on historic costs, direct material costs were computed as follows:

	£
Paper grade 1	1,200
Paper grade 2	2,000
Card (zenith grade)	500
Inks and other miscellaneous items	300
	4,000

(McLaney and Atrill, 1999: 369)

Colons are sometimes used to 'introduce' a long quotation that is set off from the rest of the paragraph by a blank line before and after it, and by a left indentation (➡ see p. 90):

Douglas describes this aspect of Hindu society in the following terms:

There are two essential characteristics of Hindu society: first, status is determined by principles independent of the distribution of authority; and

> second, the idiom in which higher or lower status is expressed is the idiom
> of purity.   (Douglas, 1975: 185)

She goes on to state that the first of these two principles is the most fundamental.

As we have seen, shorter quotations can be included in the main body of the text and don't need to be set off in the same way as longer quotations. Normally, if a quotation is included in the main body of the text, a comma is used to introduce it rather than a colon. Look at the following example:

> According to Douglas, 'status is determined by principles independent of the
> distribution of authority' (1975: 185). This is an intriguing idea in that . . .

Using semicolons

Use semicolons (not commas) in a list that appears as part of a sentence and in which each of the items is long:

> The methodology consisted of a 20-item questionnaire that all subjects were
> required to complete; a series of in-depth interviews each of which was subject
> to protocol analysis; and an analysis of subjects' personal reflections, as evi-
> denced in diaries maintained on a daily basis.

> The working party comprised Mr Sidney Rockport, MP for Dothbury; Professor
> Sharon Read, Emeritus Professor of Economics at Readham University;
> Dr Khasi Lemons, Minister for Industrial Relations; and Lord Crookshank.

Notice how, in the second example above, the semicolon also helps to distinguish each item, on the one hand, from the person and their title, which are separated by a comma. If a comma had been used in every case, the text would have been slightly more confusing to read.

Not all lists appear as part of a sentence, but semicolons may still be used. Look, for example, at the quotations from Hofstede and from Wilson *et al.*, used in the previous sub-section on colons.

Use semicolons to indicate a close connection between two ideas:

> Lack of memory for an event does not mean that it never happened; it only
> means that there is no permanent record accessible to conscious thought during
> wakefulness.   (Martin *et al.*, 2000: 304)

> Many soap operas appeal to universal human instincts and emotions; that is
> why many are so successful worldwide.

> This can be achieved by having less current in the circuit; in this way, there is
> less voltage drop.

> Heavy borrowing can be a major financial burden; it can increase the risk of
> businesses becoming insolvent.

Some models do not rely on management judgement; instead they use quantitative techniques to determine an optimal cash policy.

Use semicolons before connectors that join two ideas that are so closely linked that a full stop is not necessary. Such connectors include *however*, *nevertheless*, *moreover*, *furthermore*, *consequently*, *for this reason*, *as a result*, and *on the contrary*.

The data were limited; nevertheless, it was revealing.

The verbal reports contained numerous inaccuracies; furthermore, a series of inconsistencies became apparent once the reports were transcribed.

Using exclamation marks

There's a very simple rule that applies to exclamation marks in academic writing, and that is *don't use them*! Except in very exceptional circumstances, it is almost never appropriate to use an exclamation mark in your thesis or dissertation; it feels casual and emotive. As we've seen, these are not considered positive traits in academic writing in general, and in research in particular.

Using question marks

As with exclamation marks, the use of questions – and hence question marks – is not considered appropriate in dissertations and theses, although you may occasionally find one in other forms of academic writing such as journal articles (e.g. 'So, what are the alternatives?'). The only time a dissertation or thesis would contain a question mark might be in the context of a questionnaire or an interview that has been transcribed.

Using hyphens

Use hyphens to form compound words, particularly compound words that immediately *precede* nouns:

She was soon to become a best-selling author of children's fiction.

Her out-of-date proposals were not well received.

But:

Her proposals were out of date and poorly received, as a result.

The study involved an investigation into the dietary habits of nine-year-old children from poor socio-economic backgrounds.

The doctors showed great concern for the patients' well-being.

One sibling was over-compensating for the shortcomings of the other.

Micro-organisms display similar kinds of behaviour patterns.

Use hyphens to indicate a word-break at the end of a line.

Although word-processing programmes tend to take care of this situation for you, if you do need to break up a word, where possible try to do so *after* prefixes and *before* suffixes:

pre- . . . sentation	govern- . . . ment	sub- . . . sidiary
fore- . . . ground	high- . . . lights	un- . . . certainty
assign- . . . ment	ir- . . . relevant	method- . . . ology
ideal- . . . ism	indefens- . . . ible	success- . . . ful

TIP Try to avoid breaking up words if at all possible.

Using dashes

Dashes are longer than hyphens (– as opposed to -) and are used to identify or 'set off' parenthetical information that is incidental or additional to the main idea of the sentence. Look at these examples:

The methodology – used only once before by a team of Australian researchers – proved a great success.

Each of the research teams – the Oxford team led by Hack and Lindt and the Harvard team by Graham and Frege – completed their investigations within a month of each other.

Dashes can be preferable over commas when the incidental information they enclose contains its own internal punctuation, as in the following example:

For each of these two-year periods – 1945–47, 1967–69, 1988–90, and 2006–08 – spending was shown to be almost identical once adjustments were made for inflation.

Notice how, by using dashes, the sentence becomes easier to read and understand for the reader. Notice also the different uses of the hyphen and the dash in the example.

Using parentheses

Use parentheses to enclose information that is slightly peripheral, but not irrelevant to the main point of the sentence, and that does not fit into the flow of that sentence:

The final agreement (there were three intermediary ones that preceded it) was signed in July 2007.

George Bush Jr. (a president many regard as the worst in US history) finally left office at the start of 2009.

Use parentheses to enclose citations within a text (➡ see also p. 90):

This situation is described in detail by Hutton and Smythe (1978).

It has been stated that 'The most important factor controlling adults' speech to children is the child's attentiveness' (Martin *et al.*, 1997: 420).

TIP The information that appears in parentheses should not be punctuated with a capital letter at the start and a full-stop at the end, although you may wish to use a question mark if appropriate (➡ see page 123).

Using [square] brackets

Square brackets are used within quotations to enclose information that is not part of the original quotation but which the writer feels provides clarification for the reader in some way. It is most commonly used to enclose the word *sic*. This is Latin for *thus*, and is used when there is a mistake (factual, grammatical, spelling, etc.) in the quotation and you wish to indicate to the reader that the mistake is not yours but that of the original author of the quotation:

> In some instances and healthcare settings a generic healthcare profesional [sic] record is used in contrast to the traditional one profession one record system.

> Following the end of hostilities in 1946 [sic], the occupation of Japan by the US army was overseen by the Supreme Commander of the Allied Powers, General Douglas MacArthur.

In the following example, there is no mistake present; however, the writer feels that it needs to be made clear to the reader who he refers to. Square brackets have therefore been used:

> It was his [Tony Blair's] first suggestion that there was to be a seismic shift in policy.

> She stated: 'It [the insult] cannot not be allowed to stand; an apology must be forthcoming if negotiations are to continue in a constructive spirit.'

Using single and double inverted commas

Use single inverted commas ('. . .') to enclose short quotations that are integrated into the main body of the paragraph and which, unlike longer quotations, are not set off via indentation and a blank line (➡ see p. 90):

> Brassington and Pettitt suggest that 'The main cause of parallel trading is the price differentiating strategies adopted by manufacturers to obtain the highest price the market will bear' (1997: 460).

Use single inverted commas to express doubt or scepticism over the accuracy/ appropriateness of a word:

> The 'luxury' hotel only provided shared bathroom facilities.

By placing luxury in inverted commas, the writer implies that the word has been inappropriately used. (After all, a hotel which only provides shared bathroom facilities cannot be called luxurious!)

> The 'rigorous' study was ill conceived and utilised a fundamentally flawed methodology.

Use single inverted commas to identify words that have a specialised meaning and/or are not part of normal English:

'Nanotechnology' is one area of inquiry to which reference is increasingly being made.

'Gazundering' is a new term used in contrast to gazumping.

The environmentally aware 'greenies' see themselves as models of good and responsible behaviour.

Note that 'n'est pas' (French) and 'ne' (Japanese) do not have exact equivalents in English.

Use single inverted commas when you are specifically talking about words or phrases, i.e. when they are the focus or subject of your discussion:

'Bad' is a good example of a slang word that has taken on a meaning that is the exact opposite of what we traditionally understand by it.

Use single inverted commas to identify product names:

'Ezyclean' is one product that has taken the market by storm.

> **TIP** An alternative to putting product names in inverted commas is to italicise them.

Use double inverted commas to enclose a quotation within a quotation:

Meyerbach (2006: 77) argues stridently that 'economic status is a reliable predictor of pupils' success at school, and that "by the age of six, clever children from poor backgrounds have already fallen behind less able pupils from wealthy backgrounds"' (Carrera, 2005).

Using apostrophes

Misuse (or non-use!) of apostrophes is one of the most common errors in students' writing, yet the rules for apostrophe use are not complex; they just need learning.

Use apostrophes in shortened (contracted) forms of words in which letters have been left out: *it's*, *who's*, *she's*, *let's*, *they've*, *don't*, *they'd*, and *you're*.

As we have seen, shortened forms of this kind are generally discouraged in academic writing. There are, however, exceptions; for example, if your purpose is to transcribe precisely the language used by a subject in your study. The most obvious case would perhaps be where you are studying the use of contractions or 'casual language' as part of a linguistics degree.

Use an apostrophe *before* the 's' in a singular noun that shows possession:

The subject's responses were recorded and categorised.

Herringer's study was replicated in 1988, and similar results emerged.

The company's success was down to good accounting and strong leadership.

Use an apostrophe *after* the 's' in a plural noun that shows possession:

The students' success was the result of fine teaching.

The female executives' rise to the top took far longer.

Use an apostrophe *before* the possessive 's' in words that do not take 's' in their plural forms:

The women's reaction was one of outrage and dismay.

The children's consistent failure to achieve to the required national standard resulted in the school being put on notice.

Activity 4.11 Punctuating three texts

Add punctuation to the three texts below, as appropriate.

Text 1

companies such as apple nokia unilever p&g and philips with international distribution systems may introduce new products through global rollouts apple's iPhone first went on sale in america in june 2007 followed by the european launch in the autumn and asian roll-out in 2008 in a swift and successful global assault its fastest global rollout ever p&g quickly introduced its spin-brush low-priced battery powered toothbrush into 35 countries such rapid worldwide expansion overwhelmed rival colgates actibrush brand

(Adapted from Kotler *et al.*, 2008: 565)

Text 2

treatment programmes for drug abuse including smoking and drinking may take several forms in some cases aversion therapy is used in others less intrusive forms of therapy involving extensive counselling are used in the latter case the psychologist or therapists general aim is to teach the individual to

1 identify environmental cues or circumstances that may cause the addictive behaviour to occur or recur

2 to learn to behave in ways that are incompatible with the desired behaviour

3 to have confidence that they can overcome the addiction

4 to view setbacks in overcoming the addiction as temporary and to treat them as learning experiences in which new coping skills can be acquired

prevention programmes for people with addictive behaviours are only moderately successful many alcohol management programmes have only a 30–50 per cent success rate (Marlatt *et al.*, 1986)

(Adapted from Martin *et al.*, 2007: 787)

Text 3

in 1995 80 per cent of lords of appeal heads of division lord justices of appeal and high court judges were educated at oxford or cambridge over 50 per cent of the middle ranking circuit judges went to oxbridge but only 12 per cent of the lower ranking district judges did eighty per cent of judges appointed since 1997 were educated at a public school the appointments made by the current labour government have not broken this mould the narrow background of the judges does mean that they can be frighteningly out of touch with the world in which they are working mr justice harman who resigned in 1998 said in three different cases that he had not heard of footballer paul gascoigne the rock band oasis and the singer bruce springsteen   (Adapted from Elliott and Quinn 2008: 143)

English and Latin abbreviations

During your reading of academic literature, you will have come across a number of frequently-used English and Latin abbreviations. It is important that you become familiar with these in order both to understand their meaning when you meet them during your reading of books and articles, and to use them appropriately in your own writing. The box opposite lists common abbreviations, along with their meanings.

Activity 4.12 Scanning articles for abbreviations

Locate three journal articles related to the subject of your research. Scan them for English or Latin abbreviations. Underline any instances you find and observe the contexts in which they appear.

Headings

➡ On pages 76 and 80, we discussed the importance of good organisation in writing. In particular, we noted how good organisation allows the reader to access your ideas and follow your arguments easily. Headings can play a useful role here by signalling to the reader what your focus is at any particular point in your dissertation or thesis and helping orientate them in such a way that they know where they are in relation to the overall structure of the section, chapter and/or complete work. This is done not only via the headings themselves, but also by the numbering system employed.

In the case of the headings themselves, there are a few decisions you will need to make:

Where to position them.   Chapter titles will generally appear centred on the page and in bold typeface. Section headings will appear set left on the page.

Understanding and using abbreviations

Latin abbreviations

cf.	compare (Also see cp below)
circa	about (a specified date or number – e.g. circa 2003)
e.g.	for example
et al.	and others
etc.	and so forth
et seq	and the following (pages, material, etc.); e.g. p. 23 et seq.
ibid.	in the same book, article (used when the writer wishes to refer to a book or article s/he has already mentioned; e.g. ibid., p. 307).
i.e.	that is
infra	below or further on in a book, article etc.
loc. cit.	at the place quoted; from the same place cited before; e.g. McFarnham, loc. cit. (Note: You must give the author's name.)
op. cit.	in the book cited before; e.g. Hudd, op. cit., p. 33. (Note: You must give the author's name and a page reference.)
NB	note well
passim	throughout or at many points in a book, article, etc. (Used when a topic is referred to several times in a book, article, etc. to which you are referring.)
q.v.	look up this point elsewhere: e.g. q.v. p. 99.
(sic)	thus used; as printed or written in the original. (Used when the person you are quoting has made a mistake, such as a spelling mistake, and you want to indicate to your reader(s) that it is not your mistake.)
viz.	namely, that is to say, in other words

English abbreviations

cp.	compare this with another idea or what another writer says on the topic
ch.	chapter
ed.; eds	editor; editors
edn.; edns	edition; editions
fig.	figure
ff.	and the following pages; e.g. Haverhill *et al.*, 1998, p. 78 ff. means page 78 and the following pages of Haverhill *et al.*
ms.; mss.	manuscript; manuscripts
n.	note, footnote (nn. = plural)
n.d.	no date given, or no date available
n.p.	no place given
n.pub.	no publisher given
no.; nos.	number; numbers
p.; pp.	page; pages; e.g. Klein 2009, pp. 123–134.
para.	paragraph
supra	above; in that part already dealt with
trans.	translator/translated/translation
vol.; vols.	volume; volumes

How to format them.   A good system is to use a larger font size (say 14-point) and a bold typeface to indicate main sections, and a slightly smaller font (say 12-point) and a bold typeface for sub-sections. If these sub-sections in turn contain smaller sections, you may wish to identify these using a plain typeface or perhaps italics. Although university departments sometimes prescribe how headings should be formatted, most will leave it up to you to decide on a system of formatting that elegantly and effectively codifies the layout of your work. What is important, however, is that you apply your system consistently.

Here is one option that shows how headings can be tiered:

Heading 1

Heading 2

Heading 3

Heading 4

Heading 5

Of course, your structure will not always be so complex as to require five levels of headings! Indeed, we would advise against too many levels.

> **TIP** You may wish to use a larger font for chapter headings – 18 point, for example.

How to express the content of the chapter or section/sub-section succinctly but accurately.   The numbering system you employ for your headings will also be 'tiered' to reflect the levels of the headings themselves. The most commonly used system is the decimal system of numbering. This works as follows:

Chapter 2

2.1	Heading 1
2.1.1	Heading 2
2.1.1.1	Heading 3
2.2	Heading 1
2.2.1	Heading 2
2.2.2	Heading 2
2.2.3	Heading 2
2.2.3.1	Heading 3
2.2.3.2	Heading 3 etc

Activity 4.13 Organising information using headings

Below is some information on advertising taken from a book on marketing. Imagine you have to forge this information into Chapter 3 of your work. Use the information to make a simple plan in which you organise and tier the information, using a style system of headings, such as that illustrated above, and a decimal system of numbering. You do not need to include all the information; just create a logical system of headings under which it can be discussed.

Advertising = any paid form of non-personal promotion transmitted through a mass medium. The sponsor should be clearly identified and the advertisement may relate to an organisation, a product or a service. The key difference between advertising and other forms of promotion is that it is impersonal and communicates with large numbers of people through paid media channels.

Pioneering advertising is a form of product-oriented advertising used in the early stages of product promotion when it is necessary to explain what the product can do and the benefits it can offer. The main focus is usually on stimulating generic demand rather than beating the competition.

Competitive advertising is a form of product-oriented advertising which is concerned with emphasising the special features of a product or brand as a means of outselling the competition.

Comparative advertising. This type of product-oriented advertising makes a direct comparison between one product and another in an attempt to show the advertiser's product in a more favourable light.

Reminder and reinforcement advertising is product-oriented and tends to operate after purchase. It reminds customers that the product still exists and that it has certain positive properties and benefits. It increases the chance of repurchase or purchase in larger quantities.

Institutional advertising contrasts with product-oriented advertising. It is not product specific but aims to build a sound reputation and image for the whole organisation to achieve a wide range of objectives with different target audiences. These could include the community, financial stakeholders, government and customers.

Themes are one important aspect of formulating the advertising message. Formulating the right message requires the advertiser to know its target audience and what it wants to say to them. Sometimes, companies will use the same theme, and sometimes they may change the theme a number of times during the advertising campaign.

Message execution, or how the message is conveyed, is a complex part of formulating an advertising message, particularly when different cultures vary in their sense of humour and the extent to which they respond to emotional rather than informational content. Similarly certain things do not translate well and lose their poignancy. As a result, visual images can sometimes be more effective.

Once message content has been decided, how to get that content to appeal to the audience needs consideration.

Rational appeals centre on logical argument, persuading the consumer to think or act in a certain way.

➡

Emotional appeals influence the consumer's feelings and emotions towards what is on offer.

Product-oriented appeals seek to emphasise the importance of a product's features or attributes to the target audience.

How to solve a problem is a kind of product-oriented appeal.

Product comparison is a product-oriented appeal.

Slice of life shows how a product can help give the consumer the kind of lifestyle to which they aspire.

New facts and testimonials are a kind of product-oriented appeal and offer hard information about the product or proof through 'satisfied customers' of how it is all it's claimed to be.

Customer-oriented appeals focus on what the consumer personally gains from using the product.

Saving or making money is a customer oriented appeal and may, for example, show that a two-in-one shampoo and conditioner is more economical but as effective as buying two separate products.

Another type of customer-oriented appeal is fear avoidance – as in an anti-drink driving advertisement.

Other types of customer-oriented appeals include security enhancement, which promotes financial peace of mind, for example through life insurance; self esteem and image, which sells products based on their psychological and social benefits – the idea, for example, that they'll enhance a user's image among their peers; and usage benefits, which show how the consumer benefits from saving time, greater accuracy, minimal effort, etc.

Figures

It's probable that your dissertation or thesis will contain a number of graphs, charts, tables and other types of figures. These figures can serve a number of important functions. For example, in some cases they can be a good form in which to present summaries. Presenting information in an at-a-glance format can be particularly helpful if you're looking at similarities and differences between different sets of data, or perhaps the way in which different studies have approached a particular issue and the findings they have each generated.

Obviously, figures are employed to make information more accessible and meaning-ful to the reader. In other words, try to be discriminating about when to include a fig-ure in your work and avoid doing so merely for the sake of having a figure. Always ask yourself the questions: Does this clarify ideas and/or information for my reader? Does it serve a clear purpose? Is it transparent in what it is intended to illustrate? Does it actually illustrate what it is supposed to illustrate?

Make sure you include a key that explains any symbols you have used in the figure, and any colour- or pattern-coding.

Ensure that your figures are numbered so that, when you refer to them in the text, it's clear to the reader which figure you are discussing. Normally, figures are simply numbered sequentially, *Figure 1*, *Figure 2*, *Figure 3*, etc. Sometimes, writers will also use a decimal system that reflects the chapter in which the figure appears. For example, if there are three figures in Chapter 7, these will be numbered as *Figure 7.1*, *Figure 7.2* and *Figure 7.3*. The numbering usually appears centred, beneath the figure itself. Include a list of all figures and their corresponding page numbers at the end of your table of contents (➡ see p. 140). A sample table of contents, which includes a list of figures, can be found in Appendix 1 at the end of this book.

Finally, be sure to give titles to any figures you include. These can be positioned either immediately above or immediately below the figure.

An example figure and caption is shown in Figure 4.2.

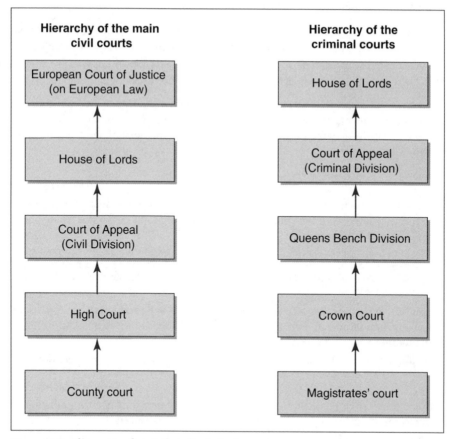

Figure 4.2 The routes for civil and criminal cases
(adapted from Elliott and Quinn, 2008)

Footnotes

The first and most important thing to say about footnotes is that while different disciplines vary to some extent in their attitudes toward them, increasingly their use is being discouraged. Nowadays, the preference is either to incorporate information within the main body of the text if at all possible, or, where appropriate, to include it in the appendices.

Assuming you are permitted to use footnotes, the conditions governing their use are as follows. Include as a footnote information that is additional but somewhat peripheral to a main idea you are discussing in the main body of the text. By treating it as a footnote, you maintain the flow of the main text and do not distract the reader from the main idea you are expressing. Generally, footnotes will be:

- fairly brief – typically one or two sentences
- an aside of some kind that would feel out of place in the main body of the text
- a point of interest related to and/or developing a point in the main text
- an additional reference or further information on a source.

A footnote is indicated by a superscript number at the relevant place in the main text. That same number precedes the footnote at the bottom of the page, thus indicating the relationship between the two texts. The footnote itself typically appears in a smaller font. Look at these examples of texts along with their corresponding footnotes:

> So it would seem that to avoid postulating endless series of inexplicable co-incidences one has to say, like Locke, that there is an unobservable public cause, or to bring in a deux ex machina to arrange a pre-established harmony of people's sensations.[1]
>
> [1]As Berkeley was tempted to do, see *Principles*, 30ff, or 61ff.
>
> (Warnock, 1967: 32)

> Therefore the fact that they do not entail the existence of their objects proves nothing: whereas the fact that verbs such as 'watch' do entail the existence of their objects, proves much.[1]
>
> [1]It is significant that Ryle actually quotes perceptual task verbs that in fact do entail the existence of their objects, though without recognizing this. So, for instance, he mentions 'watch' (p. 303) or scrutinize (ibid.): and in doing so, provides ammunition against himself.
>
> (Warnock, 1967: 48)

> Tomlin (1991) presents a cognitive model of sentence production in which subject assignment in English is tied directly to the locus of one's focal attention at the moment an utterance is reformulated.[4]
>
> [4]In this model, the traditional notion of 'theme' or 'topic' is replaced by the cognitive notion of 'focal attention', which is more amenable to empirical manipulation.
>
> (Tomlin, in Odlin, 1994: 148)

> Some suggestive possibilities emerged almost by accident from a pedagogical experiment devised by Seán Devitt of Trinity College Dublin.[2]
>
> [2]The procedures were first developed for use in in-service teacher training courses run by Authentik.
>
> (Little, in Odlin, 1994: 108)

Bibliography

A bibliography is a list of references for all sources you have consulted during the course of your research. It is an essential component of your dissertation or thesis because it provides the reader with an indication of the scope and depth of your reading, and, in turn therefore, increased confidence in its integrity. Furthermore, it allows them to follow up any of your sources and, should they deem it necessary, to check whether you have interpreted and represented them accurately. It's important, therefore, that when formatting your bibliography you follow the conventions accurately and provide all the necessary publication details. Failure to do so not only makes your work look sloppy, it can also be a source of real annoyance and frustration for your reader.

When creating your bibliography there are a few key points to remember:

- List authors alphabetically according to surname.

- Unless, for some reason, the information is unavailable, always include for each entry the author's surname and initials; the date of publication; the title of any book cited (or the book in which the work appears, if it is a chapter in an edited volume); the title of any article cited and the name of the journal in which it appears; the volume edition and page numbers in the case of a journal article; the place of publication and the name of the publisher in the case of a book.

- Where you have cited a number of works by the same author some of which are sole-authored, some joint-authored and some multiple-authored, the sole-authored works should be listed first, the joint-authored books second and the multiple-authored books last. (This applies only if the same author appears listed first in all three cases.) Multiple books listed in each of these categories should then be listed by date, with the older items appearing first.

- Where the same author has published more than one publication in the same year, a lower case letter should be used to distinguish them. Those letters should correlate with the letters assigned to the publications in the citations that appear in the main body of the text (➡ see p. 90).

In the table below is a list of different types of bibliographic entries, illustrating how each should be formatted according to the Harvard style of referencing.

Source	Bibliographic entry
Book – single author	Warnock, G.J. (1967) *The philosophy of perception*. Oxford: Oxford University Press.
Book – two authors	Keenan, D. and Riches, S. (2007) *Business law*. Harlow: Pearson.
Book – more than two authors	Kozier, B., Erb, G., Berman, A., Snyder, S., Lake, R. and Harvey, S. (2008) *Fundamentals of nursing*. Harlow: Pearson.
Edited book	Odlin, T. (ed) (1994) *Perspectives on pedagogical grammar*. Cambridge: Cambridge University Press.

➡

Source	Bibliographic entry
Book – organisation as author	National Geographic Society (1982) *Journey into China*. Washington: National Geographic Society.
Chapter or article in edited book	Bell, M. (1998) 'The journalism of attachment', in K. Matthew (ed) *Media Ethics*. London: Routledge.
A book that is not a first edition	Holden, J. (ed.) (2008) *An introduction to physical geography and the environment*. 2nd edn. Harlow: Pearson.
Undated book	Klinger, H. (nd). *Life from the front*. Unpublished Army Records. or Klinger, H. (undated). *Life from the front*. Unpublished Army Records.
Reference books	*The Oxford English Dictionary*. (1989) 2nd edn. Oxford: Clarendon.
E-book	Moore, T. and Kirby, W. (2002) *China in the world market*. Cambridge: Cambridge University Press. Available from: http://allbooks.tuj/departments/library/ebooks/default.asp [e-book accessed 9.4.08].
Different books by the same author in the same year	Mackey, H. (1988a) *The rise and fall of the tiger economies*. New York: Longman. Mackey, H. (1988b) *The bubble breaks*. New York: McGraw-Hill.
Journal article	Reder, L. (1979) 'The role of elaborations in memory for prose', *Cognitive Psychology* 11: 221–34.
Online journal article	Wilson, K. 'Facilitator talk in EAP reading classes'. *ELT Journal* 62: 4, pp. 331–338 [online]. Available from: http://eltj.oxfordjournals.org. [Accessed 23 January 2009.]
Conference proceeding	Rear, D. (2007) 'A new kind of graduate? Discourses on critical thinking', in *Challenging assumptions: looking in, looking out: Proceedings of the 33rd JALT international conference on language teaching and learning & educational materials exhibition,* (eds) Bradford-Watts, K., Muller, T. and Swanson, M., Tokyo, pp. 34–42.
Conference paper	Beretta, A. and Gass, S. (1991) 'Indeterminacy and the reliability of grammaticality judgements'. Paper presented at Second Language Research Forum, University of Southern California.
Newspaper – print	Markee, S. (2006) 'University lecturers complain of having to dumb down'. *The Times* 17 June, p. 14.
Newspaper – online	Timesonline (2008) 'Can technology spin loose from the downwardspiral?' http://technology.timesonline.co.uk/tol/news/tech_and_web/the_web/article5081652.ece [6 Nov. 2008].
Internet website	Pearce, F. (1993) When the tide comes in . . . *New Scientist*. Available from: http://www.newscientist.com/article/mg13718543.800-when-the-tide-comes-in – britains-coastline-stretches4000-kilometres-and-much-of-its-crumbling-away-what-should-be-done-strengthen-barricades-against-the-sea-or-stage-a-managed-retreat.html [6 January 2009]. Environment Agency. n.d. Diffuse water pollution. Available from: http://www.environment-agency.gov.uk/subjects/waterquality/1725838/?version=1&lang=_e [20 December 2008].

TIP The correct style for UK dates is, for example, 12 September 2009 (day/month/year). The US style is, for example, September 12, 2009 (month/day/year). Confusion can sometimes arise when you see, for example, 07/11/88. Is this 7 November or 11 July? So it's best to avoid this date version and use the full one wherever possible.

Software packages

The introduction of bibliographic management software packages in recent years has made the process of creating a bibliography far easier that it used to be, provided, of course, that you are prepared to invest a small amount of time in learning how to use such packages. It is certainly worthwhile doing so as your facility with this software can then be used with any subsequent publications you may produce and save you considerable time. Popular packages currently available include *Endnote* (**www.endnote.com**), *Reference Manager* (**www.refman.com**), *ProCite* (www.procite.com) and *RefWorks* (**refworks.com**). These packages allow you to create your own database in which you can store and organise references, and from which you can format bibliographies. They are integrated fully with word-processing packages such as Microsoft Word and WordPerfect. Consequently, you can insert references into your text (sometimes called Cite While You Write, or CWYW) and build bibliographies as you are writing. These programs also generate the bibliography in the correct style or format for publication.

Activity 4.14 Formatting sources for inclusion in a bibliography

Look at the (unformatted) list of references below. Use them to create a correctly formatted and sequenced bibliography.

Title:	Meaning in Interaction
Author:	Jenny Thomas
Date:	1995
Publisher:	Longman (Harlow)

Title:	Media Ethics
Editor:	Matthew Kieran
Date:	1998
Publisher:	Routledge (London)

Title:	Translation as interpretation
Author:	Axel Bühler
Source Title:	Translation Studies
Volume Editor:	Alessandra Riccardi
Date:	2002
Publisher:	Cambridge University Press (Cambridge)

➡

Title: Escape from the impact factor
Author: Philip Campbell
Journal: ethics in science and environmental politics Vol 8, pages 5–7
Date: 2008

Title: Tristes Tropiques
Author: Claude Lévi-Strauss
Date: 1984
Publisher: Atheneum (New York)

Title: Outsider dealing
Author: Peter Hetherington
Date: 24 January 2007; accessed 5 February 2009
Publisher: Guardian Online
Webpage: http://www.guardian.co.uk/society/2007/jan/24/
            immigrationasylumandrefugees.asylum

Title: The Annual Report of Her Majesty's Chief Inspector of Education,
            Children's Services and Skills 2007/08
Author: Ofsted
Date: 2008
Publisher: Ofsted (London)

Title: Educational issues in war and peace: some reflections
Author: Linda Peachey
Date: 2005
Source: IATEFL 2005 Cardiff Conference Selections from the 39th Inter-
            national Annual Conference Cardiff, 5–9 April 2005
Editor: Briony Beaven
Publisher: IATEFL

Title: Interpersonal Skills in Organisations
Authors: Suzanne De Janasz, Glenice Wood, Lorene Gottschalk, Karen Dowd,
            Beth Schneider
Date: 2006
Publisher: McGraw-Hill (Sydney)

Title: Liberalisation and the debates on women's access to land
Author: Shahra Razavi
Date: 2007
Journal: Third World Quarterly (online)
Publisher: Routledge
Electronic
database source: Informaworld
Website: http://informaworld.com/smpp/
                     content~content=a783868903~db=all~order=page
Access date: 18 July 2007

Acknowledgements

The acknowledgements section of your dissertation comes after the abstract (➡ see Chapter 5, p. 143). It is where you have the opportunity to thank all those institutions and individuals who have contributed to your research in some way. Typically, a researcher will wish to extend their thanks to their department and supervisor, any other external advisors, colleagues and family who offered advice and support, subjects who volunteered to participate in any empirical studies, surveys etc., and organisations who made facilities, materials and personnel available to them for the purposes of their research.

Below are two examples of an acknowledgement page, the first from a dissertation and the second from a thesis:

Example 1

I should express my gratitude to those various people and institutions that have contributed to this project in one way or another. First, the subjects who willingly agreed to take part and give their time to observing and discussing the interviews. I thank both UCLES (University of Cambridge Local Examinations Syndicate) for providing the video recordings upon which those observations and discussions were based, as well as the staff and students of the Research Centre for English and Applied Linguistics for their input. Finally, I am especially indebted to Alastair Pollitt, my supervisor, whose constant guidance and insight were invaluable and always stimulating. (Author's own work)

Example 2

I offer my deep, sincere and painfully inadequate thanks to my supervisor and mentor, Assoc. Professor Reg Cahill, for his inspiration, guidance, enthusiasm, and almost infinite patience (or so it seemed, since he rarely indicated otherwise). I will be forever influenced by his incisive wit, tenacity, and clarity of thought and I count myself most fortunate to have been afforded both his instruction and his friendship.

Heartfelt thanks, too, to my friend and colleague, Dr Susan Gunner, for her indispensable optimism, challenging discussions, pragmatic advice, and perpetual good humour.

Dr Salah Kutieleh and Dr Peter Zeegers also deserve my gratitude. As colleagues and friends, their tolerance and moral support have played no small part in this endeavour. Similarly, Dr Timothy Moss's counsel and calming influence cannot go unrecognised.– thanks for helping me across the finish line, Tim: live long and prosper!

Finally, very special thanks go to my family, whose forbearance and encouragement never faltered. In particular, my bride, Sheila, enduring more than she could have possibly anticipated yet not once wavering in her approbation, and my brother, Paul, without whose dogged goading this might still be a work-in-progress. Thank you one. Thank you all. (Klinger, 2005: xii)

Table of contents

Before submitting your dissertation or thesis, be sure to include a comprehensive table of contents after the acknowledgements page. The table of contents should show, at a glance, the structure of the work, listing the various sections and sub-sections along with their decimal numbers (➡ see p. 128). Be sure to include the page numbers that correspond to each of the sections and sub-sections, and a list of figures, abbreviations and appendices. A sample contents list is shown in the Appendix at the end of this book.

Acronyms and abbreviations

As you conduct your research, you will inevitably draw on numerous different sources of verbal and written information many of which you will want to make reference to in your dissertation/thesis. In some cases, such references will be frequent and the use of abbreviations is, therefore, a way of making this process less tedious, not just for yourself but also for your reader. For example, it can become laborious to have to repeatedly write out the United Nations Educational, Scientific and Cultural Organization, so instead people commonly refer to it as UNESCO. Although most people know UNESCO, you may well be using acronyms such as this that are only known by those involved in the particular area to which they relate; as such, you will need to spell out the acronym the first time you mention it. An acronym is one kind of abbreviation that uses the first letter of the main words that make up a name: WWF (World Wildlife Fund) is another acronym. You may also wish to use other abbreviated forms that you yourself have created and which are not acronyms. This is acceptable provided you do not overuse them and that you 'spell them out' in full the first time you use them, including the abbreviation in parentheses. Alternatively, you may wish to write '. . . hereafter referred to as X'. Furthermore, try to limit their application to the names of institutions or organisations.

Include a list of all acronyms and abbreviations on a separate page after your table of contents, along with the full forms to which they refer. The reader can then refer to this key with ease and at any time while reading your work.

Appendices

'Appendices' refers to documents and other supplementary material that is included at the end of your dissertation or thesis. Usually, material included in the appendices is too lengthy to include in the main body of the text where it would break up the flow of the text and act as a distraction. Material typically dealt with in this way includes survey instruments such as questionnaires, reports or extracts of reports, government and other official papers, lengthy tables or transcriptions, and newspaper articles. Readers are invited to refer to the appendices at the appropriate junctures in the text.

Appendices are normally placed in an order reflecting that in which they are mentioned in the main body of the dissertation/thesis. The are identified using a system of lettering (Appendix A, Appendix B, Appendix C . . .) or numbering (Appendix 1, Appendix 2, Appendix 3 . . .).

5 ▶ THE RESEARCH PROJECT

This chapter looks at the various parts of a study, each of which serves a unique and important function. The primary thought that should guide the presentation of your work is clarity; how can you present your study so that readers can easily follow your logic and appreciate the results of your work? This chapter will let you know about one way that is very commonly used, but you should treat this approach flexibly, as every study is unique and the best way to present yours may be somewhat different.

The chapter will cover:

- the abstract including keyword searches
- the introduction
- the literature review
- methodology
- the results
- the discussion
- the conclusion.

USING THIS CHAPTER

INTRODUCTION

The primary purpose of writing a dissertation is to learn more about a particular topic. Although your work must be original, it's not possible to specify exactly what that means, as everyone's work relies tremendously on previous research and the ideas of other writers. However, you can demonstrate your originality in a number of ways. First, you can show originality in your understanding of past literature. Here you can show previously unidentified gaps and/or inconsistencies in the literature, or conversely, you might identify patterns that had not been mentioned by previous writers as you carefully synthesise the ideas or results of previous studies. In both of these cases, the key is to apply independent, critical thinking when reading previous literature. In this case, critical thinking involves analysing an issue by looking at it from various angles, judging the evidence that has been presented by previous writers with a degree of scepticism, and examining the appropriateness of the inferences and conclusions that they make. Because no researcher can provide more than a part of the 'truth', and the history of science shows that we often understand an issue partially or incorrectly, adopting a questioning attitude is prudent.

A second way that you can demonstrate your understanding of an area is through your conceptualisation of the problem that you study. This might involve using a previously untried theoretical approach to investigate the problem. You might also bring in a concept or theory from another academic field. This strategy has been used successfully a great many times in some branches of the social sciences, such as in the field of education. You might also synthesise ideas from two or more writers to create a new idea that has not been explored previously.

A third way that you can show your originality is by adopting a new approach to the problem you are investigating. You might do this in your research design or your choice of analytical tools. For instance, some areas are primarily studied using cross-sectional experimental designs in which data are only collected at one point in time. The use of a longitudinal design in which you collect data over a period of several weeks or months would probably provide new and interesting information about the phenomenon. Alternatively, in areas in which either a quantitative or qualitative approach has been used predominantly, you could take 'the road less travelled'.

Ultimately, you can show convincingly the value of your study and the originality of your work by providing new findings about the issue that you are investigating; no one will argue that your study is not sufficiently original if you have results that make a real contribution to your field of study. An additional – and very important part of your efforts to produce an original piece of work – is to develop a distinctive and personalised view of the field and the issues you are studying. In other words, as noted previously, you need to develop a sense of ownership over the knowledge that you are developing.

THE ABSTRACT

The abstract is an extremely important part of your dissertation or thesis, because along with the title, the abstract is the first and sometimes the only contact that many readers will have with your work, so write it carefully. When you write the abstract, you should keep two objectives in mind. First, you want to provide enough information to inform readers about whether the study is pertinent to them. Readers need to make an informed decision about whether they would like to read your entire study, and the abstract is the main way that they will make that decision. Secondly, you want to summarise the most important points of your study and to provide information regarding how your study adds to our understanding of the problem.

A common approach to writing the abstract is to view it as a 'miniature paper' in which you open with a brief general statement that sets the scene, informs readers of the purpose(s) of your study, describes your participants and, if necessary, your methodology, and then describes your results and perhaps your interpretation of those results. As noted above, it's a good idea to state the unique contribution that your study makes to the field of study in general.

Other issues to keep in mind are that only results or information found in the body of your paper should be included in the abstract. The abstract should also be independent and self-contained in the sense that readers should be able to understand it without having to read your paper. Finally, you need to be succinct and make every word count because, in most cases, you will have a strict word limit for the abstract.

Look at the following abstract written by Robyn Gillies (2006) for the *British Journal of Educational Psychology*. It's unusual in the sense that the journal requires authors to break the abstract into six distinct categories: Background, Aim, Samples, Methods, Results and Conclusions. While it is unlikely that you would be asked to label sections of your abstract in such an explicit way, it does provide a clear model of important elements to include in an abstract.

Example of an abstract in sections

Background. Teachers play a critical role in promoting interactions between students and engaging them in the learning process. This study builds on a study by Hertz-Lazarowitz and Shachar (1990) who found that during cooperative learning teachers' verbal behaviours were more helpful to and encouraging of their students' efforts while during whole-class instruction, their verbal behaviours tended to be more authoritarian, rigid, and impersonal.

Aim. This study seeks to determine if teachers who implement cooperative learning engage in more facilitative learning interactions with their students than teachers who implement group work only. The study also seeks to determine if students in the cooperative groups model their teachers' behaviours and engage in more positive helping interactions with each other than their peers in the group work groups.

➡

Samples. The study involved 26 teachers and 303 students in Grades 8 to 10 from 4 large high schools in Brisbane, Australia.

Methods. All teachers agreed to establish cooperative, small-group activities in their classrooms for a unit of work (4 to 6 weeks) once a term for 3 school terms. The teachers were audiotaped twice during these lessons and samples of the students' language, as they worked in their groups, were also collected at the same time.

Results. The results show that teachers who implement cooperative learning in their classrooms engage in more mediated-learning interactions and make fewer disciplinary comments than teachers who implement group work only. Furthermore, the students model many of these interactions in their groups.

Conclusions. The study shows that when teachers implement cooperative learning, their verbal behaviour is affected by the organizational structure of the classroom.

(Gillies, 2006: 271–87)

Activity 5.1 Analysing an abstract

Analyse the following abstract for a quantitative study written by Heikki Ruismäki and Tarja Tereska (2008: 23–9). What are the purposes of each of the six sentences in the abstract? The first one is done for you.

This article reports on a retrospective study of Finnish pre-service elementary school teachers' assessments of their musical experiences in nursery school and real-time study of their experiences in teacher training. The participants (N = 590) had received musical instruction in five age groups (4–6 years, 7–12 years, 13–15 years, 16–19 years, 20–25 years). The assessments were most positive in the 4–6 years groups and thereafter declined until puberty in the 13–15 years group. A change in a positive direction was perceived in the 16–19 years group and also in the 20–25 years group (during teacher training). Gender differences were statistically significant except during upper secondary school. The most enjoyable activities in formal music education were singing and playing; music theory was experienced most negatively.

Sentence 1: _Tell the purpose of the study._

Sentence 2: _____

Sentence 3: _____

Sentence 4: _____

Sentence 5: _____

Sentence 6: _____

Would you consider adding any other information? As a reader, what information about this study would you like to know that is not included in the abstract?

> **TIP** Key to writing an abstract is to strive for clarity of presentation. The abstract should be easily comprehensible. Readers should be able quickly to determine whether the results of the study are of interest to them or not from the abstract.

Keywords

The vast majority of researchers and students find articles online by conducting keyword searches, many of which involve the use of clusters of keywords (e.g. 'vocabulary testing', rather than simply 'vocabulary'). For this reason, you will want to consider not only which single words can help readers locate your study, but also which phrases they are likely to use. Including the 'right' key phrases will enhance the discoverability of your study, which means that other people will be able to locate your article quickly and easily. In most cases, approximately five key phrases or between six and eight keywords is appropriate. So exactly which words and phrases should you include?

First, you might wish to include at least one keyword or phrase describing the discipline that you are working in (e.g. *education*). Secondly, if you are working in an area where standard technical vocabulary exists, be sure that your terms are consistent with that vocabulary because researchers and other students will use the standard vocabulary to search for articles. Thirdly, if you have used a particular methodology (e.g. *ethnography* or *longitudinal study*) or analytical technique (e.g. *structural equation modelling*), you might want to consider adding them to your list.

Let's look at some examples. In a study entitled 'Can the Simultaneous Experience of Opposing Emotions Really Occur?', Jack Brehm and Anca Miron (2006: 13–29) selected the following keywords: *ambivalence; emotion; mixed feelings; intensity of emotion; deterrence*. Note that with the exception of *deterrence*, their keywords have a clear relationship with the title of their paper.

This relationship between keywords and the title of the paper is a natural one given that the title is the ultimate summary of the entire paper. Indeed, some authors have considerable overlap between the two. For instance, John Sosik and Sandi Dinger (2007: 134–53) used three key words and phrases, *leadership styles, vision* and *personal attributes*, in their article entitled 'Relationships between leadership style and vision content: the moderating role of need for social approval, self-monitoring and need for social power'. Notice that the first two keywords are also part of the title.

> **TIP** Test your keywords and phrases by typing them into an internet search engine, such as Google, in order to see if the words and phrases work as expected. We find that this is an extremely useful test, as it will quickly tell you how well (or poorly) the words and phrases that you are considering actually result in the kinds of 'hits' that you're hoping for.

Activity 5.2 Write keywords for several articles in your field

Take one or more articles that you are familiar with that do not have keywords listed at the beginning. Think about the main points of the article, and then write four or five keywords or phrases for the article. Next, use those keywords and phrases to search for the article in an educational database. Could you find the article? If not, modify your keywords and phrases until you can.

Try it again with three or four different articles. Once you can write effective keywords for another person's study, you will be able to do the same for your own!

THE INTRODUCTION

The introduction of your dissertation or thesis can serve many purposes; it can set the scene for the study, establish the problem that the study addresses, target an audience, identify the relevance of the problem for the audience, define key concepts, and specify the purposes of the study.

The background of the issue

The purpose of introducing the background of the issue is to describe briefly the broad, general area in which your study is situated. One way to do this is by focusing on your area, but in a rather broad way. This will allow you to gradually narrow the discussion to your particular topic, while giving the readers a sense of the larger picture. A second possible approach is to set the scene for your study by briefly describing the history of the area in which you're working. In this approach you work from the past to the present. This allows readers to appreciate better the importance of your work, and to see how it is a logical continuation of the work that has preceded it.

Introductions typically begin with broad statements that orient the reader to the topic area. This is sometimes conceptualised as an inverted pyramid in which the broad base (the introductory statement) narrows to a sharp point (the research questions or hypotheses) – ➡ see Fig. 4.1 on p. 106. Let's look at one example of a broad opening statement from a study by Joseph Sasson *et al.* (2006: 44) of how process and human performance strategies affected typing speed and accuracy:

> Today, more than ever, organizations are under pressure to produce products and services that go above and beyond customer expectations in order to succeed. To remain competitive, companies must not only delight their customers, but they must also produce products and services efficiently. This calls for optimizing their use of resources, time, materials, and equipment.

Note that because of the general nature of this opening statement, none of the variables investigated in this study are mentioned. The opening statement simply lets readers know the larger area in which the study is situated.

Let's look at one more example from a study conducted by Terri Kurtzberg and Jennifer Mueller (2005: 335–6):

> Creativity is essential to compete in industry, and research has increasingly focused on the processes that contribute to creative outcomes for individuals in organizations. Decades of creativity research has produced several major theories of creativity . . . and each notes that some forms of interpersonal interaction can play a role in the creative process.

While the authors have not mentioned any aspects of their study directly, we can (correctly) infer that their study will concern creativity and interpersonal interaction. For this reason, we can say that these opening sentences effectively set the scene for the study that will be presented in the article.

Creating a sense of interest

In addition to informing readers of the general area addressed by the study, introductions should also create a sense of interest in the topic. While there are many ways that this can be achieved, we will focus on six techniques that are widely used in the social sciences.

The first technique involves creating a dynamic feeling through the use of powerful, emotion-laden words and phrases. This technique is nicely exemplified by John Sosik and Sandi Dinger (2007: 134) in the opening sentence of their introduction in which they use the phrases *famous charismatics*, *passionate orations* and *pursue radical change*. Let's look at the entire opening sentence:

> When one thinks of vision in terms of leadership, more often than not, it conjures images of famous charismatics who, through their passionate orations, persuade followers to believe in and pursue radical change.

The reference to *famous charismatics* may bring forth images of individuals such as Winston Churchill or John F. Kennedy, while the phrase *passionate orations* may evoke memories of Martin Luther King's 'I have a dream' speech. However, regardless of who each reader thinks about, the emotion in the phrasing lends a certain power to this opening statement.

A second technique to introducing a topic involves presenting a controversy in the field in which the study is situated. In a study on question asking, Arthur Graesser and Natalie Person (1994: 105) clearly show how experts are divided on the relationship between question asking by students and educational achievement. This division sets up a kind of tension that the study is designed to address:

> Question asking has had a controversial status in education. At one extreme, some researchers believe that question asking (and answering) are very central components in theories of learning, cognition, and education. Ideal students presumably are capable of actively self-regulating their learning by being sensitive to their own knowledge deficits and by seeking information that repairs such deficits . . . At the other extreme, however, there are researchers who have reconciled themselves to the fact that student questions do not play a central role in the normal process of learning . . . It is well documented that student questions in the classroom are very infrequent and unsophisticated.

This statement not only creates a sense of interest by highlighting the disagreement among researchers, but it also makes the point that question asking is an issue in need of further study.

The third technique that we'll look at, asking questions, is easily implemented, but care must be taken that the questions are thought-provoking in some sense. Questions invite readers to take an active role in thinking about the topic and can be a refreshing change from the 'lecture style' prevalent in most academic papers. An example of this technique is illustrated by Ben Gervey et al. (2005: 269) in their study entitled 'Positive mood and future-oriented self-evaluation':

> Thinking about one's future and effectively planning it often requires answering self-evaluative questions. What kind of field of study, job, or relationship am I suitable for? Do I possess the prerequisite skills for doing what I want? What kind of skills do I still need to acquire or improve? These questions may prompt individuals to learn more about themselves and seek diagnostic feedback about their skills.

One strength of these questions is that even readers who are very familiar or entirely unfamiliar with the topic can answer them, and they focus the readers' attention on the main idea of the study in an easily comprehensible and concrete way.

The fourth technique is particularly appropriate for researchers using qualitative methodology, as it involves writing a short, descriptive narrative of one or more participants in the study. This technique is exemplified in a study by Bryan Brayboy (2004: 125) of three Native American students attending a prestigious university in the USA. His first paragraph sets the tone for the study in a somewhat dramatic fashion:

> On many of the days that I spent with Debbie, an American Indian woman from the southwest, we met at a place not far from her apartment around 8:00 in the morning for coffee, a bagel, and a cup of yogurt. After breakfast, we

went to her class in the university museum. Although Debbie lived on the same street and only seven blocks from the museum, she did not go to class using the most direct route. Rather than walk down the street to the museum, Debbie turned away from the street (a main campus thoroughfare) after only two blocks and walked behind a large health institution. She negotiated the hidden alleys and tricky turns that travelled through and between buildings, emerging on the other side of the hospital. From there she slid down another alley and entered the museum from the rear. She took the stairs rather than the elevator, where she rarely met another soul. Although she might occasionally encounter physical plant workers and delivery people, her communication with them was minimal.

This short paragraph provides the readers with clues concerning the topic of the study, introduces Debbie, one of the participants, lets readers know a little about her life and behaviour, and invites them to speculate as to why she was avoiding contact with other people. Of course, the answer to this question is one of the main points investigated in the study. Thus, in this short opening vignette, the author effectively achieves a number of important purposes.

The fifth example is exemplified by David Blane and his colleagues (Blane *et al.*, 2007: 718), who take an effective approach to introducing their topic by presenting readers with a surprising fact in the opening sentence of their introduction:

Life expectancy at middle age in England, as in most European countries, has increased since 1970 by more than during the 20th-century's first seven decades combined.

Many readers would not have anticipated that life expectancy has changed so dramatically in recent times, so the information is interesting because it is unexpected and not widely known.

In the final technique, the author stresses the importance of the topic. Look at how Robyn Gillies (2006: 271–2) did this in the introductory paragraph in her study.

Cooperative learning is now accepted as an important teaching-learning strategy that promotes positive learning outcomes for all students, including students with a range of diverse learning and adjustment needs (Johnson and Johnson, 2002; Slavin, 1995). When children work cooperatively together, they show increased participation in group discussions, demonstrate a more sophisticated level of discourse, engage in fewer interruptions when others speak, and provide more intellectually valuable contributions to those discussions (Shachar and Sharan, 1994; Webb and Farivar, 1999).

If you carefully read other introductions, you find that other equally interesting techniques are available. Which one(s) you select depends on your own writing style, the topic you are working with and the conventions for writing in your discipline.

> **TIP** Don't select a particular technique too quickly. Try out three or four in your mind or on paper. By comparing and contrasting multiple techniques, you'll find that some are more suitable than others for your specific purpose. You may also find that a carefully-crafted combination of techniques is optimal.

Presenting key terminology

As noted above, it is not unusual for authors to present and define key terminology in the introduction of the study. You should be careful to define any new terminology, highly technical terminology or terminology that you are using in a special way, the first time it appears in your paper, otherwise some readers may have difficulty understanding some of your main points.

In their study of leadership style, John Sosik and Sandi Dinger (2007: 134) defined the term *vision* in the opening paragraph of their introduction:

> Vision represents a leader's idealized goal that is shared with followers. Vision is central to the concept of charismatic leadership . . .

Readers can easily understand what these authors understand *vision* to mean and the entire paper becomes more easily comprehensible.

Yet another way to define a term is through description. Look at the following description of an intrinsically motivated person from Csikszentmihalyi. This definition was used in a study by Dorothea Bye *et al.* (2007: 146):

> Csikszentmihalyi (1997) has described the autotelic or intrinsically motivated person as one who pays attention to things for their own sake without expecting an immediate return, is capable of sustained interest without recognition or with little support, and becomes caught up in the feedback loop between learning, interest, and enjoyment.

While intrinsic motivation is not defined using a dictionary definition in this case, the description effectively communicates what intrinsic motivation looks like, and that is sometimes better than a dictionary definition because of its clarity and concreteness.

Statement of the problem

After describing the general background of your study, focus on the specific problem(s) that you are investigating. Informing readers of the problem early in the dissertation or thesis gives them a clearer understanding of the purposes of the study and the relevance of the paper to their own interests and work. First, clearly and unambiguously explain the nature of the problem. Be sure to include the key variables in your study when you describe the problem, as this will help readers understand your paper more clearly as they continue to read. Secondly, summarise what is already known about the problem by briefly reviewing its past history; this can lead into a discussion of how the problem fits in the larger field in which it is embedded. Thirdly, explain why the problem is worth investigating. In order to do this, you may want to discuss the degree to which the problem exists (e.g. Is it always present or only intermittently so? Is it confined to any particular geographical regions?), and who is affected by the problem (e.g. men, those in lower socio-economic groups, those with high IQs). Finally, when you're finished with this section, read what you've written and ask yourself whether you are convinced by your own problem statement. Make adjustments until you are satisfied.

> **TIP** The problem statement presented in the introduction of your paper should be brief; a more detailed description of the problem should be placed before your research questions and/or hypotheses after the review of the literature.

Look at the following problem statement by Sal Mendaglio (2007: 89) from the first paragraph of his paper on perfectionism as a characteristic of gifted children:

> In the field of gifted education, the inclusion or expulsion of perfectionism among the characteristics of gifted individuals seems to depend on the type of literature one reads. In the non-empirical literature, authors generally depict perfectionism as a major characteristic of gifted individuals (Schuler, 2000), suggesting that gifted individuals possess more of this characteristic than their non-gifted counterparts. The empirical literature, in contrast, does not provide support for this contention.

In this case, Mendaglio creates a kind of 'tension' by identifying conflicting opinions among different authors regarding perfectionism. This conflict arises because of the 'problem' that he addressed in his paper.

John Sosik and Sandi Dinger (2007: 135) presented the problem that they addressed as follows:

> Whereas integrating aspects of the self into vision statements may be critical to the effectiveness of leader-follower identification processes . . . no prior research has examined the role that a leader's personal attributes play in the formation and articulation of vision statements. Failure by prior researchers to address this issue is unusual since theoretical overviews of charismatic and transformational leadership consider leadership influence to stem from the leader's personal attributes and behaviour, follower attributions, the context, or some combination of these factors.

Notice how clearly the gap is stated in the first sentence, while the second sentence suggests why the gap is an important one. This is an effective combination that you should consider using.

Purposes of the study

Following your identification of the problem that you are addressing, you can briefly state the primary purpose(s) of the paper. You generally want to do this early in the study so that readers are in a position to evaluate your methodology and analytical approach in the light of your purposes. The purpose statement should be directly based on the problem(s) that you have identified in the previous section, and readers should be able to realise immediately that your purposes are directly related to those problem(s). Considering the nature of the problem will also help you choose the best way to phrase your purpose statement. You can do this by communicating your purpose using 'action verbs', such as *describe*, *compare*, *develop* and *investigate*, which accurately indicate your research purposes.

You should consider this purpose statement as a promise to the readers in which you tell them what they will discover if they continue reading your work. The purpose statement, however, should be phrased in general terms, with specifics best handled by research questions or research hypotheses. Most purpose statements let readers know whether you are focused on making a contribution to theory, a contribution to practice or both.

Mendaglio (2007: 89) follows the problem statement presented in the previous section with this statement of purpose:

> In this article, I argue that whether or not perfectionism should be considered a characteristic of gifted individuals depends on our definition of perfectionism. If we define perfectionism in terms of the psychological construct currently used in psychological and educational research, then my answer is no: perfectionism is neither uniquely nor universally an identifying characteristic of the gifted.

Notice that the author did not use a traditional statement of purpose that begins with, 'The purpose of this study is. . . .'; instead, he informed us of his purpose simply by stating his position on the controversy surrounding perfectionism. Clearly, his purpose is to present a position and then to support that position with a persuasive argument. It's also clear that his contribution is more theoretical than practical.

Review the problem statement written by Sosik and Dinger in the previous section, and then read their purpose statement (2007: 135):

> The present study addresses this gap in the literature by examining how three personal attributes of leaders (i.e., need for social approval, self-monitoring, need for social power) influence the relationship between leadership style and themes contained in vision statements.

You can see how well the problem statement and purpose statement fit together, and how the authors clearly conveyed the main purpose of their study in a single sentence.

You might also consider mentioning information about the participants or research site, the theory or model you're using, or your analytical approach as part of your purpose statement. More complex purpose statements shed light on the breadth of your purposes in the sense that readers can gain an understanding of the degree to which your purposes are universal (applicable to all situations or persons) or local (applicable to a subset of situations and persons). They may also indicate whether your results will apply across long stretches of time or are only applicable to the present and/or immediate future.

Activity 5.3 Analyse the location and wording of purpose statements

The location and wording of purpose statements can vary according to the field in which you are working. Look at five or six articles written in your field of study and make notes about the following issues in a copy of the table below.

1 Where is the purpose statement located in the study? In the introduction section? At the end of the literature review? In another location? In both of these locations?

2 How is the purpose statement worded?

Article	Location of the purpose statement	Wording of the purpose statement

3 What do you conclude about the placement and wording of writing purpose statements in your field?

Significance of the study

After having laid out the problem that you are addressing and the purposes of your study, you are in a good position to go into some detail concerning the significance of your work. Put simply, what benefits might flow from your study? First of all, your study may have the potential to add to the scholarly literature in your field. You can explain what may be discovered, clarified or confirmed by your study. Secondly, if applicable, you can explain how your work contributes to theory development. For instance, you could state that your results will improve our understanding of a theory, they may confirm or disconfirm a theory, or they may test the theory in a new context. Thirdly, if the purpose of your paper is primarily practical, then you will want to let readers know how your results will improve or influence practice. You can accomplish this by briefly comparing and contrasting traditional or commonly used approaches with the approach that you are proposing or testing in your study. Yet a fourth possibility involves describing how your study can improve policy in a particular context.

Whatever the significance of your study might be, remember to state your case as clearly and unambiguously as possible, and be careful not to exaggerate the significance of the study. When unsure what tone to adopt in this section, we would advise that you use a conservative and slightly understated approach, as it is a serious mistake to promise more than you can deliver.

> **TIP** Don't assume that all readers will understand why a particular problem is important. Whenever you identify a 'gap' in the literature, follow that idea with a brief explanation of why the issue is important and who it affects.

Look at the following example of how two writers, Terri Kurtzberg and Jennifer Mueller (2005: 336), presented a detailed explanation of the importance of the relationship between conflict and creativity:

> Our study thus contributes to the conflict and creativity literatures in several important ways. First, previous research examining the conflict-creativity relationship has tended to treat all types of conflict alike and thus has not conceptualised conflict in a multi-dimensional way, and might thereby have obscured relevant differences in this relationship (e.g., James, Chen and Goldberg, 1992; Kold and Glidden, 1986). For another, most studies of conflict have not been able to pinpoint the effects of conflict in a natural setting and in a localized timeframe to understand the more immediate effects of conflict on one's state of mind, but instead have most often asked participants to rate the levels of conflict they experienced in retrospect (e.g., Jehn, 1995, 1997). Finally, we aim to explore a more psychological dependent measure – perceptions of creativity – instead of more tangible outcomes, to see how conflict acts in a very personalized way on this one part of the creative process. In this way, we hope to contribute to the field by examining how the experience of conflict on the same day and the day following might influence perceptions of creative performance.

Theoretical perspective

Many papers are not based on a theory, but if yours is, you need to make that clear fairly early in the paper. Ultimately, theories are needed in all fields because theories are where many variables or ideas are brought together in a unified system of causal (i.e. cause and effect) relationships. You'll want to briefly describe the theory that you are investigating by describing its key propositions and concepts, as well as the important relationships described in the theory. You will also need to indicate who created the theory and why the theory is important in your field of study.

The following example by Jack Brehm and Anca Miron (2006: 16) shows how they described their theoretical perspective in their investigation of whether people can feel opposing emotions at the same time.

> The evidence we will present is a sample of experiments that were designed for a distinctly different reason, namely, to test a theory (Brehm, 1999) built on the assumption that emotions function like motivational states. To that end, the theory assumes that distinctly different emotions, like distinctly different motivational states, do not coexist. In other words, the human system minimizes its use of resources by engaging only one motivation or emotion at the same time, and that only to the extent necessitated by the difficulty of satisfying the motive or emotion.

This statement of theoretical perspective serves several purposes. First, it provides readers with the underlying theory that this study is based on (i.e. emotions are like motivations and we can only experience one motivational state at a time), so there is no need on the part of the readers to infer what the authors are thinking. The advantage of making the underlying assumption explicit is that it allows readers to agree or disagree with that assumption. Secondly, we are provided with the Brehm (1999) reference, so we can read about the theory in greater detail if we wish. That is important because, like these authors, most of you will face page or word limitations that won't permit you to describe a theory in great detail. Referring readers to more detailed publications is therefore necessary and is a characteristic of good academic writing.

Let's look at another example from a paper by Amy Strachman and Shelly Gable (2006: 119), who succinctly describe the main ideas underlying interdependence theory:

> One of the most influential theories of relationship research is Interdependence Theory (Kelley and Thibaut, 1978). Kelley and Thibaut suggested that the outcomes of social interactions can be broken down into the rewards a person receives and the costs that one incurs. Rewards are the positive experiences that create feelings of enjoyment and happiness including emotional well-being and self-esteem. On the other hand, costs are the negative experiences that yield emotional or physical discomfort or pain. When examined in conjunction, one can achieve an overall assessment of the outcome called 'goodness of outcome.'

Activity 5.4 Examine the theoretical perspective of a study

Look at the above paragraph from the Strachman and Gable study and answer the following questions.

1 What is the name of the theory?
2 Who created the theory?
3 Where can you get more information about the theory?
4 What are the key variables in the theory?
5 What are rewards?
6 What are costs?
7 What is 'goodness of outcome'?

The audience for the study

Every study should be aimed at one or more specific audiences, and it is good for both you as the writer and your readers to be aware of who those audiences are at the outset of the study. For instance, in the field of education, possible audiences are educational researchers, teachers, students, curriculum designers, materials designers and school administrators. As you might imagine, the same topic will probably be approached in very different ways, depending on who the audiences are.

By considering the potential audiences for your study, you will be forced to consider your entire study from yet another angle. For instance, when considering what your study has to offer a particular audience, you may realise that your ideas are limited in some sense, and therefore the value of your study will be less than what you had hoped. This discovery, however, can be quite valuable as, in many cases, relatively minor adjustments to the design or analyses can produce results that are of greater value for the intended audience.

After identifying your target audiences, you'll then need to clearly explain how those audiences might benefit from your work. This will require that you think in specific ways about your study, and that is the best way to proceed when writing a thesis or dissertation. Too many generalities or vagueness will weaken your paper.

Activity 5.5 Thinking of how various audiences will benefit from your study

Think of two or more potential audiences for your study. List ways in which they might benefit from your study.

Audience	Benefits of the study for that audience

Delimitations

Because no study is designed to apply to all persons in all situations, it is necessary to state the main delimitations of your study. Your delimitations let readers know that you are aware of the scope of your study. Delimitations are primarily concerned with external validity, which is the extent to which the results of a study can be generalised to people (population validity) or settings (ecological validity) other than the one studied. When thinking about delimitations, you must consider the ways in which specific variables (e.g. IQ, language proficiency or self-esteem), participants (e.g. age, motivational level, year in school, first language or culture), settings (e.g. a laboratory, a hospital, or a particular country or region), designs, instruments, time, and analyses are used in your study and how they limit its generalisability.

Your thinking on this issue will probably be a combination of past research and commonsense. For instance, if the participants in your study are primarily women, and past research indicates that men and women do not differ greatly on the topic you are investigating, you would have a reason to conclude that the results would probably generalise to men. On the other hand, the results of some studies are probably not generalisable when different age groups and cultures are considered.

> **TIP** When in doubt about whether your results will generalise to a particular group of people or a specific situation, state that the results should be generalised with caution. It is best to be conservative in these situations.

Activity 5.6 To whom can you generalise your results?

If you're considering doing a study in which you'll gather quantitative data (many qualitative researchers are not particularly interested in generalisation), then you should certainly be clear about to which persons and situations you can and cannot generalise your results. Think about your study. To what groups of people and to what situations can you confidently generalise the results? To what groups of people and to what situations can you not do so with confidence?

I can generalise my results to the following groups of people:

_____

I can generalise my results to the following situations:

_____

I cannot generalise my results to the following groups of people:

_____

I cannot generalise my results to the following situations:

_____

THE LITERATURE REVIEW

The purposes of a literature review

The literature review serves a number of important purposes. First, as noted above, when done properly, writing a literature review is a powerful learning device because the writing process will expose you to many, diverse ideas and allows you to learn from the successes, partial successes and failures of previous researchers.

Secondly, the literature review is the first place in your own study where you can show your scholarly competence and your grasp of important issues in your field by demonstrating the breadth of your reading and the depth of your understanding. You can show your ability to distinguish well-founded, carefully argued, plausible ideas and theories from speculation and subjective opinion.

Thirdly, the literature review serves as the basis of your own study. In most cases, the overall research plan flows from an understanding of the current literature. This understanding arises from reading widely and carefully and by noticing and considering the ways in which the published literature is consistent, conflicting and partial. Based on your understanding of the current literature, gaps, inconsistencies or intellectual problems and controversies will emerge as viable areas for investigation. In the best cases, a well-written literature review relates your study to the work of previous researchers, highlights important gaps in the field, indicates where prior studies can be profitably extended, frames the particular problem that you will investigate, and acts as the basis for comparing and contrasting your findings with previous findings.

> **TIP** The gaps and contoversial issues that you identify from reading the literature can become even more compelling once you discuss them with colleagues or mentors and find that they too have unresolved questions about the issues that have caught your attention. Don't be shy – talk to your professors or others whose opinions you respect about these issues.

Reading critically

Literature reviews begin with a reading of the literature, and the quality of your reading largely determines the quality of the literature review. The key to reading well is to read critically and thoughtfully. Thinking critically is a skill that is developed over time, as it is multi-faceted and complex. It involves the ability to analyse an argument and identify its strengths and weaknesses, to consider the argument from a number of angles, to make judgements concerning the quality and quantity of evidence supporting and not supporting the argument, and – perhaps the most difficult skill of all – to be as free of personal bias as possible. Thinking critically is arguably the only way to become an intelligent and discerning consumer of research and ideas, and it is the process of thinking critically over time that eventually allows you to know your field well.

An additional reason for reading critically is because in many of the social sciences, few, if any, of the empirical findings and 'conventional wisdom' can be viewed as being absolutely established and understood. The history of science has demonstrated time and again that people have believed that they have arrived at the 'final correct answer' regarding some issue, only to later discover that the actual situation was different or more complex than understood at that time. In other words, we should assume that our efforts and those of our contemporaries, while hopefully being on the right track, are sure to fall short in a number of ways.

Finally, critical readers are active readers who are able to enter into a dialogue or conversation with whatever they're reading. This process often requires relatively slow, careful reading as well as rereading and making comparisons among the ideas and empirical findings provided by various researchers and writers. As you move through a study, you should evaluate its strengths and weaknesses in terms of how well the author has summarised the current knowledge of the area, understood key variables, theoretical positions or models, selected an appropriate methodology for studying the problem, and analysed and interpreted the resulting data.

Options for writing the literature review

You have two main options when writing the literature review. The first option, which is fairly common in some branches of the social sciences, is to write an extremely long and thorough review of nearly all literature related to your study. While it is probably a good idea to *read* nearly all of the literature related to your study, there are good reasons for taking a different approach to writing your literature review, and that brings us to the second option.

In this option, you write a highly selective literature review by discussing only literature that has direct bearing on your topic. In addition, the focus is primarily on recent studies that directly set up your research questions/research hypotheses and on studies that will help you contextualise and interpret your results in the discussion section of your paper. In other words, you need to review studies selectively, and the relevance of these studies to your study should be quite clear once readers arrive at a description of your purposes and methodology. You must also be careful that your review is up to date and that no important recent works have gone unnoticed. At the same time, don't reject literature simply because it is old, particularly if it was conducted carefully and has achieved the status of being something of a 'classic'. If you can use this second option, you will be able to complete the literature review relatively rapidly and you will then have more time to devote to explaining the rationale behind your study, carefully considering your methodology, writing the results, and interpreting those results. While this second option is typical of many of the 'hard sciences', we would argue that it is also a useful model for those working in the social sciences.

The second option does, however, present problems in terms of selecting the best articles to review – you have to prioritise them. The first way of dealing with this challenge is to list the main variables in your study and let them help guide your choice of studies to review. Obviously, you want to select studies in which the same variables have been used. The second way is to look for studies that use the same theory or model, if you are using one yourself. These articles are clearly important, as they will have a direct bearing on your study and your interpretation of your results. Thirdly, in some instances, you will want to review studies in which designs similar to yours were used. For instance, if your study is longitudinal, you will probably want to compare your results with those of other researchers who have also investigated the same issue using a longitudinal design. The final idea – and this is somewhat abstract because it involves imagining results that you do not yet have – is to think ahead to your discussion section and select articles you believe will help you to interpret your results.

How to review published papers and books

Reviewing previous studies in the literature review is primarily a summarising task, and as such, you want to summarise previous papers in a way that is easily understandable to your readers. In general, this process is relatively simple, as it requires you to follow the same standard organisational practices that the original author used. The following provides a standard model for organising a review of an article:

- State the purpose(s) of the study and/or the research question(s) or hypotheses in the first sentence.
- Provide information about the participants (e.g. *N*-size, nationality or sex)
- Comment on any important information about the methodology.
- Summarise the key results.
- Summarise the author's interpretation and discussion of those results.
- Point out any limitations or serious flaws in the study (optional) and/or how the study supports or does not support the results of other studies.

It's worth spending a moment on the final point in the list – critiquing previous studies. While a critique can show your understanding of design, analysis and interpretation, pointing out the shortcomings of previous work should be done carefully, as it can give your own work an aggressive and 'holier-than-thou' tone, and can appear disrespectful to previous researchers. One useful strategy is to show any criticisms of previous researchers to two or three other persons in order to get their feedback about the tone you've adopted and the impression you're conveying. A second strategy is to include the critiques but not place them at the end of each individual study. Instead, you summarise the strengths as well as the weaknesses that you have identified in a summary at the end of each major section in the literature review. The advantages of taking this approach are that you do not have to mention specific researchers by name, you are able to show that you are actively thinking about the quality of previous work, and when done well, this summary can constitute a valuable contribution to the existing literature.

If you choose not to point out flaws in previous studies in your literature review, you should still make notes about those flaws for your private use. These notes also make good talking points to discuss with your advisor or colleagues. Your goal should be to avoid the mistakes that have been committed by those researchers and to thereby conduct a study that is more well-conceived and well-executed than previous efforts.

Activity 5.7 Practise summarising a study

Practise summarising a study that you have read recently using the six points listed below. Use a highlighter or pencil to locate and mark the six points on the article and make notes below. Then write up the summary in one paragraph on a separate sheet of paper. Compare your summary with the article to see if you have omitted any important information.

1 Purposes	4 Key results
2 Participants	5 Interpretation of the results
3 Methodology	6 Limitations

Organising the literature review

First, we would suggest that you consider starting the literature review chapter (and perhaps your other chapters as well) with a brief one or two paragraph introduction in which the major sections of the literature review are previewed for the readers. This will alert readers to know what topics they will encounter and the order in which they'll encounter them. This can be quite helpful when readers are embarking on a reading task that spans a large number of pages, which is typical in most dissertations and theses.

TIP Organising a literature review can be one of the more complex aspects of writing a dissertation or thesis. For that reason, it's often best approached in consultation with your advisor.

The main body of the literature review can be organised in a number of ways, and we would encourage you to imagine using several of the ways that we will discuss rather than immediately settling on the most 'obvious' one. Because many organisational patterns are possible, the pattern that you choose will depend on how you believe you can best communicate the information in the clearest way possible, and in a manner that 'sets the scene' for your own study. The following are some ways in which you can organise your literature review: using mental categories or topics (e.g. intrinsic motivation, extrinsic motivation and social motivation), historical periods (e.g. modern art in the Taisho, Showa and Heisei eras in Japan), component parts of larger entities (e.g. components of intelligence: verbal-linguistic, logical-mathematical, visual-spatial), causal analyses (e.g. four causes of ageing), and an argumentative approach in which the points for a particular intellectual position are discussed and then compared and contrasted with an alternative or opposing position (e.g. innatist theories of learning versus social theories of learning).

> **TIP** A well-written, comprehensive, critical review of the literature can be a publishable piece of work and can make a valuable contribution to any field. While it is difficult to produce such an insightful and original literature review, it is a goal that you can aspire to; by aiming higher, the review will surely become more valuable.

Synthesising and summarising major sections

If your literature review is relatively long, you may wish to end each major section with a critical synthesis of the research in that domain. This gives you the opportunity to highlight major themes, areas of agreement and disagreement, paradoxes and gaps. This synthesis can be useful both to you as a writer, as it allows you to think more carefully about the literature, and to the readers, as it alerts them to issues that they may not have noticed when reading the literature.

Let's look at a brief example. After reviewing several competing models of motivation for foreign language learning, Robert Gardner and his colleagues (Gardner *et al.*, 2004: 3) made the following summary statement:

> An important feature of these models is that they all consider the concept of identity and identification with the other language community to be part of the language-learning process. This is a basic premise of the socioeducational model of second language acquisition and is why the concept of integrative motivation is considered to be an important feature of language learning.

This short summary usefully identifies the common threads running through several models of motivation – identity and identification with the other language community – and leads to a justification of the model applied in their study.

Presenting the gap in the literature

Although you should have briefly identified the problem that you are researching in the introduction of your dissertation or thesis, you will probably want to do so once again in more detail at the end of the literature review. The statement of the problem can be multi-faceted in the sense that more than one problematic issue can be identified. Let's look at a relatively complex problem statement written by Andrew

Steptoe and his colleagues (Steptoe *et al.*, 2008: 213) in their study of the relation-ship between positive affect and health:

> The psychological factors that may reduce risk and be protective in stress trans-actions include traits such as optimism and coping dispositions. Optimism has been consistently associated with subjective well-being and related constructs (Diener *et al.*, 1999; Lyubomirsky *et al.*, 2005), but again these studies have not controlled for negative affect. The coping literature has predominantly been concerned with the relationship between coping responses and positive affec-tive states in individuals exposed to particular stressors such as HIV caregivers and women diagnosed with breast cancer (Chen *et al.*, 1996; Folkman, 1997). Evidence relating positive affect with general coping dispositions is limited, and is complicated by the variety of ways in which coping has been conceptualised and measured.

As mentioned above, these gaps should flow directly from your review of the litera-ture, and the logical connection between them should be clearly evident to readers. In this way, you can enhance the sense of unity in your dissertation or thesis.

TIP To the extent possible, try to maintain a parallel organisation between the ideas in your literature review and the gaps that you identify, as this will make your writing easier to understand. For instance, if you first discuss topics A, B and C in that order, you would ideally present the gaps associated with them in the same order (A, B then C).

Stating the major purposes of the study

After identifying the gap(s) or controversies that you will focus on in your study, you are in a position to inform readers about the purpose(s) of your study. Although you may have done this briefly in the introduction to your paper, you will want to do it once again, but in a more detailed way. More details are appropriate here because at this point in your study, the readers have read your review of the literature and understood the gaps you've identified in that literature. They are therefore more able to appreciate your purposes because you have 'set the scene' by informing them about what is known about the issue and what is yet to be discovered.

TIP Gaps and purposes should always be parallel, as this will make it easier for readers to relate the two to one another. For instance, gaps A, B and C, would be accompanied by purposes listed in the same order (i.e. A, B, C).

Let's look at some examples of purpose statements. Ben Gervey *et al.* (2005: 270) stated the purpose of their study clearly in a single sentence.

> The purpose of our present research is to examine more closely how positive mood influences interest in feedback about strengths and weaknesses, and under which conditions positive mood increases self-regulation with respect to long-term improvement.

Notice how they included the key variables in their study (i.e. positive mood, feedback, self-regulation, long-term improvement) in their purpose statement. This is often a good idea because it creates a greater sense of clarity for readers.

Gerard Hodgkinson *et al.* (2008: 2) took a somewhat different approach when they wrote their purpose statement:

> The purpose of this article, therefore, is to critically evaluate the current state of scientific knowledge with regard to intuitive processing, with a view to refining the way in which the construct might be operationalized in future work.

They not only presented the main purpose of their study, but they also included a goal for the purpose (i.e. *with a view to refining the way in which the construct might be operationalized in future work*). Depending on your topic, you may find this an attractive option.

Stating research questions

As you can see from the above examples, purpose statements are somewhat general. For this reason, purpose statements are often accompanied by more specific research questions and/or research hypotheses. Let's first consider research questions.

One way to think of research questions is to view them as a contract with the reader. When we sign a contract we make a promise to do something, and it is the same with the research questions; we promise to provide answers to the questions, and this is a promise that must be taken seriously if the study is going to be seen as an example of successful research. However, when you write your research questions, it also means that you're no longer responsible for answering other questions, so, like a contract, your responsibility is limited in specific ways.

TIP Your research questions exert a tremendous influence over your study because the rest of the study, from the design, to the instrumentation, to the types of analyses that you use, are selected with an eye to answering the research questions to the best of your ability.

It's acceptable to pose main questions and sub-questions, and in some cases, this may well be the clearest way to organise your questions. You'll also want to think carefully about how many questions to investigate. This depends in part on the scope of your questions. The 'bigger' your questions, the fewer that you need to make a legitimate study. You'll also need to consider the logic of your questions – do some questions logically need to be answered before others? Do you want to place the more important ones first? Whatever your decision, be careful to put your questions in an order that you can justify if necessary.

In addition to stating your research questions, it is helpful to readers if you briefly explain why your particular questions are important, how they will move the field forward, and the possible implications for theory and/or practice that the answers to your questions will provide.

Whatever your research questions, you need to make sure that your variables are clearly defined. This typically requires an operational definition, which is a clear, context-specific statement of how you judged or identified a particular construct. For instance, if you say that you are measuring *motivation*, you'll need to specify what you mean by that term. Defining concepts or constructs in a concrete way allows them to be measured precisely and for readers to understand them clearly.

Types of research questions

A wide variety of possible types of research questions exist; you should initially consider a number of them and then select the ones that seem most interesting and worthwhile to pursue. Below we've listed nine types.

1 Existence questions

Existence questions are legitimate to ask when the existence of something is important to determine because it is related to a theory, when it speaks to a point of disagreement among experts, or when it concerns a new discovery. For instance, a palaeontologist might argue for the existence of new species of dinosaur, an archaeologist might wonder about the possibility of human habitation in a particular location or at a specific historical time, or a psychologist might wonder whether a particular personality trait exists in people living in pre-technological cultures.

2 Description questions

Once the existence of something is established, it is often necessary to determine the characteristics of the phenomenon. What is it like? How much does it vary in different contexts? To what degree does it vary? What are its distinguishing characteristics? What are its limitations? Description questions can be the basis of entire dissertations and theses, particularly those that are qualitative in nature. Case studies are good examples of this, as the researcher is often primarily interested in producing an accurate description of a person, situation, event or place.

3 Composition questions

Composition questions, such as 'What are the components of this phenomenon?', are related to description questions, but the focus is on breaking down something into its component parts and possibly determining the relative importance of those parts. For instance, a psychologist might investigate the components of personality, the components of intelligence or the components of human memory.

4 Classification questions

Classification questions, such as 'How many types of writing systems are there?', involve determining what is common and different between two more things. As things share more and more commonalities, we usually say that they belong to the same category, and as they have less in common, we usually conclude that they are members of different categories. A classification question will probably be asked whenever any new thing is discovered. For instance, new theories of memory would quickly be classified as would the discovery of a new human language.

5 Relationship questions

Once something has been described to some extent and its component parts are identified, it's possible to begin asking about the degree to which two or more things are related and the way in which they are related. For instance, many things, such as intelligence and breadth of vocabulary knowledge, have a positive relationship – increases in one are generally accompanied by increases in the other. On the other hand, some phenomena, such as self-confidence and anxiety, have negative relationships – increases in one generally are accompanied by decreases in the other. In addition to investigating the direction of the relationship, it is also often important to know the strength of the relationship. Thus, many relationship questions take forms such as, 'Do X and Y have a relationship?', 'To what degree are X and Y associated?', 'To what degree are X and Y associated when the influence of Z is considered?'

6 Comparison-contrast questions

Once a phenomenon is basically understood, it is not uncommon for researchers to compare or contrast it with other things. When comparing, we would be looking for similarities and when contrasting we would be looking for differences. For instance, we might ask whether women are more emotional than men or whether teenagers are more mentally flexible than older adults. The groups that we compare might be pre-existing (male–female; under or over 20 years of age, Asian or Caucasian) or created by the researcher through testing specific qualities (e.g. people with high or low self-esteem or lower and higher emotional intelligence).

7 Causality questions

Causality questions, such as 'To what degree does X cause/prevent changes in Y?', are extremely important in every field because they are implicitly or explicitly based on a hypothesis or theory about a phenomenon. Traditionally, demonstrating causality has been viewed as a logical as well as an experimental problem. Researchers must try to show that manipulating a specific variable is consistently followed by a change in other variables when other potential causes are controlled. For example, some researchers have been interested in determining whether giving people the freedom to make choices increases their motivation to do something.

8 Combination questions

It is also possible to combine many of the question types discussed above. For instance, *causality-comparative questions* are concerned with the effects of two or more causes of something that are compared to see which is stronger, for example,

'Does X cause more change in Y than Z?' This line of thinking can be extended to *causality-comparative interaction questions*. In this case, the effects of two or more causes of something are compared in order to determine which is stronger in a particular context, for example, 'Does X cause more change in Y than Z under condition A?'

9 Time questions

Most of the above types of questions can be addressed in a new and often important way by adding the element of time to the equation. The reason is simple – most things in this world change in important ways over time, and in order to better understand the phenomenon of interest, we need to understand how it develops over time. Thus you might use a description question to investigate the characteristics of something over some period of time, or you might investigate the degree to which one thing affects another (i.e. a causality question) over time.

Stating research hypotheses

Although research questions are widely used, and probably the norm in many fields, hypotheses are also quite common in some fields. Unlike questions, hypotheses are predictive statements about the outcome of a study, and whether they say so or not explicitly, most researchers do have some idea about how their research will probably turn out, so at least in an informal sense, most people have hypotheses about their object of study. This is quite reasonable, particularly when we consider that most hypotheses are far from being blind guesses. Our hunches are almost always based on ideas we have acquired, our experience in the area, previous empirical research, or a combination of the three. Like research questions, hypotheses should flow directly from the gap or address the problems that you have identified after reviewing the literature.

Hypotheses typically come in two forms. The first is a null hypothesis, in which the researcher states that there will be no difference between groups. An example of a null hypothesis is:

> There will be no difference in memory functioning between persons with high and low levels of self-confidence.

The second type of hypothesis is a directional hypothesis, in which the researcher predicts that particular results will occur. Although some advisors prefer null hypotheses, we prefer directional hypotheses because they place more pressure on the researcher to understand what they are doing than when using null hypotheses.

Although hypotheses are sometimes, and perhaps ideally, based on a theory, they differ from theories in the sense that they are typically far more limited and focused than a theory, which tends to be broad and stated in somewhat general terms. In addition, theories generally involve multiple variables and the relationships among the variables are specified. Because hypotheses are more focused, they are more amenable to empirical manipulation and testing. Actually, this is an important feature of a directional hypothesis; it should be directly testable.

Brandon Prins and Ursula Daxecker (2007: 29) conducted a study investigating the reasons for the persistence or termination of rivalry between nations. Let's look at some of their directional hypotheses.

Hypothesis 1: Liberal institutions increase commitment credibility and thus shorten rivalry.

H1a: Democratic institutions shorten rivalry.

H1b: Economic development shortens rivalry.

H1c: Economic development and democratic institutions together shorten rivalry.

H1d: Developing democratic institutions shortens rivalry.

H1e: International organizations shorten rivalry.

Notice that each directional hypothesis is clearly written and subject to falsification, which is a necessary characteristic of directional hypotheses. You can also see that their hypotheses are organised hierarchically, with one main hypothesis followed by five sub-hypotheses.

Terri Kurtzberg and Jennifer Mueller (2005: 339–40) presented four hypotheses in their study of three types of conflict and the immediate and delayed effects on creativity.

Hypothesis 1: Higher levels of task conflict will lead to lower levels of perceived creativity the same day.

Hypothesis 1a: Higher levels of task conflict will lead to higher levels of perceived creativity the next day.

Hypothesis 2: Higher levels of process conflict will relate to lower levels of perceived creativity the same and next day.

Hypothesis 3: Higher levels of relationship conflict will lead to lower levels of perceived creativity the same and next day.

Note again the clarity of these hypotheses. You can also see from the preceding two examples that directional hypotheses create a very different feeling compared with research questions. Research questions create an open feeling that suggests that the researcher has not formulated an answer to the question, while directional hypotheses imply that the researcher believes that they already know the answer and are simply looking for confirmation. As such, directional hypotheses will give your study a clearer direction than research questions. It is also generally more convincing to read a study in which the researcher has stated the hypotheses, rigorously tested them, and then reported that the hypotheses were supported by the results.

Let's look at one more example of directional hypotheses from a study of positive affect and health conducted by Andrew Steptoe and his colleagues (Steptoe *et al.*, 2008: 213):

> ... we predicted that positive affect would be positively associated with lower psychological distress and depression, larger social networks, and greater social support, optimism and adaptive coping responses independently of negative affect, SES, and employment status. We also expected that negative affect would be related to chronic stress experience, greater distress, impoverished social relationships, pessimism, and maladaptive coping, independently of positive affect and SES.

Notice that the authors have opted to present their hypotheses in a somewhat more informal manner by writing them in paragraph form. They have also clearly identified the key variables in their study: two variables causing change (positive affect and negative affect), the variables that are being controlled (e.g. socio-economic status (SES) and employment status), and the variables that are being affected (e.g. degree of psychological distress, number of social relationships and coping responses).

TIP In cases in which your hypotheses are not based on a theory, you should be concerned about where the hypotheses originated from, and the degree to which they are related to one another in a coherent and logical way.

If you state directional hypotheses, briefly indicate where the hypothesis leads in terms of changing current theory or practice. This ensures that you have thought through the implications of the hypotheses, and helps you identify trivial hypotheses in the early stages of your research. You want to produce hypotheses that are meaningful and that address important aspects of the phenomena that you are studying.

METHODOLOGY

The method section flows from the research questions or research hypotheses. Essentially, the methods section informs readers about the who, what, when, where and how of your research. Who are the participants, what variables are involved in the study, what did you do, when and in what order did you do it, where did the study take place, and how did you gather and analyse the data? A clearly written methods section allows readers to understand what you have done, evaluate the appropriateness of your methodology, and replicate your study if they wish to do so.

The methods section typically includes a description of the participants, instruments, procedures and the types of analyses that you will use.

Research participants

Describing the participants in some detail is important as it allows readers to interpret the results with greater confidence and to consider the generalisability of those results. Nowadays it is generally agreed that you should not refer to the people who took part in your study as *subjects*. Instead, use words such as *participants*, *individuals*, *college students* or *respondents*. In addition, it's best to use the active voice when describing what your participants did. For instance, '*The participants completed the questionnaire*' is preferable to '*The questionnaire was administered to the participants.*'

While it is impossible to say exactly what information to report about the participants, as that can change from one study to the next, the following list will provide you with some ideas to think about: the number of participants, their ages, sex, marital status, socioeconomic status, educational level, ethnicity and how they were assigned to groups.

You should also briefly explain why these particular participants were selected to take part in your study. You should select them carefully based on your problem statement and research questions and/or hypotheses; gather a sample of people that will allow you to generalise your results in the ways that you want to. Random selection from the population is ideal.

In the following example, Eugene Subbotsky (2007: 552) describes six characteristics of the participants: the total number of participants, the number of participants in each age group, where they were recruited from, their nationality, race, and social class.

---

145 participants who passed the pre-test interviews were assigned to either the magical- or ordinary-suggestion conditions. In the magical-suggestion condition there were twenty-six 6-year-olds, (M = 6.4, range 6 to 6.11), twenty-seven 9-year olds, (M = 9.5, range 9 to 9.11), and twenty undergraduates, (M = 22.1, range 18 to 39). In the ordinary suggestion condition, there were thirty 6-year-olds, (M = 6.5, range 6 to 6.10), thirty 9-year-olds, (M = 9.3, range 9.1 to 9.10), and eleven undergraduates, (M = 23.7, range 19 to 51). Children were recruited from local primary schools in the North West of England. The majority of children were British, White and primarily middle class. Adults were primarily British, White. Approximately 25% of the adult participants were international visiting undergraduates from continental Europe, Asia and the United States.

Activity 5.8 Examine the characteristics of the study participants

Here is a somewhat different example from the study conducted by Dorothea Bye *et al.* (2007: 147) in which they investigated the affective and motivational aspects of academic life for two groups of students, those 21 years old and younger and those who were 28 years of age or older. List seven characteristics of the participants described in the following *Participants* section. The first one is done for you.

A total of 300 undergraduates from a midsized urban university were recruited from a booth set up in the lobby of the main campus library. Each participant received 10 dollars for completing a questionnaire battery. Comparisons of the characteristics of this study's participants (N = 300) with those of the total university's population (N = 26,226) confirmed that it was a representative sample of the total university population in proportional terms of faculty enrolment, gender, and age. Of the participants, 50% were registered in the faculty of arts and sciences, 20% in the business faculty, 20% in engineering, and 10% in other programs. A total of 56% of the study participants were male. Participants' age ranged from 18 to 60 (M = 25, SD = 6.64), and 74% were attending university on a full-time basis. Of the 61% of participants who were working in addition to going to school, 13% worked 21 hours per week or more, and 48% worked 20 hours per week or less.

1 *The total number of participants in the study.*
2
3
4
5
6
7

Instrumentation

After describing the participants, you'll need to describe any instruments that you used in your study. Instruments are devices, such as laboratory equipment or video recorders, as well as things such as tests, questionnaires, interview prompts and observation categories. In the latter case, it is a good idea to put a copy of the test or questionnaire in an appendix if possible, as that will provide interested readers with all the details they should require. If, however, the instrument is copyrighted and you cannot show it in an appendix, tell readers where they can get more information about the instrument. This might be in the form of a reference to a book or academic article that describes or actually shows the instrument, or you might provide an internet address where interested readers can get more details about the instrument.

The reasons for carefully describing your instrumentation concern the issues of allowing readers to understand more fully your study, replication and operationalisation. Readers cannot adequately understand what you have done without fairly detailed knowledge of the instrumentation that you have used. In addition, other researchers cannot replicate your study unless they know exactly what instruments you used. Finally, the instruments that you use often show how you have operationalised your variables. For instance, the motivation to do well in school can take many forms; only when readers see the exact questions that your participants answered can they understand how you have operationalised motivation in your study.

> **TIP** Your instrumentation is directly related to your research questions, hypotheses, models and/or theories because your instruments are the tools that you use to bring abstract ideas to life. For that reason, you should take the quality of your instruments very seriously.

When describing a test or questionnaire, you'll first need to explain your rationale for using the instrument. You will then want to describe what it is designed to measure, who developed it, the types of items on the instrument, how it is scored, and important statistical information related to reliability or validity. Just because a previous researcher used a particular instrument successfully, it doesn't guarantee that the instrument will work well with your participants. That is why you need to take the time to establish that the instrument worked as intended with your participants.

While using an established instrument is the easiest route to take, it is unlikely that an instrument created for a different group of people and in a different context will be wholly appropriate for your participants. For this reason, some adaptation of an existing instrument is recommended. However, if you've adapted an instrument in any way, you'll need to let readers know about what you did and why you did it. In addition, you should be aware that adapting an instrument generally requires some technical expertise because it often involves writing new items, piloting them, and statistically analysing them. The decision to use an instrument 'off-the-shelf', adapt an existing one, or create an entirely new one boils down to the benefits that will flow to your study in terms of validity and reliability and the practical issues of time and expertise. Whatever you decide, one thing is for certain: the instrument that you use is a crucial part of your study because it will produce the data that form the basis of your results and conclusions. Any weaknesses in your instruments will be translated into weaknesses in your results and potentially in your interpretation of those results.

Helen Sullivan and her colleagues (Sullivan *et al.*, 2006: 159) described one of their survey sections in the following way:

> Lockwood *et al.*'s (2002) scale of regulatory focus was used to measure promotion focus and prevention focus. Participants rated nine statements about their promotion focus (e.g., 'I often think about the person I would ideally like to be in the future') and nine statements about their prevention focus (e.g., 'I often think about the person I am afraid I might become in the future') on a 9-point scale (1 = not at all true of me, 9 = very true of me). Cronbach's alpha was .84 for the promotion focus scale and .87 for the prevention focus scale.

The name of the instrument, its purpose, the number of items on the instrument, sample items, the type of scale used and the reliability of the instrument are all provided. In addition, the creator of the survey and the date of the original publication are provided.

Activity 5.9 Analyse the description of an instrument used in a study

Now look at the following description of a different instrument from the same study (Sullivan et al., 2006: 159). List six pieces of information included in their description. The first one is done for you.

> Participants were asked to describe five goals that they had for an introductory psychology class. They were given the following instructions: 'Please describe the five most important goals you will be working on for this course over the next semester.' Two raters coded each goal as either an approach goal (e.g., 'Get an A') or an avoidance goal (e.g., 'Never miss any classes'). Approach goals were also coded as either performance (e.g., 'Get an A') or mastery (e.g., 'Learn about psychology') goals. Disagreements were resolved through discussion. Inter-rater reliability was .97. . . .

1 _What the participants were asked to describe._

2 _____

3 _____

4 _____

5 _____

6 _____

What are two more pieces of information that might be usefully added to the description?

1 _____

2 _____

When a large number of instruments are administered, the description might be very short. For instance, Gardner et al. (2004: 12–14) administered a questionnaire measuring 11 variables, so the description of each one was short and included the name of the variable, its abbreviation, reliability indices, a one-sentence description of the variable and one example item.

Motivational intensity (MI; $\alpha = .70$, $\alpha = .79$). A high score represents considerable effort expended to learn French. Sample: I keep up to date with French by working on it almost every day.

Desire to learn French (D; $\alpha = .78$, $\alpha = .88$). A high score reflects a strong desire to learn French. Sample: I would like to learn as much French as possible.

Attitudes toward learning French (ALF; $\alpha = .85$, $\alpha = .92$). A high score indicates a positive attitude toward learning French. Sample: I really enjoy learning French.

Procedures

After describing the participants and instrumentation, you are now in a position to let readers know what you did and the order in which you did it, that is, the procedures that you followed. Your goal in this section of your paper should be to describe the procedures that you followed clearly enough and in sufficient detail so that interested readers can replicate your study. Procedures include such issues as any instructions you gave your participants, the language(s) that you used when communicating with them, how and when groups were formed, and the steps that you followed as you conducted your study. These steps should usually be summarised in chronological order and the times between steps specified when appropriate. Here is an example description of research procedures from the study by Gardner *et al.* (2004: 11):

Participants were tested on six different occasions throughout the academic year in their regularly scheduled French classes. During the first session in September, they completed the AMTB (adapted from Gardner, 1985), a questionnaire asking for demographic information, and a form requesting their permission to obtain their grades from their instructors. Administration of these measures required about 20 min. The second, third, fourth, and fifth testing sessions were conducted in October, November, January, and March and took approximately 5 min each to answer six questions dealing with state motivation and state anxiety halfway through each class. The final session required 20 min, during which time the AMTB was readministered. This last session took place near the end of March, approximately three weeks after the fifth testing session . . .

As you can see, the researchers indicated how many times the participants were tested, which tests were completed and when they were administered, and the approximate amount of time required to complete each test.

Activity 5.10 Analyse the procedures described in a study

Now look at the following description of the procedures used by Steptoe *et al.* (2008: 216). Do you confidently feel that you could replicate this study given the following information? If not, what further information do you require? List your ideas on the following page.

Participants attended a medical assessment session during which clinical and cognitive measures were obtained . . . Height and weight were measured, from which body mass index (BMI) was calculated. The questionnaire containing the socio-economic and demographic measures and assessments of social isolation, social support, financial strain, the GHQ, social support and sleep problems was completed. The additional questionnaire, containing the CES-D and measure of neighbourhood stress, optimism, and coping, was distributed, and participants were asked to return it by mail, along with the booklet of rating sheets.

1 _____

2 _____

3 _____

4 _____

5 _____

Analytical approach

Researchers who use statistics to analyse their data sometimes include an analysis section in their paper, as this alerts readers to how the data will be treated and makes understanding the upcoming analyses – a task that is often complex and difficult – somewhat easier. This section is frequently placed immediately after the procedures section because it is at that point that readers know who has participated in your study, how you have measured variables and the steps you took while carrying out the study. Thus, readers are logically in a position to be informed about how you plan to analyse the data. Your analytical methods must be consistent with your research questions. For instance, in a quantitative study, if your research question asks about a relationship, then calculating a correlation coefficient might be appropriate.

TIP When using an unconventional statistic or analytical approach, describe it fully, provide references so that readers can get more information, and state the advantages of the statistical or analytical approach. Comparing it with more conventional approaches might also be warranted.

The second main kind of analysis that you can do is based on qualitative data, which includes all non-numerical data. These kind of data include observations that take place in natural settings, such as a high-school classroom or at a company, field notes that you have taken in order to describe a situation in detail, transcripts of face-to-face or telephone interviews with individuals or groups of people, public documents such as newspapers or official reports, or private documents such as personal diaries, letters or email, and audiovisual materials, such as photographs and audio and video recordings.

TIP The time to think about how you'll analyse your data is before collecting it. Careful and detailed planning is one of the keys to conducting high-quality research; your entire analytical approach needs to be specified in advance because not doing so runs the risk of not collecting the right kind of data, not collecting enough data, or omitting important kinds of data that you later realise you need in order to do the study properly.

THE RESULTS

The results are what everything we've discussed so far has been leading to; they are the fruit of all your efforts to design and implement a worthwhile study. The results should directly answer your research questions and clearly indicate the answers to your research questions or, if you are using hypotheses, whether they were fully supported, partially supported or not supported. When writing the results section, you'll want to consult frequently with your advisor, because this is often a complex section to write, even for seasoned researchers.

In most cases, it is best to report your results succinctly and clearly, particularly if you have a discussion section in your study, as that is where you can go into detail about your interpretations of the results. Be sure to emphasise both those results that turned out as you had hoped and those that ran counter to your hypotheses. In other words, avoid the temptation to trumpet your successes and downplay your failures, because the parts of your study that did not turn out as planned can be informative and excellent opportunities for both you and your readers to learn more about the topic that you are studying.

TIP A guideline applied in some universities is to use the past tense when describing results (e.g. 'Anxiety *decreased* significantly . . .') for the simple reason that you are describing actions that occurred in the past.

Organising the results

In general, the best way to organise your results is to use your research questions or research hypotheses, as this will allow you easily to maintain parallel structure as you move from one part of your study to the next. It's also often a good idea to restate your research questions or hypotheses, particularly if your study is long or complex, and then to present the results that apply to that particular question or hypothesis. For instance, you might restate research question 1 and present the results for that question, restate research question 2 and present the results for that question, and continue in that way until you have answered all of your research questions. The reason for this is that if your research questions or hypotheses were first stated, say on page 30, and your results section begins on page 60, most readers will not clearly remember what the questions or hypotheses are. Restating them makes the readers' task easier.

Let's look at an example of how John Sosik and Sandi Dinger (2007: 145) reported the results pertaining to their research hypotheses:

Hypothesis 1 was fully supported; charismatic leadership was more positively related to inspirational vision themes . . . than contingent reward . . . and laissez faire . . . leadership. Hypothesis 2 was also supported; contingent reward leadership was more positively related to instrumental vision themes . . . than charismatic . . . or laissez faire . . . leadership . . . Hypotheses 3a and b were supported; the relationship between charismatic leadership and inspirational vision themes was significantly more positive in the low need for social approval manager sub-sample than in the high need for social approval manager sub-sample. Moreover, the relationship between contingent reward leadership and instrumental vision themes was significantly more positive in the high need for social approval manager sub-sample than in the low need for social approval manager sub-sample.

The results are clear and easy to comprehend because each hypothesis is addressed separately and succinctly.

TIP If your results chapter is long, you should consider writing a one or two paragraph summary of the results, as this may help some readers to understand more clearly what you have found. In complex results chapters, it's easy to 'not see the wood for the trees' because of all of the detailed information; a summary can alleviate this problem.

Using tables and graphs to present results

As we saw ➡ in Chapter 4, page 132, you should use tables and figures as needed, always remembering that they should be included in order to make the results easier for the readers to understand. In addition, figures such as charts and graphs should generally supplement rather than duplicate information provided in the text of your paper or in any tables that you provide. Any table or figure that you present should be introduced and at least briefly discussed in the body of the manuscript. Because many tables and figures are somewhat complex, you'll want to draw the readers' attention to the most important parts of the tables and figures. In other words, don't leave it up to the readers to try to figure out why the table or figure has been included; tell them clearly.

THE DISCUSSION

After presenting your results, you'll need to interpret them. When done properly, the discussion section is often the most difficult part of the study to write because it involves a great deal of complex thinking. Many results, and especially quantitative results, are factual. For instance, if you report that the average score on a test is 51.37, barring an error in calculating the average, there is little room to argue that the average score is not 51.37. However, that same score of 51.37 can mean many different things to different people. Some people may consider it to be a rather high score while others strongly believe that it is a low score. The point is that what you primarily need to do when you discuss your results is to interpret what they mean to you and that means that you need to think very carefully about your results. This is yet another section of your dissertation or thesis where consultation with your advisor or other knowledgeable people is strongly recommended. It makes little sense to try to interpret your results in isolation; it is far better to make your own interpretations, and then get reactions from others. They may well expose weaknesses in your interpretations or provide convincing alternative interpretations that didn't occur to you. In either case, your study and your educational experience will be enhanced.

> **TIP** One way to look at research is to see it as an extended conversation involving many people living in diverse geographical locations who hold differing views of the same phenomenon. Your results and your discussion of those results are your contribution to this conversation.

In order to maintain parallel structure throughout your dissertation or thesis, you will probably want to organise this chapter using your research questions or research hypotheses. You may want to begin the discussion by briefly summarising the results pertinent to that question or hypothesis, and then proceed to interpret those results.

> **TIP** Generally, you should use the present tense when discussing your results. For instance, you might write, 'The results for research question 1 *indicate* that . . .' or 'This finding *suggests* that . . .'. The reason is that the discussion section is your *present* understanding of what your results mean.

The following are some ideas to keep in mind when interpreting and discussing your results.

Relate your results to previous research

Whether you are using a theory or not, you will want to compare and contrast your findings with those of previous researchers. What is the same? What is similar?

What is quite different? While similarities should be noted, it is more important to discuss and try to explain the areas where your results differ from those of previous researchers. The purpose here is to move beyond the relatively narrow confines of your study by framing your results in the larger field.

Steven McCafferty and his colleagues (McCafferty *et al.*, 2001: 293) investigated how an implementation of activity theory influenced the learning of foreign language vocabulary. They first discussed how their findings supported previous research results:

> Results for the true-experimental condition, then, are supportive of previous claims that increased mental effort (Hulstijn, 1992; Mondria and wit-De Boer, 1991) and the productive use of new words (Joe, 1995) may positively affect learning and retention. In particular, they provide support for Newton's (1995) claim that task-essentialness may lead to gains in vocabulary.

The authors then went on to point out a difference between their results and those of previous research (2001: 293):

> The difference of exposure in the true-experimental condition versus the quasi-control condition suggests, contrary to Elley (1989), that mere exposure to words in meaningful contexts may not be sufficient for learning and retention. Task-essentialness, then, can be seen as deriving from the role of an item within an activity and, specifically, its relation to the goal.

As you can see, this is where your review of the literature and your familiarity with a large body of literature becomes indispensable. As we mentioned in the section on writing your literature review, one criterion for selecting which articles to include in your review of the previous literature is the degree to which they will help you interpret your results. Including research that allows you to compare and contrast your results with previous results is a key part of how of you can engage in the 'academic conversation' that we mentioned earlier.

The theoretical consequences of your results

If you are using a theory or model, frame your results by placing them in that theory or model. Where do they support, partially support or not support the theory? Try to explain why the results, and particularly the results that do not support the theory, turned out as they did. However, even for results that supported your initial hypotheses, you should consider alternative reasons for the results.

In a study testing the model of generative learning (Wittrock, 1974, 1990) Merlin Wittrock and Kathryn Alesandrini (1990: 499) discussed the results of their investigation of the effects of the generative model on reading. Notice how the results are specifically related to the generative model in this part of their discussion:

> With one exception, the data supported these hypotheses. As predicted in the first hypothesis, the Generate Analogies group and the Generate Summaries group each produced a higher mean learning score than did the Read Text group. The rank order among the treatment means was also as predicted . . . However, the Generate Summaries group mean was only two points higher than the Generate Analogies group mean, a difference which was not statistically significant.
>
> With this one exception, these data agree with the predictions, and with the results we have obtained in earlier studies discussed in the introduction to this article. The data imply, in agreement with the model, that when learners relate the text to their knowledge and experience, their learning increases. In this study the generation of analogies was designed to make use of this part of the model.
>
> The data also imply that when learners relate the propositions of the text to one another and to their knowledge, their learning increases. The generation of summaries, as we specified them, was designed to make use of this part of the model.

The practical consequences of your results

It is also important to indicate how your results contribute to the advancement of any practical issues in the field. How might practice improve as a result of your findings?

TIP Go beyond the concrete results that you've reported in your results chapter and make inferences based on what you've found. Be sure to explain clearly how your results resolve the problems that you set out to solve.

In the same study by Merlin Wittrock and Kathryn Alesandrini, the authors also indicate how teachers might use the results of their empirical study to improve the learning of their students (1990: 500–1):

> Leaner generation of the types of summaries and the analogies used in this study appears to be a practical way that teachers can use to stimulate construction of these relations, which are important for comprehension and retention . . . teaching procedures, such as instructions to generate analogies and summaries, can facilitate comprehension and knowledge acquisition by stimulating learners to use their analytic and holistic abilities to develop one or both of these two types of relations.

The study by Wittrock and Alesandrini show the best of both worlds: they both tested a theoretical model and then made concrete suggestions about how that model can be used to enhance learning in classrooms. While this is not an obligatory characteristic of a good study, it is something to consider as you plan your dissertation or thesis.

New contributions of your study

Your study should have made a substantive contribution to the field in which you're working. You'll want to make the unique and original contributions of your study clear in the discussion section.

Ultimately, doing research means that you have to take a public stand, and you should do that strongly and clearly. Provided that you have confidence in your design and methodology, it's inappropriate to express your original contributions in a vague or understated way.

Look at how Terri Kurtzberg and Jennifer Mueller (2005) let readers know about the contributions of their study of conflict and creativity. Note their use of phrases such as *The most important contribution that this study provides . . .* and *Our findings contribute to this growing stream of research . . .* to clearly mark where they have added new knowledge to the field (2005):

> The most important contribution that this study provides is that specific types of everyday events that occur within teams actually do have effects on individuals in quantifiable ways . . . This study encourages us to think about teams not only as a series of important moments, but as a continuous process during which critical things can happen at any point, and even events that seem mundane on a daily level can lead to predictable individual reactions.
>
> More specifically to the study of conflict, our results suggest that conflict events do have local effects in terms of timing . . . Recently, some research (e.g., Jehn and Mannix, 2001) has begun to look at the temporal dimension of conflict in teams longitudinally, and has found that when separated into beginning, middle, and end time periods, the temporal location of different kinds of conflict can have differing effects on performance. Our findings contribute to this growing stream of research by demonstrating effects on the daily level.

Ben Gervey *et al.* (2005: 293) also make their contribution clear through their use of the phrase *Our current research goes beyond these findings by . . .* This clearly signals to readers that they have produced new and important findings.

> Earlier research on mood as a resource has shown that positive mood increases participants' interest in weakness-focused feedback as compared to strength-focused feedback, indicating that participants in a positive mood were more likely to choose a self-evaluation strategy that was more in line with long-term self-improvement goals (Raghunathan and Trope, 2002; Trope and Neter, 1994). Our current research goes beyond these findings by examining how mood changes the perceived relationship between means and goals. Positive mood buffers against the short-term affective costs of negative information when it is perceived to be useful for serving long-term learning goals. However, when the information's utility is lower for learning goals than for affective goals, positive mood enhances individuals' interest in information that serves the latter.

Although you should make your original contributions clear, you also need to qualify your findings and interpretations when appropriate because it is often the case that results do not apply to all people in all contexts. Let readers know to whom and to what extent your results can be applied and why you think so. While you are free to speculate and interpret ambiguous results, you should clearly relate your speculation to your data or theory. This is basically an exercise in logic in which you give reasons for your views and explain each link in your chain of reasoning.

Let's look at one final excerpt from a discussion section from a study in which Tania Lombrozo (2007) investigated why some explanations were judged to be more believable than others. She shows how results can be qualified through her use of phrases such as *it could be that, If this account is correct*, *simplicity may enjoy*, and *if the world is believed to be simple*.

First, it could be that simpler explanations are judged more probable in virtue of making for better explanations. On this view, simpler explanations receive elevated prior probabilities because they are judged more explanatory, not because of their simplicity per se. If this account is correct, then other explanatory virtues like consistency, scope, and fruitfulness may also lead to elevated prior probabilities. Alternatively, simplicity may enjoy probabilistic privilege for reasons not mediated by explanation. For example, if the world is believed to be simple, then simple explanations are more likely to be true not because they're more explanatory, but because they're more likely to describe the world.

THE CONCLUSION

The conclusion section of your dissertation or thesis should generally be quite short and serve to wrap up the study and give readers a sense of closure. You will want to first summarise the main findings and your interpretations of those findings. Then depending on your advisor's preferences, you might add a discussion of the limitations of your study and suggestions for future research. Finally, you will want to make your closing remarks. Let's look at each of these sections in turn.

Summarising your findings

Before anything else, you will want to summarise your findings briefly – be succinct and to the point because you have already presented your results in considerable detail and discussed those results thoroughly.

Let's look at how Bryan Brayboy summarised his study of three American Indians attending prestigious universities in the USA (2004: 17):

In this article, I explain the strategic uses of (in)visibility to illustrate that these three individuals were able to manipulate certain campus structures to their benefit. Whether an out-of-the-way route to class or a strategic use of office hours, their choices highlight thoughtful, complicated responses to oppressive institutional structures. However, it is clear that they were not always able to control how, and in what ways, they were made (in)visible. The power of the institutions and their agents to define the identities of American Indians illustrates the individuals' lack of control. Ultimately, these students' experiences show that visibility can lead to surveillance, marginalization, and ostracism, while simultaneously having positive consequences that are directly related to strategic forms of activism, advocacy, and the maintenance of cultural integrity.

In one paragraph, he has communicated the essence of his findings and reminded readers of the key points in his study one last time.

Robert Gardner *et al.* (2004: 28) summarised their key findings in only two sentences:

Taken together, the results of the four sets of analyses paint a clear picture of the interplay of affective variables and second language learning. The investigation of the potential for individual change assessed in terms of the analysis of absolute difference scores demonstrated that the possibility of change is not great, but it is larger for variables directly associated with the classroom environment than for more general variables.

This summary serves a useful purpose for readers because quite often, they cannot remember the myriad details that are presented in a dissertation or thesis; they often take away the main points, and that is exactly what these summaries represent.

Limitations of the study

No study is perfect, and one form of intellectual honesty involves pointing out areas where your study could have been better. Whereas delimitations concern external validity, or the generalisability of your study, limitations concern internal validity, which concerns the believability of your results. Various kinds of problems can plague a study and make the conclusions suspect, but some of the more common ones concern the use of a flawed research design, inappropriate participants, too few participants, variables that were not included in the study but that appear important in hindsight, and instruments with reliability or validity problems.

TIP Developing your ability to identify problems with your study is an important part of your educational experience, and is yet another area where you can demonstrate your knowledge. Be critical of your ideas in the planning stage so you won't have to write a long limitations section!

Look at the following example in which three researchers working in the field of foreign language learning, Tomoko Yashima, Lori Zenuk-Nishide and Kazuaki Shimizu discussed the limitations of their study (2004: 144):

Limitations of the current study need to be discussed. Neither Yashima (2002a) nor this study sufficiently addresses the relationship between L2 competence and L2 self-confidence. This needs to be explored further. Methodologically, it will be necessary to reconstruct for adolescent learners a few of the variables used in the current study whose reliability indices were not high enough, including interest in international vocation/activities. Alternative methods of assessing frequency/amount of communication as a behavioural manifestation should be considered, for example, classroom observation and observation of communicative events. Combining other's ratings and self-ratings will result in a more comprehensive assessment of reciprocal communication behavior.

Notice how they critique an issue related to two of their variables (i.e, *Neither Yashima (2002a) nor this study sufficiently addresses the relationship between L2 competence and L2 self-confidence*), the reliability of their instruments, and the assessment methods that they used. Their message? If they can improve these points in future studies, their results will be more trustworthy and accurate.

Timothy Curby *et al.* (2008: 741) investigated how task orientation and peer sociability during kindergarten and first grade influenced their chances of enrolment in a programme for gifted children in the USA. Look at the limitations that they identified in their study:

Three limitations require mention. The process of gifted enrolment occurs through a few sequential steps. Teachers nominate children, children take tests, parents advocate for their children, and resources in a particular school fluctuate. With this in mind, the first limitation is that the present study does not account for all the modes or factors involved in this selection process ... Second, because this study had fewer children from the lower SES background than the original longitudinal sample these findings may not generalize to those students that are most transient in a district. Third, the district had a higher enrolment rate than state and national averages. Thus, many children in this district were given the opportunity to participate in the gifted program whereas many fewer children might have been afforded this opportunity in other districts. Therefore, these findings may be less generalizable to districts with substantially lower enrolment rates.

Their first limitation (*the present study does not account for all the modes or factors involved in this selection process*) is the same as the study by Yashima *et al.*: they left some potentially important variables out of their study. Their second limitation concerned a sampling problem – there was an insufficient number of children from the lower SES background in the study. Their third limitation concerned a second sampling problem – the school district had a higher than average enrolment rate.

As you can see, limitations can take many forms, and every study will be plagued by one or more of them. The best that we can do is to become aware of them in advance and eliminate as many as possible before starting the study.

Suggestions for future research

A final way in which you can demonstrate your understanding of the area that you've studied is to make specific recommendations for future research and to follow each recommendation with a brief explanation of the value of that recommendation. Each recommendation should be directly related to your study. While the recommendations are of obvious value to your readers and others working in the same field, they also show that you're able to move from the concrete (your study) to the abstract (studies yet to be) and that you understand your area well enough to point to where the next steps forward can be found.

Here is how Timothy Curby *et al.* (2008: 741) went on to make a number of recommendations for future studies:

> New research questions emerge as a result of these findings. How do teachers' perceptions of task orientation change during the early years of school, and what are the influences of these fluctuating perceptions on the decisions that they make for young children? From a developmental perspective, what are the typical social competence profiles of gifted children? Further, how do these profiles change during the early years in school both as a function of development and early school experience?

While they used questions to point the way forward, it is also possible to write the recommendations as statements. Look at the following recommendations made by Khanh Bui (2007: 330–1).

> Future studies can examine whether these results would generalize to other measures of academic achievement (e.g. course grades) and to students of various sociocultural backgrounds. Such studies would shed further light on how to promote both high educational expectations and high academic achievement among all students.

Notice how this writer not only pointed out areas for future research, but also indicated why the studies would be useful. This is a combination that we would recommend you use, as it shows that you are not simply thoughtlessly listing possible studies; you are listing studies that have real value for the field.

Final conclusions

At the end of your dissertation or thesis, you will probably want to write one or two paragraphs in which you make final – and probably general – comments about the

185

area that you've studied. The tone that you adopt will probably be determined by the tone generally adopted in your field of study and by the preferences of your advisor or faculty that have input into your dissertation or thesis.

One approach is to end with a factual tone about the general contributions of your study. This is the type of final remarks made by Gabriele Oettingen *et al.* (2005: 264–5):

> Two experimental studies described self-regulatory strategies that cause fantasies and expectations to corroborate in forming strong goal commitments. Specifically, fantasies made expectations relevant for goal commitment if the fantasies were contrasted with reflections on impending reality . . . Finally, the present research showed that mental contrasting makes people consider expectations in forming goal commitments, irrespective of whether the fantasies pertain to a positively-perceived or a negatively-perceived future.

A second approach is to invite readers to think for themselves about your findings. This is often achieved through the use of a question. Let's look at an example of this approach from the study by Brian Brayboy (2004: 18):

> Ultimately, Tom, Debbie, and Heather highlight the power (in)visibility for marginalized students in institutions of higher education. How do we – as academics, policymakers, students, and teachers – examine and help resolve the tensions these students face in their lives in a fair and equitable manner?

One more approach is to end the study with an optimistic tone by expressing your confidence that continued progress will be made in your field and that the progress will provide benefits to certain groups of people. Here is an example of this approach from Tomoko Yashima *et al.* (2004: 145), who conducted a study of students' willingness to communicate (WTC) in a foreign language (L2):

> Communication is a process in which people influence each other. Intercultural communication is the sharing and construction of meaning through interaction with dissimilar others. Through learning an L2 or FL, we can expand our communicative repertoires and make the construction of shared meaning easier. WTC in an L2 involves readiness to initiate this process, which will hopefully lead to mutual understanding and trust.

TIP Notice how researchers in your field end their studies and the techniques they use. Do they present facts? Do they attempt to end with an inspirational tone? Remember that your study needs to 'fit' the field in which you're working in terms of the tone you adopt.

This chapter looks at some of the practicalities involved in finishing your dissertation or thesis, preparing it for submission, arranging for suitable examiners to evaluate it where necessary, the possible outcomes of that evaluation, and strategies for dealing with any oral examination. Finally, it offers advice about how to go about presenting and publishing your research so that you and others can benefit from it.

The chapter will cover:

- submitting your dissertation/thesis
- selecting your examiners
- getting your dissertation/thesis bound
- the viva (oral examination)
- the outcome
- publishing and presenting your research.

USING THIS CHAPTER

SUBMITTING YOUR DISSERTATION/THESIS

Students often wonder when they should submit their dissertation or thesis. After devoting months or years to their research and investing huge amounts of energy and emotion in it, many feel uncomfortable with the idea of finally drawing a line under it and saying to themselves 'this is as good as I can make it' or 'this is as good as it's ever going to be'. There is a lot at stake and most people feel they can always improve on what they have done, even though they might not know how exactly. However, most students seem to recognise when it's time to submit their work. There comes a saturation point when it seems as though any attempts to further polish the project feel like tampering, and risk spoiling it. This is often accompanied by the realisation that while there must always be room for further improvement, there is not much more they personally can give to the project. And, of course, this is another instance where your supervisor can play an important role. Their experience can help with what is a crucial judgement call. Like you, they too want to be sure that the dissertation or thesis submitted, and of which they have overseen the development, is of a high quality and well regarded by the examiners.

Once you and your supervisor are happy to submit your dissertation or thesis and confident that it will stand up well to critical scrutiny, you will need to choose your examiners. Let's conclude, then, with a look at what is involved in these processes, at the possible outcomes of the examination of your research, and at opportunities and strategies for publishing it.

SELECTING YOUR EXAMINERS

Dissertations are generally examined internally by members of the department with which you are registered. Normally, you will have no say in who examines your dissertation, although you will almost certainly know the individual(s) concerned; indeed, the project may well have been overseen by them in the early stages of its development. It's not uncommon, for example, for a dissertation to be linked to a particular course that you have taken as part of your degree studies, and for the course tutor to help you in formulating a suitable research question. Once your dissertation has been completed and submitted, the same tutor may well even be involved in examining it.

Theses, in contrast, are typically examined by two examiners, one internal (from your own or another department of the university) and one external, from another university. The external examiner is normally considered to be the primary examiner and as such will take the lead role in the examining process. In other words, they will typically co-ordinate meetings between themselves and the internal examiner in order to discuss your thesis; they will co-ordinate written feedback on the thesis and take the lead in the oral examination (something we'll discuss in a later section (➡ see p. 190)).

Unlike dissertations, theses are examined by academics considered suitably quali-fied to evaluate the research concerned. In consultation with your supervisor (➡ see also Chapter 1, p. 19), you will need to decide, therefore, which individuals have the expertise and knowledge needed to understand, evaluate and comment usefully on your particular area of inquiry. In terms of the external examiner, this will probably be a person whose work you have drawn on in your research and quite possibly some-one with whom your supervisor has a good professional relationship. Whoever you decide to invite to examine your thesis, though, they need to be rigorous but fair-minded and objective. Furthermore, they need to be sympathetic to what it is you have attempted to achieve, even if they do not necessarily agree with all your opin-ions. You will probably also want to choose somebody with good interpersonal skills and who you will not feel overawed by in the viva.

Once you have selected your examiner, they will need to be approached. This is often done by your supervisor, who will also arrange a suitable date for the oral exam-ination and co-ordinate this according to the availability of the internal examiner.

Activity 6.1 Considering suitable examiners

Below, list the names of three academics who you feel might be suitable for exam-ining your thesis.

1 _____

2 _____

3 _____

GETTING YOUR DISSERTATION/THESIS BOUND

Once your have settled on an examiner, it is your responsibility to get a profession-ally bound copy of your thesis to them. You will probably also need to get one addi-tional copy made which will reside in your university's library. If you wish to have your own personal hard-bound copy – and most students do – you may want to wait until after your thesis has been examined and you have made any amendments nec-essary before ordering it. That way you have the most polished version for your own library and avoid the cost of having two versions of your thesis hard-bound.

TIP In the case of a dissertation, a hard-bound copy of your work is not nor-mally required; a spiral bound copy is generally considered adequate. If you are submitting a thesis for examination, it can be a good idea to have a spiral-bound copy made for the purpose of the viva; it is easier to flick back and forth through the pages. Furthermore, you may wish to annotate your thesis before going into the viva.

THE VIVA (ORAL EXAMINATION)

What is a viva and what is its purpose?

Whether your research successfully results in your being awarded a PhD degree depends on how favourably it is judged by your examiners. That judgement is based on two criteria: the quality of the thesis and the confidence and effectiveness with which you address queries and defend it against criticism during your viva. If you do both of these things to the satisfaction of the examiners then, all other things being equal, you will be recommended for a PhD.

Your examiners cannot award you the PhD; they can only recommend that the *university* award you the degree. Although, in theory, the university can ignore their recommendation, in practice this very rarely happens. The university has to approve the examiners initially, and it would only be under very exceptional circumstances, therefore, that they might choose to act contrary to the decision of those examiners. A case of plagiarism or other ethical misconduct, for example, that was brought to the university's attention subsequent to the viva and which was not identified by the examiners themselves might well provide grounds for such drastic action.

Your written thesis is evaluated according to the quality of the writing, the conceptual rigour, elegance and soundness of application of your research methodology, the depth and insight of your argument and analysis, and the originality of the study and the extent to which it contributes new knowledge to its field (➡ see also Chapter 1, p. 3). The viva provides a further means of assessing these things. Because it's interactive, it allows the examiners to check their understanding of points in the thesis that may be in need of clarification and to pursue their lines of questioning through discussion with you directly. In this way, they are able to tease out information and finer points of detail to their satisfaction. Furthermore, the viva provides them with an opportunity to gauge your control of the study, to test your knowledge of the literature relating to it, and to determine whether and how you addressed or circumnavigated problems and challenges which presented themselves during the design and implementation of your research. Finally, the viva gives the examiners a chance to measure your own level of confidence in the study and your capacity to think on your feet and respond knowledgeably, clearly and relevantly to questions and queries of those considered expert in your field.

It is generally agreed that a student cannot fail their PhD on the basis of a poor viva. If, after reading your thesis, the examiners feel it to be of sufficiently high quality for them to recommend the award of the degree by the university, then the viva is highly unlikely to change that decision. If all goes well and you have a strong viva, then it will either:

- serve to confirm the examiners' belief that the thesis is strong and deserving of a pass, or
- ensure that your thesis is passed despite there being reservations prior to the viva based on the examiners' reading of the thesis. In other words, the viva can be

critical in borderline cases by allowing you the opportunity to reassure the examiners that, despite real or apparent flaws in the work, it is nevertheless sufficiently strong and deserving of a pass.

If, on the other hand, the viva goes badly, then it will either:

- confirm the examiners' belief that the work is not good enough for them to recommend awarding the degree, or
- simply be put down to a poor oral performance, despite the obvious quality of the work. In this case, the viva effectively has no bearing on the decision whether or not to recommend award of the degree.

Preparing for your viva

Obviously, before going into your viva you will not know the examiners' view of your thesis and you will want to do everything you can to ensure that the interview goes well. So, how can you prepare for it? Here are a few points to help you.

Strategies for preparing for your viva

- Read through your thesis a few times so that you have it virtually committed to memory and know where different elements are in relation to one another. This will help convey a sense of control by helping you navigate the thesis more efficiently in response to questions and queries raised during the viva.
- Try to identify areas of actual or perceived weakness in your research and try to prepare a rebuttal of any criticisms of these aspects of your work.
- Identify points in your thesis that might invite requests for clarification, and decide how you will respond to such requests.
- Have a spiral-bound copy of your thesis to hand for quick and easy reference.
- Annotate your thesis by writing notes in pencil in the margins. These might be cues or reminders to help you respond to issues raised by the examiners.
- Arrange a mock viva with your supervisor. This will give you some sense at least of what the viva might feel like and of your ability to respond 'on the hoof' to questions and queries. It can also further help you to identify weaknesses in the thesis and in your presentation of it.
- Prepare yourself psychologically. Although it's easier said than done, try to stay calm and see the viva as an opportunity to show off your work and demonstrate the pride you take in what you have done. Try to look forward to discussing your ideas with your examiners, getting their take on things and exchanging views as equals on issues that arise.
- Remember to invite your supervisor if you feel their presence will give you added support and confidence.

Activity 6.2 Identifying weaknesses; anticipating and preparing for questions

Read through part or the whole of your dissertation or thesis. Try to identify any gaps or weaknesses and, where possible, rectify them. If you are writing a thesis and cannot easily rectify any weaknesses you find, try to anticipate the questions they might provoke in the examiners. Then, note down how you might address each such question in an effective and convincing fashion.

What to expect in the viva

It's difficult to be specific about what you can expect in your viva because they can vary quite significantly from one to another depending on the way the department chooses to conduct them, the individual styles of the examiners, the candidate's own personality, and the chemistry between the candidate and the examiners. However, a fairly typical scenario runs as follows.

Following the appointment and approval of your examiners, your supervisor will generally have made all the necessary arrangements for the day, normally in consultation with you. A time and venue will have been agreed for the viva with you and the examiners. It will typically take place in your supervisor's office, partly for the sake of convenience and partly because it will be familiar to you and should therefore help you feel comfortable. After all, it is here that you will probably have had many discussions with your supervisor about your research. You will probably be advised to come to the department's administration office about half an hour in advance of the viva. This is often the time when candidates begin feeling quite nervous and you may therefore find it helpful to have a coffee and chat to members of the department just to distract yourself.

TIP Not only will your examiners have been in communication with one another in the weeks leading up to your viva in order to exchange views on the thesis, it is also likely that they will have discussed you and your work informally with your supervisor over coffee or lunch prior to meeting with you on the day. During that discussion it may well be that the examiners give some indication of how they feel about the thesis. In fact, if they feel very positively about it, they may even let your supervisor know in advance of the viva itself that they intend to pass the thesis and recommend that you be awarded a PhD. In this case, they and your supervisor may well also agree to tell you the good news right at the start of the viva, so as to put you out of your agony and settle you down. However – and this is important – don't count on this; and do not assume that just because they don't tell you at the start of the viva that they intend to pass your thesis that they are not satisfied with it.

Note: The fact that examiners will sometimes tell candidates at the start of the viva if they plan to recommend them for a PhD emphasises the fact that you cannot usually fail your PhD based on your viva performance alone.

Eventually, you will be invited (probably by your supervisor) to meet the examiners and begin the viva. Needless to say, all examiners are aware of nerves and most are sympathetic, even if they do not always show it! As such, they will typically start with some pleasantries and perhaps ask you about the background to or motivation for your research, rather than talk immediately about the content of the thesis. Gradually, of course, they will direct the discussion toward the thesis itself.

Possible questions

Although it is impossible to predict the specific questions you might be asked in a viva, the following are some examples of generic question types that typically feature:

- Can you explain a little bit about what motivated your study?
- What was your rationale for doing X in the way you did?
- Have you read X's article on . . .? Given your findings, how would you respond to the questions she raises concerning . . .?
- Did you consider using a different approach/methodology? Why did you decide not to adopt that approach/methodology?
- Can you explain what you mean by xxx on page 000?
- What, in your view, is the relationship between A and B?
- I'm unclear how you . . . Can you explain further?
- If you were to conduct this research again, how might you do it differently?
- Do you have any plans to build on this research? If so, how?
- How do your findings compare with those of . . .?
- Can you summarise what your study has contributed to our understanding of . . .?
- What do you think are some of the practical applications of your findings?

Activity 6.3 Preparing for typical, more generic questions

Look at the bulleted list of questions above. Think about how some of these questions might apply to your own research. Consider:

1 How you would answer them?
2 Other questions that might arise given the nature of your particular project.

Of course, the examiners will also ask you more detailed questions – for example, about your methodology, your analysis of data or how your own findings fit with those of other scholars. However, do not suppose that the viva will consist merely of a series of questions and answers. Often the examiners will make comments and observations of their own, and you may well find that these generate discussion among the three of you. This can actually make the viva a stimulating and enjoyable experience and help 'loosen you up' by taking the focus off you and allowing you to contribute to the discussion on your own terms. This, in turn, will allow you to present yourself and your research to greatest effect. If your supervisor is present – and many students feel it a courtesy to invite them to attend – they may also contribute to these discussions, but only if invited to do so by the examiners.

Often – usually toward the end of the viva – examiners ask the candidate what their future plans are and frequently offer suggestions as to how they might go about publishing their research. This latter stage of the viva often reflects the early stage in that it tends to be 'lighter' and consist of more pleasantries.

Strategies for success

It can be useful to have a few techniques to hand to help you to cope with the demands of the viva. Listed below are a range of strategies that have been used by students to get them across this final hurdle successfully whilst minimising their stress levels.

The final stage of the viva normally consists of asking the candidate to leave the room and wait outside (usually in the departmental office) while the examiners deliberate on the candidate's performance and on the recommendation they wish to put forward to the university regarding the awarding or otherwise of the degree. This process will typically last between 10 and 30 minutes, at which point they will invite the candidate back into the room and inform them of their decision. Let's, then, look now at the possible outcomes of the PhD examination.

The viva: strategies for success

- Know your thesis back to front.
- Annotate your thesis with cues, points to remember, and answers to anticipated queries, criticisms and questions.
- Go in with a positive attitude. See the viva as an opportunity to show off what you have achieved and try to relish the chance to discuss it with other scholars who come at it from a fresh perspective.
- Try to enjoy the experience of talking about and defending something with which you almost certainly have a greater familiarity than anyone else. As they say in the acting profession, this is 'your moment'. Take it, and enjoy discussing your work with experts in the field. And try to *look* as though you're enjoying it!
- Don't get defensive, even if you feel the examiners are being aggressive or unreasonable. Be measured and thoughtful in responding to their queries and always remain courteous.
- Convey a sense of calm, confidence and self-assuredness.

- Don't be arrogant, but equally don't feel intimidated. You have absolutely no cause to be either.

- Don't be afraid to accept criticism and acknowledge weaknesses where you really feel they are legitimate. No study is perfect, and the examiners will not expect perfection. Unless the weaknesses are catastrophic, the chances are they will appreciate your ability to be objective and to recognise and acknowledge them.

- Make the most of any opportunity to take the pressure off yourself momentarily. For example, if the examiners and/or your supervisor begin to discuss an issue amongst themselves, this can allow you a chance to relax and collect your thoughts. And don't be bashful; contribute to the discussion, for these moments are an opportunity to 'show off' on your own terms without being under pressure of questioning.

- Where you feel it's appropriate, ask your examiners questions. For example, if they ask you a question to which the answer is by no means clear cut, you may, after having a stab at answering it, ask them, 'How would you deal with this issue?' or 'What's your view on this?' Once again, this can help alleviate the pressure on you while instilling in you a sense of being in control of the situation and of discussing your work with the examiners on equal terms.

THE OUTCOME

The table below illustrates the possible outcomes of your PhD examination, along with any subsequent action that may need to be taken by you.

Meaning	Action needed
Unconditional pass	
The examiners are satisfied with the thesis as it is and do not require any amendments.	None. The examiners will submit a report recommending that you be awarded a PhD degree. You will be formally notified of the result.
Pass with minor amendments	
The examiners are essentially satisfied with the thesis but require you to make some minor changes and to 'polish' it slightly. These changes will often reflect points raised in the viva concerning the thesis, but many may simply be presentational – correcting typographical errors, formatting, etc. In general, most changes required are fairly superficial in nature.	Because these amendments are only minor, they can generally be completed in a short space of time. A date is usually agreed for a resubmission of the thesis – usually a month at most, depending on the candidate's personal circumstances. The examiners do not generally request that they see the amended version and are normally happy for the supervisor to oversee this process and to defer to the supervisor's judgement as to whether or not the amendments have been completed satisfactorily by the candidate. Once approval of the amended version is given, a formal notification is sent to the university recommending award of a PhD degree.

➡

Meaning	Action needed
Pass with substantial amendments	
The examiners are not entirely happy with the thesis in its current form and require more significant, larger-scale amendments. These will probably, though not necessarily, be concerned with more fundamental conceptual problems that can only be addressed through a reworking of certain parts of the thesis.	An approximate date is usually agreed for a resubmission of the thesis. The date decided will depend on how substantial the amendments are and the anticipated timescale for completing them. A more definite date is normally agreed as the amendments are nearing completion. Generally, examiners will not require candidates to sit a second viva following resubmission of the thesis; however, this is at their discretion. More typically, the examiners will read through and consult together on the amended version of the thesis and come to a decision as to whether or not to pass it. Normally, the candidate's supervisor will inform the student of their decision.

If the examiners decide not to pass it, they may either request further changes or, if they feel that further improvement is unlikely, recommend the award of a MPhil degree. |
Fail of PhD but unconditional award of MPhil	
The examiners feel that the thesis is not strong enough to justify the award of a PhD degree and believe that it is not salvageable either because of a lack of breadth and depth, or because they judge the candidate to be incapable of implementing the changes necessary to bring the thesis up to the required standard. They believe, however, that its qualities and the extent of the research undertaken are such that they justify the award of the MPhil degree, without the need for any amendments.	None. The examiners will submit a report recommending that you be awarded a MPhil degree. You will be formally notified of the result.
Fail of PhD but award of MPhil subject to amendments	
The examiners feel that the thesis is not strong enough to justify the award of a PhD degree and believe that it is not salvageable either because its weaknesses are too fundamental or because they judge the candidate to be incapable of implementing the changes necessary in order to bring the thesis up to the required standard. However, with modifications, they believe that it qualifies for the award of an MPhil degree.	An approximate date is usually agreed for a resubmission of the thesis. The date decided will depend on how substantial the amendments are and the anticipated timescale for completing them. A more definite date is normally agreed as the amendments are nearing completion. Generally, examiners will not require candidates to sit a second viva following resubmission of the thesis for the MPhil degree; however, this is at their discretion. More typically, the examiners will read through and consult together on the amended version of the thesis and come to a decision as to whether or not to pass it. Normally,

Meaning	Action needed
	the candidate's supervisor will inform the student of their decision. If the examiners decide not to pass it, they may either request further changes or, if they feel that further improvement is unlikely, recommend that the student not be awarded the MPhil degree.
Complete fail	
The examiners feel that the thesis, and the research on which it is based, is critically undermined by fundamental conceptual flaws that cannot be rectified even by substantial amendments to the thesis. They will almost certainly also feel that the candidate does not have sufficient potential to produce and present research of the required calibre.	The examiners will submit a report advising the university that they feel unable to pass the thesis and award the MPhil degree. You will be formally notified of the result and the reasons for their decision.

Let's assume that your dissertation or thesis has met with the approval of the examiners and that you have subsequently been awarded your degree. Now what? The next section looks at how you can make the most of your research to enhance your profile and improve your career prospects.

PUBLISHING AND PRESENTING YOUR RESEARCH

All too often, and despite having invested months or years in bringing their dissertations or theses to fruition, students then leave them in their bookcases to gather dust. Particularly in the case of theses, this is often because, with it having dominated their lives for such a long time, they are simply tired of it; they want a break and feel unable to countenance any further activity directly associated with it. They have reached a kind of saturation point and frequently want to move on to other things, things they may have shelved while completing their degrees and which have been beckoning. This, of course, is perfectly understandable and most students need and deserve a break – a moment to bask in their success and enjoy life without their research hanging over their heads. However, the danger is always that the longer that rest continues the more distant you become from your research and the more difficult it is to re-engage with it, either because you've lost the motivation, lost touch with the research itself and the thinking underlying it, or because developments in the field have overtaken it. For many, such re-engagement never happens. Particularly for those pursuing or intending to pursue academic careers, this is a lost opportunity.

Today, more than ever before, academic status and opportunities for promotion are in large part dependent on an individual's publication record – both the quality and quantity of their publications, and the reputation of the journals in which they appear. This climate of 'publish or die', as it is sometimes characterised, means that you need to take every opportunity to showcase your work in books and journals that are held in high professional regard, as well as at conferences. Your dissertation or thesis provides a rich source of material for papers and presentations and you should take full advantage of it. Although you may only get one paper out of a dissertation, most theses can feed two to four papers, often with quite minimal reworking. In this section we will look at how to get published and how to present materials sourced from your dissertation or thesis.

Publishing in journals

It's not easy get your work published in journals, particularly the more prestigious ones; standards are high and the competition is strong. Everyone is trying to do the same thing in order to further their own careers and professional standing and you will therefore need to be as well prepared and strategic as possible if you are to maximise your chances of success.

Almost all good journals are peer-refereed. This means that an editorial board has been set up to oversee and maintain the quality of the journal by ensuring that only the best articles get published. This is normally done through a system of blind refereeing whereby all articles submitted to the journal are sent out to reviewers to be assessed for their suitability for publication in the journal. Those reviewers are themselves respected individuals within the profession and well placed to comment on your contribution. An article will typically go to two reviewers and sometimes a third if those two reviewers have opposing views on whether or not the article should be published. From the time you submit your article it may well take three months for the review process to be completed and for you to hear back from the editor(s) notifying you of their decision. Typically that decision will consist of one of the following:

- an agreement to publish your article
- an in-principle agreement to publish your article provided you make a few changes in accordance with the reviewers' recommendations
- a rejection of your article. Often this will occur either because the reviewers feel it is not and cannot be turned into an article of the required standard, or because they feel the journal is not a suitable forum for the article.

If your article is rejected, you will be sent comments from the reviewers on what they regarded as its main strengths and weaknesses. Although it can be difficult, try to view these comments constructively as they can prove very helpful should you choose to rework your article and submit it to another journal.

If the journal decides to publish your article, they will give you an indication of when the article will appear in the journal (often as much as two years later) and you will get the opportunity to see the proofs before it goes to press. As a contributor, you will normally receive two free copies of the journal issue in which your article appears.

> **TIP** Bear in mind that journals reserve the right to make minor changes to your article in order to make it more readable or to ensure that it conforms to the journal's formatting requirements.

So, we have seen that success does not come easily with journal publications. What, then, are some of things you can do to increase your likelihood of having your article accepted?

First of all, be sure that it's well structured and has a clear focus. If there's no clear point to your article and it just seems to meander from one idea to the next, it will not be well received. Any journal will require an abstract (➡ see p. 143) of around 150 words for articles submitted, and if you find yourself unable to do this with some ease then the chances are that your article lacks focus and you need to carefully reevaluate it. If you submit it in its current form then you will almost certainly be wasting your time.

If possible, divide your article into sections with sub-headings. This is not only a good way of helping you check its structure and ensuring the logical progression of your thinking, it also helps, along with the abstract, to provide the reader with an overview of the article and to orientate them as they read through it.

Try to avoid overly long and dense sentences that make your writing hard work to read and difficult to understand. Most journals today prefer writing that is straightforward, clear and concise. Furthermore, unless absolutely necessary, do not overload your article with technical language that may make it inaccessible, particularly to non-specialist readers or novices to the field. There will, of course, be times when technical language most definitely is required and nothing else will serve as an adequate substitute. However, always keep in mind that you are not trying to blind the readers with technical jargon but rather attempting to convey facts and ideas in a way that is accurate and comprehensive but also most easily understood. Journals are a forum for exchanging ideas and not for showcasing your knowledge of jargon and mastery of complex English sentences!

Make sure you research your journals carefully. Each journal has its own focus and target audience and you do not want to waste your time and the editors' time submitting articles that are unsuitable for the particular journals concerned. It is normal practice for a journal to include a statement on its website or in each issue – or in every few issues – explaining its interest focus and readership. This should give you all the information you need in order to determine whether or not it would be a suitable home for your article. You may well find that there are a number of journals each of which would be suitable, so how do you go about deciding which one to select? One useful strategy is to list all the possible journals, placing the most prestigious at the top and the least prestigious at the bottom. Take advice on this if you need to. Having done this, you then need to decide whether you want to publish in one of the top journals or in one of the more modest ones. This is a matter of careful judgement and of being honest with yourself. If you feel your article is strong and able to compete with the best competition and successfully make it through the rigorous review process of the most prestigious journals, then go ahead and submit it to one of the journals at the top of your list. If however, you have rather less confidence in it, then it may be better to submit it to a journal lower down your list. This way you will not lose time by waiting for the review process of a prestigious journal to take its course, only to find that your paper is rejected. Once again, it can be helpful to run your article by an experienced academic in your field who has a good publication record and will help you make the best judgement about who to submit your article to and when.

In making your decision about where to try and get your article published, you need to be aware that journals generally do not like you submitting your article to a number of different journals at the same time, and they will often ask you whether you have done so at the time of your submission. Why are they uncomfortable with this? First, there is the issue of pride in their own publication. All journals like to feel that they are an author's first port of call because of the quality and prestige of their product. Secondly, and perhaps more importantly, journals need to plan ahead. As we have seen, as the pressure on academics to publish is increasing, so too is the number of articles being submitted to journals, with the result that actual publication times can be in excess of two years. Journals, therefore, need to be able to plan ahead with confidence and to be able to confirm with their authors when they can expect their articles to appear in print. This is difficult to do if they know that other journals are considering the same articles and that, ultimately, despite themselves accepting a particular article, the author of that article might receive and accept another offer of publication elsewhere.

Once you've decided on a journal, make absolutely sure before you submit your article that it conforms to the journal's submission guidelines. Along with details of its research focus and readership, these will be spelt out clearly in hard copy issues of the journal as well as on its website, so check these carefully. Remember: guidelines vary between journals with respect to such things as formatting requirements, word count, the number of references permitted, the length of the abstract and the method of submission.

Although, with online submission becoming increasingly common, incorrect submissions are less likely to occur (often you cannot submit until all information has been correctly entered), there is still room for error. Make sure, therefore, that you check everything one final time before you press the 'submit' button. It's all too easy, for example, to attach an earlier draft of your article rather the final one, or to forget to include a word count or, where required on initial submission, your biographical information (your qualifications, professional affiliations, publications and experience).

Finally, don't feel too downhearted if your article is rejected; this happens all the time to some of the finest, most respected academics, even if you don't always hear about it! It may well be that your article isn't bad, but others were considered better or slightly more appropriate for the particular journal concerned. Just consider how you might further improve the article and then move on to the next journal on your list.

Getting published in journals: strategies for success

- Ensure that your article has a clear focus and is making a clear point.
- Consider dividing the article into headed sections so as to give the reader an 'at-a-glance' picture of its overall structure.
- Keep your language clear and concise and avoid dense, complex sentences.
- Keep technical jargon to a minimum.
- Target your journals carefully – which are the most suitable for your article in terms of prestige and content?
- Submit your article to one journal at a time. Do not submit it to a number of journals simultaneously.
- Submit your article to the most prestigious journals first and work your way down.
- Ensure that your article conforms precisely to the journal's 'guidelines for submission' (check previous issues and the journal's website).
- Have a colleague read through your article to check for accessibility (reader-friendliness) and conceptual soundness.
- Don't lose heart if your article is rejected. It may actually be quite good and merely be in need of some slight reworking before submission to a more suitable journal.

Activity 6.4 Identifying possible journals

Think about the content of your dissertation or thesis and try to decide which sections of it lend themselves to publication. Once you have done so, try to identify suitable journals to which you might submit articles. As you work through the various journals, identify their foci and guidelines for submission.

Publishing a book

Just as your dissertation or thesis can provide material for journal publications, it can sometimes also be turned into a book, although it will almost certainly need considerable reworking. Many successful PhD students are understandably keen to turn their years of hard work into a published book of which they are sole author and which can increase their professional profile significantly.

In some respects, publishing a book is quite similar to publishing a journal article. It will, for example, be subjected to a process of rigorous evaluation and require dedication, self-belief and a good deal patience on your part. As with a paper, it needs to have a clear focus and be well written; and even then there is certainly no guarantee that a publisher will accept it and offer you a contract.

Before outlining the process of getting a book published, here, in brief, is a summary of some of the factors that can determine whether or not you meet with success:

- Does the book have a clear focus?
- Is it based on a good idea?
- Is it conceptually sound?
- Does it offer something unique?
- Does it improve on the competition?
- Is it timely in terms of where the field is currently and what is generating interest?
- Is the proposal well received by reviewers? (very important)
- Is there a market for the book? or Is there a gap in the market?
- Are you able to define that market clearly?
- Does it fit with the publisher's publishing plans/marketing strategy?
- Does the publisher publish books of the kind you are proposing?
- Does the book fit into an established series?
- Is there room for a sister book or a series of similar books?
- Will it sell?
- Is it well written?
- Have you previous experience of publishing your work?
- What are your professional affiliations?
- Are you a well-known and respected academic?

Of course, no book proposal ticks all of these boxes but it will have to tick enough to make your book seem an attractive and worthwhile proposition for the publisher concerned.

Activity 6.5 Assessing the possibility of book publishing

If you are thinking of publishing your research as a book, think about how you and your proposed book meet, or fail to meet, the criteria listed above by filling in the table below.

Criterion	Don't know	No	Yes	How
Has a clear focus				
Based on a good idea				
Conceptually sound				
Offers something unique				
Improves on the competition				
Is timely				
Has a clear market				
Responds to a gap in the market				
Fits in with publisher's plans				
Fits with publisher's book type				
Fits into an established series				
Could lead to a pair/series of books				
Potential to sell				
Well written				
Previous publishing experience				
Relevant professional affiliations				
Well-known, respected academic				

Writing a proposal

The first step to getting your research published is to write a proposal. All publishers have guidelines about what your proposal should look like and what elements you need to include, and although these might show some degree of variation they tend to be very similar. The following elements typically feature:

- a synopsis of the book's vision/philosophy
- a synopsis of the subject matter of the book including a detailed table of contents
- analysis of the competition, including strengths and weaknesses, and a description of features that distinguish your book from the competition
- target audience for the book

- where appropriate, course(s) for which the proposed book would be suitable
- key features of the book, e.g. learning aids, case studies, illustrations, examples, exercises, summaries, readings
- supplementary material that you would prepare for lecturers or students
- where relevant, any new theories or developments in the subject that you intend to cover
- present state of the project (i.e. idea, partial manuscript, lecture notes, etc.)
- estimated final number of pages, words, diagrams, tables, etc.
- any sample material you may have including chapters, preface, etc.
- your curriculum vitae – including previous publications.

The review process

Having received your proposal, the first thing the publisher will do, usually via a commissioning editor, is send it out to reviewers (usually two or three) and get their impressions of the proposal based on what you've submitted. Along with the proposal, they will also send the reviewers a list of specific areas they would like them to comment on, along with the opportunity to express any other views they may have about the book.

The review process is probably the most crucial stage in the life of your book, for what the reviewers say will strongly influence the publisher's decision whether or not to publish. If there is a general feeling among the reviewers that the proposal is well conceived and well written, and would be well received, make a useful contribution to the field and tap a potential market, then the chances are the publisher will go ahead and offer you a contract. If, on the other hand, reviewers exhibit serious concerns about the proposal, the publisher's decision is likely to go the other way.

Even if the reviews are positive, they will almost certainly include indications of the proposal's weaknesses, along with suggestions for improvement. Before offering you a contract, therefore, it is likely that the publisher will request that you respond to the reviewers' feedback, either by making changes that address some of their concerns and suggestions, and/or by providing a rationale for why you may disagree with them. A revised proposal is then submitted and considered by an in-house editorial panel or committee, and a decision taken to award or withhold a contract. Normally, by this stage, provided that you're seen to have been open to reviewers' suggestions and responded reasonably, the likelihood is that the publisher will 'go to contract'.

Writing the book

Once you have a contract, the serious business of writing the book begins. As we've seen, just because you have a dissertation or a thesis on which the book is based does not mean that there is not substantial work still to be done. The requirements of a book and its publisher will mean that you may well have to reorganise and rewrite parts of your work, as well as add new sections to it, change the tone, add graphics and other features, and make it more appealing and accessible to a wider audience. You will also need to write according to the publisher's 'style guide' – essentially a set of instructions on how to prepare the manuscript for submission: how to format the text, present any artwork specifications, clip art and other illustrations, etc. Furthermore, you will now be working to the publisher's timescale and therefore be under some pressure to have a completed manuscript by an agreed date, often specified in the contract.

Although it depends on the nature of the book and at what stage your manuscript is, a 12–15 month turn-around time for a manuscript is quite typical. While the date itself is negotiable to some extent, the publisher will often push for a book to be in print by a particular deadline – often a particular time of the year. Publishers plan ahead and base their marketing plans on assumptions about when new books will be available and in the bookshops. For example, in the case of books written for undergraduate students, they will often try to get these into print by springtime so that students can buy them ready for the upcoming academic year in the autumn. The marketing of those books will begin happening even earlier, with catalogues being printed and sales reps visiting schools and universities in order to showcase them.

This all means that the publisher may, periodically, wish to see evidence of how you are progressing with the book. They may ask to see some of the completed material in order to check that it's developing in the way envisaged, and to make suggestions where they feel this would be helpful and make for a better book. A developmental editor will be assigned to the project to oversee it and provide you with any assistance you may need. Reviewers may also be involved in commenting on chapters as your writing progresses.

Even after the manuscript is complete and has been submitted, some (not all) publishers send it out to reviewers one final time. As a result, you may be asked to consider making a few last-minute and normally fairly minor changes to it. Once those changes have been incorporated and accepted, the main part of your job has been done, although at various points in the production process the publisher may come back to you with requests for clarification or questions concerning your preferences for certain elements of the book, for example. Eventually, after it has been typeset and before it goes to print, you will be asked to read through the 'proofs' of the book. The proofs are essentially all the pages of the book almost exactly as they will eventually appear in the final product, on the bookshelves. This is your last opportunity to make any changes to the manuscript and correct any of your own or the typesetter's errors, so the proofs need to be read with great care and any necessary adjustments meticulously and clearly noted. The publisher will normally advise you on how to annotate the manuscript appropriately with any amendments you may require.

Once the proofs have been annotated and submitted, your involvement in the production of the book will be minimal, although you will be consulted on the design of the book cover and the biographical data you would like included. Hopefully, the next iteration of your manuscript you get to see will be the completed book, and this typically happens within three to six months of the final submission of the manuscript. The publisher will normally send you a few gratis copies of the book; indeed, this is usually written into the contract along with a precise number. Once again, you can feel proud of your research, and enjoy what it has helped you achieve!

Presenting your research

In Chapter 1 (➡ see p. 17), we talked briefly about attending research seminars, conferences, local chapters and special interest groups as a way of networking, becoming involved in the academic community, and generating and getting feedback on ideas for your research. Of course, these fora also provide excellent opportunities to disseminate your research.

As with journal articles, your dissertation or thesis can provide material for a number of presentations. These will probably – though not necessarily – mirror the journal articles that your research generates. Often, academics will present their papers at conferences only after they've been accepted for publication; this helps give the papers standing or credibility and the presenters themselves added confidence. In contrast, others see conference presentations as proving grounds; as opportunities to test their papers on their peers and to get feedback that may help improve their work prior to submitting it to journals.

Presentations, then, bring with them a number of potential benefits, many of which they have in common with journal articles. These include:

- enhancing your professional profile
- generating interest in an area in which, by virtue of having successfully completed your dissertation or thesis, you have become something of an expert
- generating feedback that may help clarify your thinking and improve your work
- providing you with ideas for 'spin offs' – research projects, other papers, etc. that build on the research on which your are reporting
- presenting opportunities to network with others in the profession who share similar interests
- forcing you to reflect on your own ideas.

Finally, although presentations do not, as a rule, command as much respect in academic circles as books or papers published in well-regarded, refereed journals, they do nevertheless carry weight and tend to be a somewhat easier route to getting your research 'out there' and into the wider academic community. What's more, they constitute an important – some would say crucial – element in the development of any academic career.

AND FINALLY . . .

However you choose to showcase it and use it to your and others' advantage, your research, as recorded in your dissertation or thesis, will always remain as a testament to your intellectual ability, creativity and perseverance. It is an achievement of which you can be justly proud.

Sample table of contents (1)

Table of contents

(Source: Klinger, 2005)

Sample list of figures (1)

List of figures

➡

(Source: Klinger, 2005)

Sample table of contents (2)

➡

Chapter 3

THE STATE AND STATUS OF COMMUNICATIVE LANGUAGE TEACHING (II): SOME PROBLEMS AND CONTROVERSIES

Chapter 4

THE EMERGENCE AND DEVELOPMENT OF COMMUNICATIVE COMPETENCE THEORY

Chapter 5

ASSESSING THE UTILITY OF FRAMEWORKS OF COMMUNICATIVE COMPETENCE

➡

Chapter 8

COMMUNICATIVE LANGUAGE TEACHING AND THE JAPANESE
ENGLISH LANGUAGE CLASSROOM: INCOMPATIBILITIES,
RESOLUTIONS AND THE PRACTICAL APPLICATIONS OF
A NEW PERSPECTIVE

Chapter 9

FOSTERING A NEW TEACHER ATTITUDE: THE CHALLENGE
FOR LANGUAGE TEACHER EDUCATION

(Source: Author's own work)

Sample list of figures (2)

List of figures

(Source: Author's own work)

SELECTED ANSWERS TO ACTIVITIES

Activity 4.1 Avoiding clichés and using alternatives

Here are some possible answers.

1 The fall of the Berlin Wall and the historic meetings between Gorbachev, Reagan and Thatcher were clear indicators that change was not just inevitable but already under way.
or
The fall of the Berlin Wall and the historic meetings between Gorbachev, Reagan and Thatcher were clear indicators of change.
or
The fall of the Berlin Wall and the historic meetings between Gorbachev, Reagan and Thatcher both heralded change.

2 With the advantage of hindsight, the years following Armistice Day represented a brief interregnum before war once again broke out, and on a scale never before seen.

3 In the initial weeks following the Watergate scandal, some constitutional experts were confident that President Richard Nixon's downfall was inevitable.

4 Research has shown that people of different social, educational and professional backgrounds share similar attitudes to violent crime.
or
Regardless of their background, all people share similar attitudes to violent crime, according to the research.

5 Throughout history, mankind has sought to explain his world and give meaning to his existence.
or
Man has always sought to explain his world and give meaning to his existence.

6 One common perception was that the vast majority of politicians are dishonest and self-serving.
or
One common perception was that politicians who are honest and not self-serving are rare.

Activity 4.2 Integrating and formatting long quotations

Possible answer:

While it is widely acknowledged that an understanding of law is a crucial part of the social worker's toolkit, one that both informs their practice while also affording them protection against legal action, as Wilson *et al.* note, its notoriously ambiguous nature means that it can be difficult to navigate:

To practice social work effectively it is necessary to have a critical understanding of law and to recognise its limitations alongside its strengths. A common misconception about law is that it is clear-cut and provides unambiguous answers or solutions. In fact some provisions of the law lack that clarity and may be open to interpretation. When new legislation is introduced it is sometimes necessary to wait for clarification on meaning of certain provisions from the courts. In other situations law may appear to lack clear direction because it allows discretion for practice within broad boundaries.

(Wilson *et al.*, 2008: 191)

Activity 4.3 Integrating and formatting short quotations

Possible answers:

Text 1

Without doubt, marketing is considerably more sophisticated today than it was even thirty years ago. This is in part due to technological developments that allow for more complex analyses of markets and buyer behaviour. One particular area of buyer behaviour that has recently been a subject of discussion in the literature is that of the so-called cyclical nature of purchasing, where, according to Kotler *et al.*, 'People's attitudes and lifestyles are influenced by past purchases, and each passage through awareness interest, desire and action influences all other purchase decisions' (1996: 44). This notion contrasts with the linear view of consumer behaviour, where . . .

Text 2

What emerges from most studies that look at attainment levels of high school pupils is that there is a clear correlation between both socio-economic status and ethnicity and academic success. Although there are efforts being made to reduce attainment gaps, these, as Davies notes, 'are reliant on government funding and initiatives, and rely on a national vision and drive to counteract disadvantage and deprivation' (2006: 55). Unfortunately, that vision and drive is frequently inadequate to bring about change of the magnitude required to really make inroads into the problem.

Text 3

One of the biggest challenges facing new teachers is to deliver material in such a way that it engages and develops all pupils in a class regardless of their different capacities. These teachers quickly need to find ways to ensure that 'pupils who are finding the topic easy will be able to develop and enrich their learning and not be held back' while 'those who find the topic or area of work more challenging will be supported so that they will in time get to a competent level of understanding' (Davies, 2006: 19). To achieve this requires careful planning, sensitive and strategic implementation, and above all experience.

Activity 4.4 Paraphrasing a text

Possible answers:

This view accords with that of Smith (1988), who believes that despite the emergence of new technologies – most obviously the computer – and the enormous sums of money invested in efforts to find an ideal method for teaching reading, those 'traditional' methods and materials we have always used cannot be significantly bettered.

Wray *et al.* (1998) explain the popularity of closed questions in terms of the ease with which they can be scored, and the range of formats for tallying and comparing responses that they permit.

Activity 4.5 Quoting secondary sources

Possible answer:

According to research conducted by Vennard (cited in Elliott and Quinn 1996), acquittal rates in the Crown Court tend to be significantly higher than those in magistrates' courts. This confirms the belief of many defendants that they are more likely to be acquitted in the Crown Court.

Activity 4.6 Writing an introduction 1

Possible answer:

- Advances in technology – flight and information technology in particular – have created a 'smaller', more inter-dependent and more homogeneous world.
- This has led to the emergence of a global society which in turn has resulted in the interaction of different ethnic groups both within and outside the workplace.
- Multiculturalism is increasingly a reality for most businesses. As such they need to be able to respond to that reality.
- Intercultural awareness and intercultural communications skills are part of that response.
- Good intercultural communication helps ensure understanding is maximised, conflict minimised and efficiency increased.
- Good intercultural communication helps ensure that individuals clearly understand and are therefore able to fulfil their roles in the organisation.
- Good intercultural communication helps ensure that the organisation is able to draw on and benefit from the diverse talents of all its employees and business associates.
- Good intercultural communication means recognising and maximising business opportunities.

Activity 4.7 Constructing and positioning thesis statements

Possible answers (with thesis statements underlined):

Statement at the end
The incidence of depression among teenagers is on the increase. Research spanning the past ten years and focusing on the records and anecdotal evidence of health professionals, including Counsellors, GPs, psychiatrists and psychologists, suggests that more young people than ever are requiring treatment for the disorder – a trend particularly evident in the developed world. Furthermore, it seems that teenage girls are more susceptible to depression than teenage boys.

One of the costs of this unfortunate trend is the enormous toll it can take on the psychological wellbeing of the parents of children who suffer from depression and who themselves can, in more severe cases, sometimes end up requiring support in dealing with the stress and anxiety associated with trying to ensure their children manage the disorder.

In light of the increasing incidence of depression and the sometimes severe disruption it can cause in the lives of sufferers and their families, <u>the following pages will provide some insights into the causes of teenage depression and how, if at all, it might be prevented or at least alleviated.</u>

Statement at the beginning

<u>This chapter considers some of the underlying causes of a disorder that has been on the increase among teenagers over the last ten years, according to research that has investigated the records and anecdotal evidence of health professionals, including Counsellors, GPs, psychiatrists and psychologists. That disorder is depression</u>, and the evidence suggests that it is noticeably more common in the developed world and among teenage girls.

Another, perhaps unsurprising finding that emerges from this research is the often enormous toll depression can have on the parents – and indeed the wider family – of those suffering from the disorder. It is often the case that these 'carers' themselves have difficulty in coping with the stresses and strains caused by the worry associated with their child's condition and trying to ensure that they are given every possible support in trying to manage it effectively.

Activity 4.8 Writing an introduction 2

Possible answers:

Given the increasing incidence of depression and the sometimes severe disruption it can cause in the lives of sufferers and their families, there is good reason to consider some of the possible causes of teenage depression and how, if at all, the disorder might be prevented or at least alleviated.

If the problem of teenage depression is to be successfully addressed, the question needs to be asked: 'What are the underlying causes of depression?'

Activity 4.9 Writing an introduction 3

Possible answer:

Although the notion of a 'global village' has become something of a cliché, like many clichés, it reflects reality and offers us an insight, a glimpse into some aspect or perception of the world. Undeniably, the Earth today is indeed a far 'smaller' place than it was a century ago, with people from almost every culture interacting in a way and to an extent unimaginable to our grandparents. This has led to the development of something verging on a homogeneous world culture, where people listen to the same bands, wear similar clothes, look up to the same icons and aspire to similar lifestyles. In sum, it has resulted in a sea change in the way we view ourselves both as individuals and as part of human society in general.

Two key factors that have brought about this change are flight – its development and affordability – and the revolution in information technology. These two things have meant that we can traverse huge distances quickly and easily, communicate almost instantaneously with others anywhere in the world, and access the vast resources of the World Wide Web at the mere click of a mouse button. The consequences for migration, social integration and, ultimately, cross-cultural interaction, have been enormous, and these in turn have had major repercussions on the world of work. It is rare indeed for today's businesses and other organisations not to have at least a proportion of workers from various ethnic backgrounds; indeed, legislation is increasingly requiring them at the very least to be open to the notion of a multicultural workforce. Furthermore, employees are increasingly aware of the benefits such a workforce can bring to their organisations.

As 'the multicultural workforce' becomes more widespread, the role of intercultural skills in the workplace takes on a new significance and raises important questions concerning language proficiency, work ethics and attitudes, and an understanding of behavioural norms. This chapter looks in particular at the issue of language and cross-cultural communication, both in terms of the challenges it presents as well as the various ways in which organisations have sought to meet those challenges such that workers' cultural traditions are valued and respected, and the company's ethos and efficiency maintained.

Activity 4.10 Summarising a text

The expression of environmental concern by ordinary people in Iran is severely constrained by its authoritarian clerical government which leaves dissenters, who exist and are tolerated to an extent, with little or no voice alongside the green, government-sanctioned NGOs. This carefully crafted situation helps maintain oligarchic control by the theocracy while simultaneously allowing the people some semblance of controlled participation, and women in particular, a voice they have been lacking since the revolution of 1979.

In Burma, on the other hand, environmental issues are linked to human rights, leading to a discourse of 'earth rights'. Dissent is not tolerated and can only find a voice via military insurgency or international fora.

In both these non-democratic regimes, then, the brand of environmentalism exported by the West has had its character changed through the process of importation. Yet their mutated forms may still help shape societal change in the future, particularly in Burma, where the environment and human rights have been linked more strongly in struggles for survival.

Activity 4.11 Punctuating three texts

Text 1
Companies such as Apple, Nokia, Unilever, P&G and Philips with international distribution systems may introduce new products through global rollouts. Apple's iPhone first went on sale in America in June 2007, followed by the European launch in the autumn, and Asian roll-out in 2008. In a swift and successful global assault – its fastest global rollout ever – P&G quickly introduced its SpinBrush low-priced, battery-powered toothbrush into 35 countries. Such rapid worldwide expansion overwhelmed rival Colgate's Actibrush brand.

(Kotler *et al.*, 2008: 565)

Text 2
Treatment programmes for drug abuse, including smoking and drinking, may take several forms. In some cases, aversion therapy is used; in others, less intrusive

forms of therapy involving extensive counselling are used. In the latter case, the psychologist or therapist's general aim is to teach the individual to:

1 identify environmental cues or circumstances that may cause the addictive behaviour to occur or recur;

2 learn to behave in ways that are incompatible with the desired behaviour;

3 have confidence that they can overcome the addiction;

4 view setbacks in overcoming the addiction as temporary and to treat them as learning experiences in which new coping skills can be acquired.

Prevention programmes for people with addictive behaviours are only moderately successful. Many alcohol management programmes have only a 30–50 per cent success rate (Marlatt *et al.*, 1986).

(Adapted from Martin et al., 2007: 787)

Text 3

In 1995, 80 per cent of Lords of Appeal, Heads of Division, Lord Justices of Appeal and High Court judges were educated at Oxford or Cambridge. Over 50 per cent of the middle-ranking circuit judges went to Oxbridge but only 12 per cent of the lower-ranking district judges did. Eighty per cent of judges appointed since 1997 were educated at a public school. The appointments made by the current Labour Government have not broken this mould. The narrow background of the judges does mean that they can be frighteningly out of touch with the world in which they are working. Mr Justice Harman, who resigned in 1998, said in three different cases that he had not heard of footballer Paul Gascoigne, the rock band Oasis and the singer Bruce Springsteen.

(Elliott and Quinn, 2008: 143)

Activity 4.13 Organising information using headings

Possible answer:

3.1   Introduction: What Is Advertising?
3.2   Types of Advertising
3.2.1   Product-Oriented Advertising
3.2.1.1   *Pioneering Advertising*
3.2.1.2   *Competitive Advertising*
3.2.1.3   *Comparative Advertising*
3.2.1.4   *Reminder and Reinforcement Advertising*
3.2.2   Institutional Advertising
3.3   Formulating the Advertising Message
3.3.1   Themes
3.3.2   Message Execution
3.4   Audience Appeal
3.4.1   Rational Appeal
3.4.2   Emotional Appeal

3.4.3 Product-Oriented Appeal

3.4.3.1 *Problem Solving*

3.4.3.2 *Product Comparison*

3.4.3.3 *Slice of Life*

3.4.3.4 *New Facts and Testimonials*

3.4.4 Customer-Oriented Appeal

3.4.4.1 *Saving or Making Money*

3.4.4.2 *Fear Avoidance*

3.4.4.3 *Security Enhancement*

3.4.4.4 *Self Esteem and Image*

3.4.4.5 *Usage Benefits*

Activity 4.14 Formatting sources for inclusion in a bibliography

Bühler, A. (2002) 'Translation as interpretation', in A. Riccardi (ed.) *Translation Studies*. Cambridge: Cambridge University Press.

Campbell, P. (2008) 'Escape from the impact factor', *Ethics in Science and Environmental Politics* 8: 5–7.

De Janasz, S., Wood, G., Gottschalk, L., Dowd, K. and Schneider, B. (2006) *Interpersonal skills in organisations*. Sydney: McGraw-Hill.

Hetherington, P. (2007) 'Outsider dealing'. http://www.guardian.co.uk/society/2007/Jan/24/immigrationasylumandrefugees.asylum [5 Feb. 2009].

Kieran, M. (ed.) (1998) *Media ethics*. London: Routledge.

Lévi-Strauss, C. (1984) *Tristes tropiques*. New York: Atheneum.

Ofsted (2008) *The Annual Report of Her Majesty's Chief Inspector of Education, Children's Services and Skills 2007/08*. London: Ofsted.

Peachey, L. (2005) 'Educational issues in war and peace: some reflections', in *IATEFL 2005 Cardiff Conference Selections from the 39th International Annual Conference Cardiff, 5–9 April 2005* (ed.) Beaven, B. IATEFL.

Razavi, S. (2007) 'Liberalisation and the debates on women's access to land', *Third World Quarterly* 28(8): 1479–1500 [online]. Routledge. Available from Informaworld: http://informaworld.com/smpp/content~content=a7838688903~db=all~order=page. [Accessed 18 July 2009.]

Thomas, J. (1995) *Meaning in interaction*. Harlow: Longman.

Activity 5.1 Analysing an abstract

Sentence 1: Tell the purpose of the study.

Sentence 2: Describe the five age groups.

Sentence 3: Tell the results for the most positive assessments and the trend thereafter.

Sentence 4: Tell more results for the groups that changed positively.

Sentence 5: Tell the results for gender differences.

Sentence 6: Tell the results for the most and least enjoyable activities.

Activity 5.4 Examine the theoretical perspective of a study

1 Interdependence theory.

2 Kelley and Thibaut.

3 From the Kelley and Thibaut, 1978 article.

4 The rewards a person receives and the costs that the person incurs.

5 Rewards are the positive experiences that create feelings of enjoyment and happiness including emotional well-being and self-esteem.

6 Costs are the negative experiences that yield emotional or physical discomfort or pain.

7 An overall assessment of the outcome that is arrived at by combining rewards and costs.

Activity 5.8 Examine the characteristics of the study participants

Possible answers:

1 The total number of participants in the study.

2 The type of school the participants were attending.

3 How the participants were recruited.

4 The payment the participants received.

5 The representativeness of the sample.

6 The participants' majors.

7 The percentage of male participants.

Activity 5.9 Analyse the description of an instrument used in a study

Possible answers:

1 What the participants were asked to describe.

2 The instruction the participants were given.

3 The number of raters coding the goals.

4 The types of goals that were coded (i.e. approach and avoidance goals).

5 The two types of approach goals.

6 How disagreements were resolved.

Activity 5.10 Analyse the procedures described in a study

Possible answers:

1 Exactly what "clinical and cognitive measures" were obtained in the medical assessment session?

2 In what order were the questionnaires and assessments administered?

3 How long did it take the participants to complete all of the questionnaires?

4 How many of the participants returned the additional questionnaire?

5 How soon did the participants return the additional questionnaire?

REFERENCES

Anderson-Levitt, K. M. (2006) Ethnography. In J. L. Green, G. Camilli and P. B. Elmore (eds), *Handbook of complementary methods in education research*, 279–95. Mahwah, NJ: Lawrence Erlbaum.

Blane, D., Netuveli, G. and Bartley, M. (2007) Does quality of life at older ages vary with socio-economic position? *Sociology* 41/4: 717–26.

Brayboy, B. (2004) Hiding in the ivy: American Indian students and visibility in elite educational settings. *Harvard Educational Review* 74/2: 125–52.

Brehm, J. and Miron, A. (2006) Can the simultaneous experience of opposing emotions really occur? *Motivation and Emotion* 30/1: 13–29.

Bui, K (2007) Educational expectations and academic achievement among middle and high school students. *Education* 127/3: 328–31.

Burbules, N. C. and Warnick, B. R. (2006) Philosophical inquiry. In J. L. Green, G. Camilli and P. B. Elmore (eds), *Handbook of complementary methods in education research*, 489–502. Mahwah, NJ: Lawrence Erlbaum.

Bye, D., Pushkar, D. and Conway, M. (2007) Motivation, interest, and positive affect in traditional and non-traditional undergraduate students. *Adult Education Quarterly* 57/2: 141–58.

Connelly, F. M. and Clandinin, D. J. (2006) Narrative inquiry. In J. L. Green, G. Camilli and P. B. Elmore (eds), *Handbook of complementary methods in education research*, 477–502. Mahwah, NJ: Lawrence Erlbaum.

Cresswell, J. W. and Plano Clark, V. L. (2007) *Designing and conducting mixed methods research*. Thousand oaks, CA: Sage.

Crookes, G. (2003) *A practicum in TESOL: professional development through teaching practice*. Cambridge: Cambridge University Press.

Csikszentmihalyi, M. (1997) *Finding flow: The psychology of engagement with everyday life*. New York: Basic Books.

Curby, T. W., Rudasill, K., Rimm-Kaufman, S. E. and Konold, T. R. (2008) The role of social competence in predicting gifted enrollment. *Psychology in the Schools* 45/8: 729–44.

Davies, S. (2006) *The essential guide to teaching*. Harlow: Pearson Education.

Douglas, M. (1975) *Implicit Meanings: essays in anthropology*. London: Routledge & Kegan Paul.

References

Doyle, T. and Simpson, A. (2006) Traversing more than speed bumps: green politics under authoritarian regimes in Burma and Iran. *Environmental Politics* 15/5: 750–67.

Elliott, C. and Quinn, F. (2008) *English legal system*. Harlow: Pearson Education.

Ellis, R. (1985) *Understanding second language acquisition*. Oxford: Oxford University Press.

Feldon, D. F. and Kafai, Y. B. (2008) Mixed methods for mixed reality: understanding users' avatar activities in virtual worlds. *Educational Technology Research and Development* 56: 575–93.

Gardner, R. C. (1985) *Social psychology and second language learning: the role of attitudes and motivation*. London: Arnold.

Gardner, R. C., Masgoret, A.-M., Tennant, J. and Mihic, L. (2004) Integrative motivation: changes during a year-long intermediate-level language course. *Language Learning* 54/1: 1–34.

Gervey, B., Igou, E. and Trope, Y. (2005) Positive mood and future-oriented self-evaluation. *Motivation and Emotion* 29/4: 269–96.

Gillies, R. M. (2006) Teachers' and students' verbal behaviours during cooperative and small-group learning. *British Journal of Educational Psychology* 76: 271–87.

Graesser, A. C. and Person, N. K. (1994). Question asking during tutoring. *American Educational Research Journal* 31/1: 104–37.

Hodgkinson, G. P., Langan-Fox, J. and Sadler-Smith, E. (2008) Intuition: a fundamental bridging construct in the behavioural sciences. *British Journal of Psychology*, 99, 1–27.

Hofstede, G. (1984) *Cultures consequences*. London: Sage Publications.

Jenkins, J. (2000) *English as an international language*. Oxford: Oxford University Press.

King's College London (2006) *Handbook of Academic Regulations for Research Degrees*. London: King's College London.

Klinger, C. (2005) Process physics: bootstrapping reality from the limitations of logic. PhD thesis. Flinders University.

Kotler, P., Armstrong, G., Wong, V. and Saunders, J. (2008) *Principles of marketing*. Harlow: Pearson Education.

Kurtzberg, T. R. and Mueller, J. S. (2005) The influence of daily conflict on perceptions of creativity: A logitudinal study. *The International Journal of Conflict Management* 16/4: 335–53.

Little, D. (1994) 'Words and their properties: arguments for a lexical approach to pedagogical grammar', in T. Odlin (ed.) *Perspectives on Pedagogical Grammar*, 99–122. Cambridge: Cambridge University Press.

Lombrozo, T. (2007) Simplicity and probability in causal explanation. *Cognitive Psychology*, 55, 232–57.

Macaro, E. and Masterman, L. (2006) Does intensive explicit grammar instruction make all the difference? *Language Teaching Research*, 10(3), 297–327.

Martin, G., Carlson, N. and Buskist, W. (2007) *Psychology*. Harlow: Pearson Education.

McLaney, E. and Atrill, P. (2008) *Accounting: an introduction*. Harlow: Pearson Education.

McNair, B. (1994) *News and journalism in the UK*. London: Routledge.

Mendaglio, S. (2007). Should perfectionism be a characteristic of giftedness? *Gifted Education International* 23: 89–100.

Oettingen, G., Mayer, D., Thorpe, J. S., Janetzke, H. and Lorenz, S. (2005) Turning fantasies about positive and negative futures into self-improvement goals. *Motivation and Emotion* 29/4: 237–67.

Pearson, J. C. and Nelson, P. E. (2000), *Perception, self-awareness, and self concept, an introduction to human communication: Understanding and sharing*, 8th edn. New York: McGraw-Hill Education.

Prins, B. C. and Daxecker, U. E. (2007). Committed to Peace: Liberal institutions and the termination of rivalry. *British Journal of Political Science* 38: 17–43.

Ruismäki, H. and Tereska, T. (2008) Students' assessments of music learning experiences from kindergarten to university. *British Journal of Music Education* 25/1: 23–39.

Sarroub, L. K. (2001). The sojourner experience of Yemeni American high school students: An ethnographic portrait. *Harvard Educational Review* 71/3: 390–415.

Sasson, J. R., Alvero, A. M. and Austin, J. (2006) Effects of process and human performance improvement strategies. *Journal of Organizational Behavior Management* 26/3: 43–78.

Smith, F. (1978) *Reading*. Cambridge: Cambridge University Press.

Sosik, J. and Dinger, S. (2007) Relationships between leadership style and vision content: The moderating role of need for social approval, self-monitoring, and need for social power. *The Leadership Quarterly* 18: 134–53.

Steptoe, A., O'Donnell, K., Marmot, M. and Wardle, J. (2008) Positive affect and psychosocial processes related to health. *British Journal of Psychology* 99: 211–27.

Strachman, A. and Gable, S. (2006) Approach and avoidance relationship commitment. *Motivation and Emotion* 30: 117–26.

Subbotsky, E. (2007) Children's and adults' reactions to magical and ordinary suggestion: Are suggestibility and magical thinking psychologically close relatives? *British Journal of Psychology* 98: 547–74.

References

Sullivan, H. W., Worth, K. A., Baldwin, A. S. and Rothman, A. J. (2006) The effect of approach and avoidance referents on academic outcomes: A test of competing predictions. *Motivation and Emotion* 30: 157–64.

Tomlin, R. (1994) 'Functional grammars, pedagogical grammars, and communicative language teaching', in T. Odlin (ed.) *Perspectives on Pedagogical Grammar,* 140–78. Cambridge: Cambridge University Press.

Tsui, A. (2007). Complexities of identity formation: A narrative inquiry of an EFL teacher. *TESOL Quarterly* 41/4: 657–80.

Tubbs, S. L. and Moss, S. (2000) *The verbal message: human communication*, 8th edn. New York: McGraw-Hill.

University of South Australia (2008) *Academic regulations for 'Higher Degrees by Research'*. Adelaide: University of South Australia.

Vavrus, F. (2005) Adjusting inequality: education and structural adjustment policies in Tanzania. *Harvard Educational Review* 75/2.

Warnock, G. J. (1967) *The philosophy of perception*. Oxford: Oxford University Press.

Watson, J., Kelly, B. and Izard, J. (2006) A longitudinal study of student understanding of chance and data. *Mathematics Education Research Journal* 18/2: 40–55.

Wilson, K., Ruch, G, Lymbery, M. and Cooper, A. (2008) *Social work: an introduction to contemporary practice*. Harlow: Pearson Education.

Wittrock, M. C. (1974) Learning as a generative process. *Educational Psychologist* 11: 87–95.

Wittrock, M. C. (1990) Generative processes of comprehension. *Educational Psychologist* 24: 345–76.

Wittrock, M. C. and Alesandrini, K. (1990) Generation of summaries and analogies and analytic and holistic abilities. *American Educational Research Journal* 27/3: 489–502.

Wray, A., Trott, K. and Bloomer, A. (2006) *Projects in linguistics: a practical guide to researching English*. London: Hodder Arnold.

Yashima, T., Zenuk-Nishide, L. and Shimizu, K. (2004) The influence of attitudes and affect on willingness to communicate and second language communication. *Language Learning* 54/1: 119–52.

Yin, R. K. (2006) Case study methods. In J. L. Green, G. Camilli and P. B. Elmore (eds), *Handbook of complementary methods in education research*, 111–22. Mahwah, NJ: Lawrence Erlbaum.

INDEX

Index

Index